Hands-On UX Design for Developers

Design, prototype, and implement compelling user experiences from scratch

Elvis Canziba

BIRMINGHAM - MUMBAI

Hands-On UX Design for Developers

Commissioning Editor: Amarabha Banerjee
Acquisition Editor: Noyonika Das
Content Development Editor: Jason Pereira
Technical Editor: Rutuja Vaze
Copy Editor: Safis Editing
Project Coordinator: Sheejal Shah
Proofreader: Safis Editing
Indexer: Rekha Nair
Graphics: Jason Monteiro
Production Coordinator: Nilesh Mohite

First published: July 2018

Production reference: 1310718

Published by Packt Publishing Ltd.
Livery Place
35 Livery Street
Birmingham
B3 2PB, UK.

ISBN 978-1-78862-669-9

www.packtpub.com

`mapt.io`

Mapt is an online digital library that gives you full access to over 5,000 books and videos, as well as industry leading tools to help you plan your personal development and advance your career. For more information, please visit our website.

Why subscribe?

- Spend less time learning and more time coding with practical eBooks and Videos from over 4,000 industry professionals

- Improve your learning with Skill Plans built especially for you

- Get a free eBook or video every month

- Mapt is fully searchable

- Copy and paste, print, and bookmark content

PacktPub.com

Did you know that Packt offers eBook versions of every book published, with PDF and ePub files available? You can upgrade to the eBook version at `www.PacktPub.com` and as a print book customer, you are entitled to a discount on the eBook copy. Get in touch with us at `service@packtpub.com` for more details.

At `www.PacktPub.com`, you can also read a collection of free technical articles, sign up for a range of free newsletters, and receive exclusive discounts and offers on Packt books and eBooks.

Contributors

About the author

Elvis Canziba has over 12 years of digital experience, the bulk of which came from working in the highly competitive industry.

He is a UX designer and frontend developer with a passion for technology and a knack for creating order out of chaos. He previously worked with different companies in the United States and Europe, and has moved to Dubai within the last two years. In that time, he has produced fantastic results in UX design and has managed various companies as Lead Developer, producing a high ROI every time.

About the reviewer

Basil Miller is the co-founder of Devlight and an Ivano-Frankivsk-based leading Android developer. Since 2014, Android developers all over the world have observed his progress and are using free products that he has developed as an open source Android UI widgets provider. Those libraries have reached the top of the popular trend charts. Being a co-founder and developer by nature, Basil is able and willing to collaborate in work on new business projects and startups. Also, it is easy to contact Basil in order to involve him in projects as a mobile development consultant.

> *Thank you to Packt Publishing and Sheejal Shah for involving me in this project. This is the third time you have given me a chance to use my skills and boost myself in different directions.*
>
> *Thank you, author, for deciding to write this book. I hope everyone will read it and improve their daily UX experience.*

Packt is searching for authors like you

If you're interested in becoming an author for Packt, please visit authors.packtpub.com and apply today. We have worked with thousands of developers and tech professionals, just like you, to help them share their insight with the global tech community. You can make a general application, apply for a specific hot topic that we are recruiting an author for, or submit your own idea.

Table of Contents

Preface

The **User Experience** (**UX**) field is growing rapidly, and most businesses are realizing that achieving their goals requires a level of product presence that is aligned with that of customer needs. UX is an essential part of product creation today, but the process of it can be long and costly. So, in this book, we are going to explain everything UX—from the complete basics right up to the advanced stuff.

If you want to learn about the processes, tools, and techniques that are required for creating a great UX design, this hands-on guide has you covered.

We'll start off our journey by understanding what UX is in the first place, why we need UX, how to do UX, and how to handle discovery, planning, research, and design with good UX in mind. Then, we will explain the full stack design dilemma and, more importantly, we will dive deeper into explaining the development side of an UX project.

With this book, you will gain the ability to think like a UX designer and understand both sides of product development, both the design and coding parts. You'll master how to create engaging, human-centered design practices, UX methodologies, the UX process itself, animation, and interaction. Finally, you'll prepare your portfolio and find yourself having become an expert in the UX field.

Who this book is for

This book is mainly for developers who want to enter the UX design field, but is also for product owners, entrepreneurs, and even beginner designers who would like to learn more about UX design and become professionals in this field.

What this book covers

Chapter 1, *What is UX*, will explain what UX design is, the main differences between UX and UI design, and the path to becoming a UX designer. Once everything is clear regarding the tasks of the UX designer, we will move on to explain the simple process of UX design and its various stages. Besides this, we will explain what full stack design is and how to become a full stack designer.

Chapter 2, *UX Design Process*, will discuss the most important things that we need to know to become a UX designer. The UX design process is a key thing that everyone in the UX industry is undertaking, but they are all doing so differently. So, we will dive deeper inside the UX design process and its stages to fully understand them. After that, we will move on to explain how to do UX project planning and proposals, and look at how to create a UX strategy. Also, to create a good UX, we need to understand the client business, competitors, and customers, and this will be covered during this chapter.

Chapter 3, *User Behavior Basics and User Research*, talks about how, as UX designers, we need to think about more than just what our product looks like. We will need to encourage users to engage with our product or service. So, to do this properly, we have to observe how the users behave with our product, and, for this, fortunately, we can use some psychology principles to analyze how our users think, behave, and interact with our product. So, this chapter will cover the user behavior basics, including psychology principles and how to conduct a proper user research.

Chapter 4, *Getting to Know Your Users*, explores how, to deeply and clearly understand why people use specific products and how they use them, we first need to know them. To create outstanding products, getting to know our users is an important thing. In this chapter, we will explain the importance of knowing the users during the process of UX design and how, by knowing more about users, we can easily create successful products. So, during this chapter, we will cover the areas that are important for us to know when it comes to users, as well as UX research methods and how to conduct an interview.

Chapter 5, *User Personas*, will help us achieve our goal of creating a great user experience for our targeted users by explaining the need for creating user personas. They are important to us because we can easily know who our user is during the product design process. This chapter will cover everything related to user personas, including why we create them, why we need them, and how to create a proper structure of user personas.

Chapter 6, *Designing Behavior*, will explain what drives users to behave in a certain way or take certain actions. Besides the BJ Fogg model, we will cover a few other behavior models that are worth knowing and understanding. We will cover topics such as behavioral design models, the factors that compel users to take certain actions, and how to create designs that will change user behavior.

Chapter 7, *Visual Design Principles and Processes*, goes into how, when we want to speak about the language of design, we need to provide a proper visual design for the users so that they can understand what we are trying to tell them. So, in this chapter, we will go through the basic elements of visual design, looking at what they are and how to use them. This is one of the most important chapters of this book when it comes to understanding UX and UI design together. We will cover everything, ranging from the basic elements of visual designs, such as colors, shapes, and lines, up to design principles such as repetition, balance, contrast, hierarchy, and spaces.

Chapter 8, *Wireframes and Prototyping*, continues in helping you learn the skills and methods for creating and designing interactive wireframes and prototypes, which will help us in the process of visual design, especially when it comes to creating better UI designs. I will share different examples on how wireframes can be created, what kind of tools we can use, and what kind of wireframes we can create to enhance our product design process. Here, we will cover everything from the basics up to the advanced concepts of wireframes and prototypes. Then, we will move on to explain in detail the different types of wireframes that we can create and the different ways of creating them.

Chapter 9, *UI Design and Implementation*, will explain what UI design is, where it can be used, and how we can create it. This chapter will explore what the process for creating a good UI design for our product is.

Chapter 10, *Frontend UI Implementation and Process*, explains the process of how to hand product design over to the frontend development team, what kind of assets should be provided to them, and what kind of tools we can use to make the process easier for both the design and frontend development sides of the story. After that, we will move deeper and explain the frontend development discipline—what languages and tools they use, and what areas of development they cover. So, this chapter will cover the complete process of UI implementation on the coding side of things, starting from the UI hand-over process and going right up to the organization of HTML, CSS, and JavaScript code.

Chapter 11, *Post-launch UX Activities*, goes into how, after we launch the product, we will need to learn more about those who will be using our product—we need to reach them, listen to them, and improve the product for them. We will talk more about what kind of metrics we should get from our customers, which parts of these metrics are important for us to know, and how we can use those metrics for our benefit. Areas such as A/B testing, gathering user metrics, and performing user interface accessibility testing will be covered during this chapter.

Chapter 12, *Designing for Big Data*, looks at how today's world is experiencing a growing amount of big data, which is all being collected from different sources, such as e-commerce businesses, social network platforms, search engines, and even small online businesses. Throughout this chapter, you will gain a better understanding of those points and the role of big data when it comes to UX. We'll also look at how we can use big data in design and why big data matters.

To get the most out of this book

In order to get the most out of this book, you should have some experience in developing products or services, besides knowing the basics of UX. It might be good as well if you have some knowledge of using design tools. Although this book will show you a few great tools to use, this is not a book focused on tool or software tutorials. Be prepared to use not only online tools, but papers, sticky notes, pens, paper templates, canvases, whiteboards, and whatever walls you can write on.

Download the color images

We also provide a PDF file that has color images of the screenshots/diagrams used in this book. You can download it here: https://www.packtpub.com/sites/default/files/downloads/HandsOnUXDesignforDevelopers_ColorImages.pdf.

Conventions used

There are a number of text conventions used throughout this book.

CodeInText: Indicates code words in text, database table names, folder names, filenames, file extensions, pathnames, dummy URLs, user input, and Twitter handles. Here is an example: "As you may have noticed, using the grid-column CSS property, we define the starting and ending points of each column that we have."

A block of code is set as follows:

```
<button class="f1 br1 ph3 pv4 white bg-red hover-bg-light-
red">Search</button>
```

Bold: Indicates a new term, an important word, or words that you see onscreen. For example, words in menus or dialog boxes appear in the text like this. Here is an example: " To choose one of them, we need to simply go under the **File** menu of Sketch, open the **New From Template** submenu, and choose one of available UI templates, as follows ."

Warnings or important notes appear like this.

Tips and tricks appear like this.

Get in touch

Feedback from our readers is always welcome.

General feedback: Email `feedback@packtpub.com` and mention the book title in the subject of your message. If you have questions about any aspect of this book, please email us at `questions@packtpub.com`.

Errata: Although we have taken every care to ensure the accuracy of our content, mistakes do happen. If you have found a mistake in this book, we would be grateful if you would report this to us. Please visit `www.packtpub.com/submit-errata`, selecting your book, clicking on the Errata Submission Form link, and entering the details.

Piracy: If you come across any illegal copies of our works in any form on the Internet, we would be grateful if you would provide us with the location address or website name. Please contact us at `copyright@packtpub.com` with a link to the material.

If you are interested in becoming an author: If there is a topic that you have expertise in and you are interested in either writing or contributing to a book, please visit `authors.packtpub.com`.

Reviews

Please leave a review. Once you have read and used this book, why not leave a review on the site that you purchased it from? Potential readers can then see and use your unbiased opinion to make purchase decisions, we at Packt can understand what you think about our products, and our authors can see your feedback on their book. Thank you!

For more information about Packt, please visit `packtpub.com`.

What is UX? 1

Simply put, **UX** means **User Experience**. In this chapter, we'll explain how to choose the right approach for UX. Then we'll move on to what a UX designer is. We will cover the process of UX design, where we'll give you guidelines and tips on how to become a better UX designer. Finally, we will move on to the main topic of this book: full stack design. Also, we will discuss the processes and tools being used, and areas of design and development that are part of the full stack design process. Finally, we'll discuss how to become a full stack designer.

In this chapter, we will cover the following topics:

- UX design and the difference between UI and UX
- Who is a UX Designer?
- UX designers, their role, and the processes they have to follow
- Full stack design and the role of a full stack designer
- Becoming a full stack designer

What is UX design?

Just knowing what **UX Design** stands for is not the same as really understanding the details of what it is. UX design is mainly focused on the overall experience of your product and not just on its look.

When it comes to UX design there is no general definition for it, because UX design covers a lot of different areas inside it, such as designing, branding, research, usability, accessibility, and function.

So, a proper definition of UX design might be the following:

UX Design is the process of designing physical or digital products that are useful, easy to use, and provide a great experience in interacting with them.

In short, it's everything that involves *why*, *what*, and *how* the product is being used by its users.

We will start with *why* because it involves the user's desire to use the product. The desire might be to finish a specific task or to add value for themselves by using it. The *what* explains the things that people will do with the product's functionalities or the features that are provided with it. Finally, *how* relates to the user's way of accessing the product's functionality through its design or interface.

Think of an app that you use daily, that you love, makes sense when you open it, and provides you with great value when you are using it; that's a good UX.
Every app that you have on your devices has a UX, but it may be a good or bad one.

However, a bad UX design has consequences. If your app has a bad UX design, users will have a hard time using it, and they will need training to use the app. As soon as they find a similar, better app that accomplishes the same task, they will move on because no one wants difficulty in completing a simple task.

Losing users means losing revenue. An improved UX design increases revenue because people will pay more for premium services if it makes their life easier. It's really important to understand the difference between what UX design is, and what it is not.

UX Design versus UI Design

Some of you might be confused about what exactly the difference is between UX and UI design. As mentioned earlier, UX looks at the overall experience of the product, whereas UI is focused more on the look and feel, such as fonts, colors, buttons, layout, and spaces.

Let's take an example of a booking website. Let's say that we need to book a flight from India to somewhere in Europe; booking in this case is the main *content*, the main thing that we want to accomplish; the website itself provides us with an UI with the options of searching the flights and choosing the one that we need. However, the whole process where we interact with the UI, from searching to choosing, and in the end, booking the flight, is the UX process, where the main content, booking in our case, is done.

The following image aims to explain the difference between a UI and UX design:

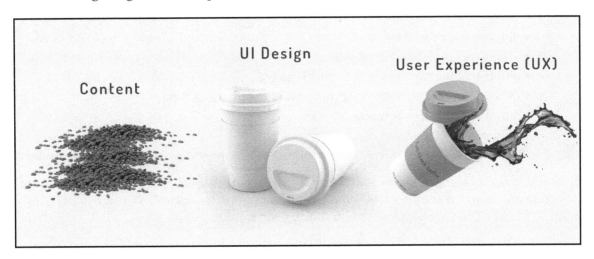

Although we have mentioned this several times, it is important that we explain this topic further for clarity.

It is really important for UX to be involved from the first phase of the product development; it will reduce the cost, since you can detect issues in the early phase and fix them, rather than doing so later.

UI supports UX, UI extends the UX, and, for sure, UI is the vehicle for UX. UI is the **user connection** to your application, which needs to be as simple and as clear as possible for your user. It must allow your user to do their work in a pleasing, easy, and efficient manner.

Why is UX so important?

UX can be in a wide range of features; even smaller parts of the application could prevent you from losing your audience.
Let's say that two companies have a very similar product but one of the products offers a better UX, which means that this product will attract a greater number of users and will provide a better return-on-investment to the company. You can find this similarity in various products nowadays, such as web applications, video games, mobile apps, and, of course, even on physical products.

Specifically, the UX Professionals Association mentions the following six key benefits that business can derive from UX design:

- It increases productivity
- It increases sales and revenue
- It reduces the cost of support and training
- It reduces the cost of development and development time
- It reduces the cost of maintenance
- It increases customer satisfaction

UX design, as its name suggests, is about designing the ideal experience of using a service or product. As such, it can involve all types of products and services, for instance, about the design involved in a museum exhibition. However, mainly the term UX design is used in relation to websites, web applications, and other software applications.

Since late 2000, technologies have become increasingly complex, and the functionalities of applications and websites have become far broader and more intricate. Early websites were simple static pages that served information to feed curious searchers; however, a few decades later, websites became more interactive, offered a richer feel for the users globally, and more information as well. If we also count responsive websites, real-time applications, and mobile apps, we can see how easily users get the information that they need nowadays compared to earlier times.

But there is one interesting thing: if we boost UX and UI too fast, the users will not get used it, so everything should take place in a natural, discrete, ordered way.

As I mentioned earlier, the biggest mistake new start-ups or companies make is that they don't start their UX planning at the beginning of a project. Usually, you will hear comments such as, *"We need to launch the product or services first, and we'll think about its look and feel later."*

Well, I can say that this is totally insane.

It is like an architect saying, *let's start the house, finish it, then later we'll think about its look;* crazy, right?

Why? It sounds absurd for hundreds of reasons, as follows:

- You will not know whether there is a need for your product or service in the first place
- You will not have a single clue about whether you have done it right

- It will cost you a lot of money
- It will cost you time

That is why UX should be involved right from the beginning, that is, from the first phase of your product or service design, in order to avoid making these mistakes and to have a better return-on-investment (ROI).

A good UX design starts at the very beginning of your product, well-planned UX will help the development to move faster. Everything should be produced by general product guidelines.

Usually, my biggest challenge is when I am being asked by clients to improve their UX just before they go live. That is really difficult, since most of the time it is really late and almost impossible to change anything.
Since their app is almost ready, its architecture is done and the budget has diminished, and, even worse, you don't have the option to make any changes without affecting their product because most of its parts were not created with the users in mind; the team just wanted it to work on the functionality side.

When users can't understand how to use a product, they will require instructions and training to use it. Such a product will be problematic for someone who has to use it on a daily basis. Due to this, they will look for alternative options.

Besides the user's involvement from the beginning of the product design/development, it's important to understand that all other teams in the company need to be involved on the UX design process, should have a good relationship among each other, and should help other teams for a better final result.

For example, the marketing team can get user feedback on issues they are having when using the product and send it to the UX team.

Hopefully, by now, your knowledge of UX design has increased, and you have a clear understanding of what it stands for, how it is used, and when you need to use it.
Now, it is time to move on to explain what a full stack designer is.

 However, before we go there, just keep this in mind:
BETTER USER EXPERIENCE (UX) DESIGN = HAPPY TEAM = HAPPY USERS = MORE USERS = MORE REVENUE.

Who is a UX designer?

A UX designer is someone <u>who investigates and analyzes how users feel about the products offered to them</u>. UX designers then apply this knowledge to product development in order to ensure that the user has the best possible experience with that product. UX designers conduct research, analyze their findings, inform other members of the development team about their findings, monitor development projects to ensure that those findings are implemented, and do much more.

People usually presume that product design was simpler in the past. Well, they thought it was simpler because designers or product owners had a particular design in mind and built their products in a way that they thought was good and hoped their clients would like.

However, it was different because online competitions for solving specific problems were not as prominent as they are today, so even if the people didn't like a product much, they were forced to use it because there was no other option available to them. That is the reason why most of products used to be designed without users in mind.

UX increases the chances of a project's success when it finally comes to market, not least because it doesn't gamble on users taking to a product just because it's a brand name.

UX design can be found in a variety of project environments nowadays. The more complicated the project, the more essential its UX design is. Too many features handled the wrong way can deter users like nothing else.

You may not find dedicated UX teams in a start-up, but UX is always part of the objective. High-tech start-ups developing innovative projects need to understand how their users feel even more than established companies do.

The bigger the project is, the more resources it consumes, so UX becomes even more important to deliver a return on the investment.

The main methodology used to guarantee the UX in most projects is **user-centered design**. Simply put, user-centered design is all about designing with the user's needs and expected behaviors in mind.

We can say that if the heart of UX design is the concept of constant iterative optimization, then the problem is the blood the heart is pumping.

So, the approach for our future customers or users should be to find the problem that they are dealing with and then solve it for them. We have to find the problem and define it–feel the same pain that our users feel–and eliminate it for them. That is the highway to providing a great UX.

To stay on the right path, we will need a lot of analytical and intuitive skills, because one of the trickiest parts with problems is that when we have something that troubles us, it is difficult to define it.

In the past, the role of a UX designer was a bit more difficult, because we always had to prove the value of UX to the company we were working for, and it was a real struggle to explain to companies why UX is important and why they need to start focusing on it. However, nowadays, companies and start-ups have become aware of the importance of UX and take this user-centered design approach seriously.

UX design process

Like most other disciplines, UX design has its own process. UX design follows the user-centered design process, which looks like this:

- Discovery and planning
- Strategy
- UX Research
- Analysis
- Design
- Production

We will go deeper into each one of these in the later chapters of this book, but I will clarify a small point here: what each of this phases includes. To have a successful product result in the end, it is really important to follow all this stages strictly:

- **Research**: By research, we mean that a statement of work is delivered to the client, with details such as the project's cost, timeline, and what its end result will be. Also, at this stage, team-planning will be included, so this is the initial preparation before starting the project and going deeper into it.
- **Strategy**: This is the first phase, where we define what goal we want to achieve in this process. It deals with understanding what the benefit of the final product will be.

- **Discovery and Planning:** This is usually referred as the Discovery phase, and will include a lot of sub-phases inside its life cycle, such as interviews, user research, competition research, observations from users, and different surveys.
- **Analysis**: Here, you write the insights on the data that you collected from the research phase and then define how UX design can help you with that data.
- **Design**: This comes after you define clear goals and flows from the previous three phases and put your product to life by visualizing it and designing all the specific flows, refine them, and get input from the users by doing paper prototypes, wireframes, interactions, and UI designs.
- **Production**: This phase is where all the visual designs are finished, and you validate the product with stakeholders and go through user testing sessions. In this phase, the UX design team has to collaborate a lot with the developers team and guide them to produce a high-quality product.

So, all these six stages of the UX process include the **user feedback** from the beginning of each stage and during the entire product life cycle.

Full stack design

Since we now understand what UX stands for, it's time to dive deeper into a trending topic that is getting a lot public attention, the full stack design.

As an example, let's look at designing a new logo. Usually, a graphic designer will create a bundle of graphical elements to give a better presentation to their client. For example, they will include the good and bad practices of logo use, negative logos, how it can be used in horizontal, and vertical space, favicons, and so on.

The idea of web frameworks, such as Bootstrap, Foundation even Google's Material Design guidelines, is similar; just like a graphic designer who has to provide all the rules, guides, and best practices of use for a logo that they created, the full stack designer provides web style guides, animations, graphical assets, interactions, and UI elements that will be used across the platform.

Today, a lot of companies, even larger ones, have built their own custom design frameworks to keep track of their product's UI.

So, creating this kind of framework, from A to Z, from the UX Research process to the final UI components that represent the core of your product concepts on many areas, I call this the full stack design process.

Who is a full stack designer?

It is important to clarify that the word full stack doesn't mean to do it all from designing, coding, database or management; it means that a person has developed multiple skills, which allow them to complete a design or a development project on their own.
A full stack designer is someone who can work through the entire life cycle/process of the design phase, starting from conception, research, and wireframes to UI design and Visual Design. They will be involved in the prototyping process using specific tools, such as Marvel, InVision, or Sympli, and will finalize the process by providing frontend style guides and UI Prototypes and animations using HTML/CSS, WebFlow, Framer.js, SVG Animation, and so on.

By involving the frontend code, I don't mean that you have to be a great coder like you are on design side, but you should understand how the frontend code works and what technologies are behind it; in the following diagram, I have added the frontend code on both areas, that is, Design and Development:

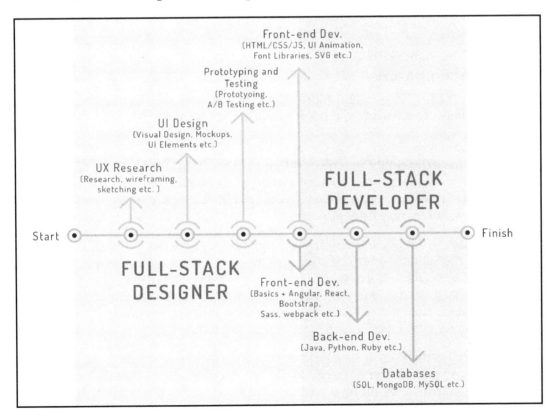

A good designer does not focus only on the UI or on the Design itself, but also on other things that are connected to it. A designer needs to realize the influence of different factors that can affect the product result. So, the more you are involved in these connected or related areas, the better a full stack designer you will become. And one of the biggest benefits is to involve developers from the beginning stage of UX.

The difference between a regular designer and a full stack designer is the ability to think of the bigger picture, because a full stack designer will be involved in the UX Process, design patterns, critical thinking, coding techniques, and a lot of other tools that will help them to finish the project, while a regular designer is involved in a specific area of design only.

A roadmap to becoming a successful full stack designer

There are tons of things that you can do to become a full stack designer, but I would suggest these five points as a roadmap to becoming successful in a full stack designer career:

- Learn the right **skills**
- Learn the right **tools**
- Show your work and gain some **experience**
- Learn how to **network** and get connected with people
- Build trust

We also should have the ability to receive different input from informations data, content, product requirements, feature requests, and so on, and develop different series of sketches and wireframes that will follow the best practices of UX design, solve problems, and, more importantly, create user-friendly experiences.

We need to be able to understand wireframes and design and every other UI component around them because this needs to be aligned with our client branding, that is, solving visual problems by providing a complete visual view and presentation of the product. Finally, we will need to be able to take these finalized UI designs and convert them into working prototypes, frontend code, or at least pieces of interactions just to show clearly our thinking for interactivity, functionality, and product look (UI).

Another thing that confuses people a lot about the full stack design field is the separation of frontend tasks. Usually, I prefer to clarify to the full stack developer that their task is to get the product to come to life by filling it with real data and add its interactivity to the backend and database by following the framework that was provided to them by the design team.

Usually, I see a lot of blogs written about the full stack designer as a designer who can code, but the central idea is not coding, but combining the framework, the toolset, and the assets of all the research that has happened on UX process phases into one complete bundle for the full stack developer to follow.

Also web frameworks such as Material Design Guidelines, Bootstrap Framework, Animation showcases, and clear actions and functionalities can be also included in this bundle.

The word *stack* usually refers to the layers of technology in an application.

So you can think of this as if you were to *stack* all design technologies on an application, starting from UX. It would look something like this:

- **UX design** (Research, Wireframing, and Prototype): Using tools such as Balsamiq, Pen and Paper, and sketching
- **UI design** (Visual Design, mockups, icons, and assets): Using tools such as Photoshop, Illustrator, SketchApp, and Adobe XD Design
- **Interaction Design** (prototype of UI, animation, human interaction): Using tools such as Principle, Adobe After Effect, InVision, and FramerJS
- **Frontend side**: This includes the following two areas:
  - HTML and CSS for User Interface Design
  - JavaScript + Advanced CSS features for Interface Interaction and Animations

So, putting this simply, you can see that a full stack designer is someone who can research, design, implement, prototype, mock up, and code or slice (HTML/CSS). They are knowledgeable about all types of designs starting with graphics, web, mobile, software, or more specific areas of a new product design.

A full stack designer is a designer who has a multi-set of different design skills, and who is able to understand, design, and maintain an awareness for the entire product structure. Also, this kind of designer can customize their list of skills for a specific project.

For example, one project might require their skill on visual design and create interaction examples to solve a specific problem, whereas the other challenge for them might be to think through information data and develop clear UX design flows and solutions. So, this kind of designer will have all the necessary skills for solving both challenges and they choose the right ones for a specific task.

Having this kind of skill makes their process really seamless and allows them to have higher expectations when it comes to finalizing the product. Plus, it can save them a lot of time and money.

If we talk about the difference between a full stack designer and a full stack developer, it is really simple, because full stack developers are more focused on understanding a different range and wide spectrum of technologies so that they can improve on the engineering side. On the other hand, full stack designers are more focused on understanding the process for creating the product so that they will be able to deliver a better design, better UX, and a better product.

So, in being a full stack designer for creating a digital or physical product, it is important to concentrate on the following core aspects:

- **Usability**: We have to create and provide a clear and really easy-to-use product
- **Utility**: The product itself needs to provide useful content and solve a user problem
- **Accessibility**: The product needs to be accessible to different user categories
- **Desirability**: The product is attractive and creates a good UX

The advantage that you will have by becoming a full stack designer is not about how to make things look beautiful; instead, you will be able to research human behaviors and needs. You will also understand how to structure the information collected by the research so that it makes sense when your team reads it, and you will be involved in prototyping and getting validation from whether real people find value in your product before you build it.

A lot of companies are starting to realize the value of these skills and what they mean to their business, so no matter your job title, if you have these skill in your toolbox, you are highly desired in the market.

However, on the other hand, if you choose not to expand your overall skill set, the end result will be really disappointing for your overall growth potential, which means you are essentially setting yourself up to fail in the long run, as nowadays, in the tech world, designers are expected to do rather more than just design things.

If you really want to become a better designer, you have to stop caring only for the design itself and start checking out the other parts that are connected to it, such as users, technologies, and the product itself.

When you start improving yourself on the other design-related parts, you will realize just how much of the big picture you were missing before, and you will even start understanding the key part of the development process that depends on the design itself.

By this, your work and your product design will become much better because of your overall realization that you've got around different processes that are related to design. This is how the mindset of a full stack designer actually works. Also, in the last few years, full stack designers essentially started to become extremely cross-disciplinary and increased in number at an astounding pace.

The moment that you choose to become a full stack designer is the moment that you decided to help everyone on your team, as well as the users, in creating a specific product.

Besides financial rewards, the biggest benefit of being a full stack designer is the opportunity to expand your skills.

Let me tell you a true story, something that happened to a really amazing Visual Designer that I knew and worked with. When I say amazing, I mean it. This guy's portfolio on the visual side was incredibie, and it was a pleasure to work with him; however, even though everything that he designed looked really good, almost none of his designs ever came to life simply because they were without sense when you wanted to code or animate them based on your requirements.

Why? Because he never cared for the other side of the process and design-related stuff design, such as research, user testing, user feedback, and coding.
When we tried to implement his design on the coding side, most of the time it was so messy. Even after we brought it to life, it simply would not work for the users when we put that app or web service online. We just got a bunch of bad feedback because of its usability. We tried to convince him to make an effort to understand the other parts of the process, but it wasn't working so we had to let him go; we didn't have a choice.

He joined another reputable company; they were so happy to have him on board, but a few months later, other team members–mainly developers–started leaving the company. It was simply because it didn't work for them to work with someone who cared only for the product to be amazing and beautiful on the visual side when its real-life implementation wasn't working at all, and wasn't making sense.

Why am I am telling you this? Because, if you want to stick just with the design side, OK, that is your choice, but you will not achieve anything with that; without understanding the other parts connected to design, you will just fade away.

In the worst scenario, few years back, these guys would last longer in the big companies because people were taking into consideration their amazing portfolios without checking their general knowledge on the implementation side or understanding what process they use for designing or developing a product.

Lately, a lot of blog posts have been written; too much confusion has been added by saying that a full stack design is not making sense, and they are mixing up this discipline by comparing people who only code, or who only design, with people which can do both of them.

Actually, this discipline has nothing to do with this comparison; in the end, a new bunch of skills added to your toolbox will not hurt you. It is not about being a generalist, but about understanding the complete design process and all the parts connected to it.

So, if you are feeling too lazy to learn how to write some lines of codes or a new prototyping tool, such as Principle, framer.js, or any other tool that will make your design process easier and better, then this is your call.

Keep in mind that knowledge is one of the most valuable things you can have. Happiness and usefulness depend upon it. Knowledge is the acquisition of facts and the application of them to life.

As a full stack designer, you will be able to recognize the limitations and expectations of the project during the plan of the UX Process or UI design itself. You will be able to know what will and will not work on your project in its early phase because you'll develop more realistic expectations of outcomes before you start to push the code or any visual design.

So, by this, you can see that having a full stack designer in your company does not only benefit the design team, but also all the other teams inside the company, even the employer. Apart from increased knowledge and an expanded set of skills, another benefit of a full stack designer is that they know exactly what to expect from visual designs that they have come up with in the coding stage because they are aware of what is possible and what is not in the coding phase itself, whether it is a bad or good approach, whether it will work for that specific UI or not, and much more.

Summary

The demand for designers who work on more than just the design side is on the rise; gone are the days when web designers were sitting in front of their computers with their heads buried in their sketchbook or Photoshop, not worrying about how the design will be implemented.

We already covered all the basic parts in this chapter for becoming a good UX designer and the roadmap for becoming a full stack designer. It is important to not misunderstand the difference between UI design and UX design; if necessary, read this chapter again, especially the first part, to get a better understanding of it.

We also covered the basic process of UX here, so in the next chapter, we will go more deeply into each stage of the UX process, which is one of the most critical steps for you to become better in the UX design field.

2
UX Design Process

In this chapter, we will discuss the most important thing that we need to know to become a UX Designer. The UX design process is a key part that everyone in the UX industry is undertaking, but they are all doing it differently.

Like any other discipline, UX also has its own stages and processes for doing it right. In this chapter, we will cover the following topics:

- UX design process
- Discovery and planning
- Project proposals
- Project objectives and methodologies
- The UX strategy
- Understanding competitors and customers
- Discovering your own UX strategy framework
- UX research

UX design process

Like every other discipline has its own stages or process of development, UX also has its own process for doing it right. However, the problem with the UX process is that it's not always the same; it depends on several factors, such as the size of the project, the category of the project, the targeted users (audience), the problem that you want to solve, your client, and the budget and timeline of your product.

So, you as a UX designer, or the UX team, can define your own process, depending on the factors mentioned in the preceding paragraph. I will walk you through the main stages, which are always important to cover in the UX design process and that depend on your expertise level or on the experience gained while developing your product. You can go back and redo some of the UX process stages or even try to involve some new ideas in your process during the roadmap to product design.

You have to keep in mind that, as a UX designer, you need to have great communication with other teams that will be involved in the process of product development, such as the development team, the marketing team, stakeholders, and, most importantly, your users.

As we said in the first chapter of this book, if we ask 10 different experts to define the meaning of UX design, you will get 10 different answers. Also, the same goes for the UX process itself. Each company has its own UX process, depending on their project. However, do not panic; we will cover the practices that each UX team should follow for every project. The practices that we'll learn in this chapter include conduct product-planning, product research, and analysis, which are principles in every part of the UX process itself and can be customized based on your project's needs.

The UX process that we will cover in this chapter is as follows:

- Discovery and planning
- UX strategy
- UX research
- Analysis
- Design
- Production

Refer to the following diagram:

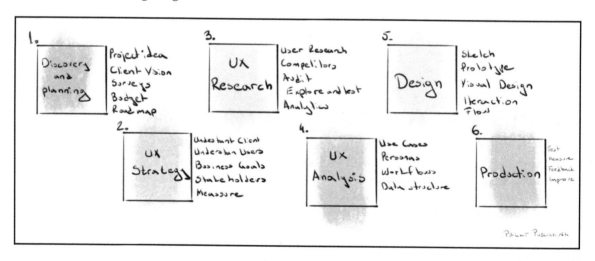

So, let's start explaining the first stage of the UX process.

Discovery and planning

This is the first stage of the UX process where we first touch on/discuss the idea behind our product. It's always a good approach to involve the client here immediately and introduce them to our UX team. Then, together, we can start defining the product scope.

We will start by listening to the client's idea, putting their idea on paper, and trying to understand their idea acutely. In order to understand their idea acutely, we will need to get answers to questions, such as what they want to achieve with this product, their goal, and their targeted audience. This will help the UX team and the client to start giving shape to the product together.

The goal of this stage is that our team should have a clear idea about the product that they will design and develop.

The discovery phase can take up to a few weeks for our team to clearly understand the client idea, their business, their product idea, the problem that they want to solve, and what is important to their users. The UX team's goal here is to be perfectly aligned with the client and have an absolutely clear idea of what the client wants to achieve with this product or service.

During the discovery phase, we, as a UX team, get involved in the client's world. We meet with our client, have conversations with them, and try to understand why and how they came up with this idea. Then, we will try to learn whether they have any specific competitor or other competitors with similar ideas and listen to their stories about why they are involved in this category of business; we do research to better understand our client and their needs. However, more importantly, we need to clearly understand their company's vision and their vision for the product that they want to build.

Understanding the market is also a key part of the discovery phase. One effective way of getting an overview of where your market stands is through surveys. By getting the survey results, we can understand other parts of the market, such as how big our target market is, identify market segments, and define the demographic details of the market and other different market segments. Another good part of having surveys is that we can learn more about our users and their behavior before initiating the designing of the product.

After we finish the process of getting clear goals from the client for their product, we start creating a document with requirements and specifications for starting the product design and development. Now, by having a document in our hand, that lists the clear requirements and specifications for the product, we will have a better idea of timelines, team sizes, budget, basic product sketches, and wireframes. This will go under the planning stage, which, as a UX team, we will be involved in creating in this first stage of the UX process.

So, now we move on to the planning phase of the UX process.

The planning phase

The planning phase is about understanding what you have been asked to do and documenting all the requirements from the discovery phase. Using the results and data that you got in the discovery phase, you can start creating clear documentation for the project, including answers to questions such as:

- What is the required budget for this project?
- What will be your team size?
- What is the timeline of the project and the deadline for each stage of the launch?
- What are the other related resources that need to be involved in the development of this project?

Having documented all that data, now it is even easier for us to provide a final estimation, budget, and expectation to our client.

Here, we can have the following two cases:

- The first case involves defining all the requirements for project development on the UX side, such as timing, budget, resources, and team sizes. Provide all these documents to the client and explain clearly to them what you, as a UX team, will achieve with this and also what you will provide to them. You need to be confident that the tools and techniques you choose will be the right ones to give you the insight you need within the constraints of the project.
  So, in this first scenario, *you* are providing the required time, budget, and resources to the client and asking them to provide what is needed to agree on that road map.

- The second case is where you have a limited time and budget provided by the *client*. However, you have to understand that it is your job, as a UX professional, to deliver the best user experience within the available time and budget. Also, you have to explain to the client that for a better product and better user experience, your suggestion is to go with the preceding approach. The good part of the UX project is that there is always a way you can add value to the project, regardless of the budget.
All clients like to start with a small budget and tight timing, but if you're able to justify why you need a better timeline and budget, it is more likely that you can get it from the client.

The tools and techniques you select are usually determined on the basis of timeline, budget, and the challenges that the project has. It is obvious that a different approach is required to design and develop a microsite from scratch compared to making a large-scale usability implementation on an existing huge web application or a product.

Often, you have to deal with clients and businesses that are unfamiliar with the importance of UX design for their product, and it often can be difficult to get the budget you want to involve users from the first stage of the process. However, it's really important for you, as a UX designer, to teach your client what a good user experience is and why it is always important to involve users from the beginning of product development.

As mentioned in the first chapter of this book, you can point out the following elements to the clients about why involving the user from the beginning is a good idea:

- It will cost less because you can note mistakes from beginning, and it will be easier to fix them right away
- We will get more time by finding what works and what doesn't at the beginning, instead of finding something in the last stage of the product development
- We will see the problems your users have during the first phase of trying to use your product
- We will realize whether the idea is worth creating with our initial approach or whether we need to customize the idea and adopt a different direction to solve that specific problem

In other words, we can say that it is better to test a product at the beginning phase with one user rather than at the end of it with hundreds of users.

The project usually begins with a lot of research into its users and, especially, competitors. This can give us unique insights into what the competitors are doing right or wrong, how they are doing it, and also why specific users are using their products.

Project proposals

Having all the pieces of data in place now will make it a bit easier for us to create a proposal and provide it to the client. It is always challenging to manage projects and client expectations at the same time, but we need to have an appropriate agreement in place, otherwise we will find ourselves in really tough situations later on.

After we have an agreement with the client for the project, it will be easy for both sides to have a bigger picture of how much time this project will consume, the money that will be spent, team sizes, resources, and deadlines. Keep in mind that you should always write proposals before starting a new project.

The sooner we have an approved, and signed, proposal, the sooner we can begin the work, and, more importantly, we begin to get paid for the work now.

The following are the key components that a proposal should have:

- A title page
- A revision history
- The project overview
- The project approach
- The scope of work
- Assumptions
- Deliverables
- Additional costs and fees
- Ownership and rights
- The project pricing
- The payment schedule
- An acknowledgment and sign-off

It is really important to understand that the client is hiring you or your company because they believe that you are an expert in that specific field; however, ensure that you are always clear about the proposal content that you write, such as the estimation, budget, final result, and your client's expectation. Otherwise, if you miss the main parts of their product idea or don't provide the result that was expected, the client will come back to haunt you.

Project objectives and methodologies

Project objectives and methodologies are a key part when you want to kick off the project. It is important for the project itself and for our team, because as a team we want to know the clear goals of this project, its importance, the approach that we will use, and much more. Usually, this part has to be defined by our UX leader, or, in most cases, by a project leader, but it is really important for us to understand this too.

Usually, when we start a project, we must schedule a meeting with the full team, where we give a general overview of the project to the entire team, and by the end of the meeting, we answer the following questions:

- What is the importance of this project to our company?
- How will stakeholders determine the project's success?
- What approach or methodology we will use during the development of this project?
- What is the project timeline, which resources will we be using, and who will be involved in this?
- Do we have any pending information that we need from the client or stakeholder or any other requirement that is necessary before kicking-off the project?
- And always be ready to add new requirements that might appear during the development process that we were not able to recognize in the first discovery phase.

So, your goal for this meeting or session is to have clear objectives for the project.

If you find that the objectives are unclear and some parts will prevent us from starting the project, then we can help the project team understand the business-related context of the project by holding a workshop with them.

Then, during the workshop, we can let them know about the missing part for the project to start, the company's weakness and its strength, and more importantly, your approach, as a UX team, to the project.

Understanding the approach or methodology of a project is a really important part. The project methodology can depend on many things, for example, the structure and location of the project team, the technologies that will be used in the project, and the teams that will be involved in it. Defining this is a project-management responsibility, but it is really important for us–as a part of the UX team–to fully understand the methodologies that we will use for our product; for example, it might be the Waterfall approach, the Agile approach, or some other project-management approach. The main thing is for us to understand the approach so that we will have a clear idea of how to start the UX process and align with other team members, project-management teams, and the client themselves.

The team should be from different areas because everyone will contribute unique ideas.

Their differing viewpoints and opinions will spark the team's creativity. Don't be afraid to switch members between projects.

Now that we're clear on the discovery and planning phase, we can move on to the second phase of the UX process, which is strategy.

The UX strategy

Let me start this part of the chapter with a real-life story. Almost 10 years ago, I joined a company that was working on creating a new mobile application. The idea behind that product belonged to the company's owner. He'd been facing a problem for a long time and had found a way to solve it. He wanted to try to help other people with the same problem through this application. He was so enthusiastic about his idea and was sure that people would need his mobile application and would love using it.

By the time I joined, the product was almost finished and the owner had spent a lot of time and money developing the product. The only things remaining were some enhancements on design and working on the marketing campaign. After the product went live, nobody was actually interested in his product and those who tried it only did so for a short period of time before they deleted the app. So, in other words, nobody was interested in his service and application.

The difficulty was that the owner solved a problem that he was facing and thought that others would need to, too. However, that was the wrong approach. It doesn't matter how good his idea was, he never did the research to check whether other people were facing the same problem and whether they needed that solution, and why his way of solving the problem seems better than what users were already doing.

So, that is where the UX strategy takes place. Before you start building any kind of digital or physical product, you will need to have a strategy first, a plan for your product to succeed.

In the UX process for building a digital product, the strategy begins at the discovery phase. This is where our teams perform deep research related to the idea that was provided by a client to create the idea that we want to build for ourselves.

The UX strategy is the process that we start immediately after we are done with the discovery and planning stages for a project. So, by this, it is clear that we start the UX strategy process before the design or development of the digital product.

We know that UX design covers different disciplines. The UX strategy also stands inside the UX design process, but usually a part of it is also aligned with business strategy. In other words, it can be said that UX strategy is a plan of action for how to find out whether the user experience of a product is aligned with business goals or objectives, as can be seen in the following diagram:

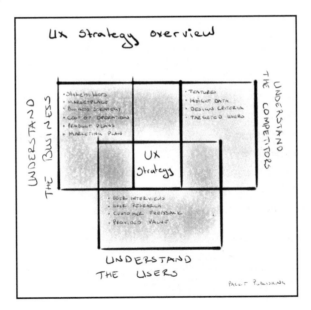

In the UX strategy process, we will need to include all the pieces of data that we have collected from the first phase of the UX process by also adding the business and product goals on it. So, we create the UX strategy as documentation for guidelines and rules that will outline how the design team will try to achieve the business and product goals.

However, we have to understand that the UX strategy itself depends on a number of different factors, such as:

- Understanding our client's business
- Understanding our competitors
- Understanding our users

Understanding the client's business

We touched upon understanding the client's business in the first phase of the UX process. This is essential for the UX strategy; we have to understand how our design can impact our client's business results.

To do that, we should obtain answers to questions such as:

- Where is the client positioned on the marketplace?
- Where will their product be positioned on the marketplace?
- What is the cost of operating? What can impact their product?
- What is the competitor doing, more or less, that is different than us? What does the customer value in our competitors' products?
- What changes are we going to make with this product, and how will this help our customers?
- How can we achieve a steady rise in customers?

Also, we should obtain answers to the technical side of the questions, as follows:

- How do the technologies that we will use to create this digital product drive our customers' attention?
- How will our design of this digital product grab the attention of customers?
- What can we design better, or which feature can we add to make life easier for our customers in comparison with our competitors' products?
- What kind of promotional approach can our marketing team use for our product?

In many cases, if the UX leaders do not have answers to these kinds of questions, or, even worse, they don't ask these kinds of questions at the beginning of project, then we have a problem–not just us as a UX team but also the product itself can get stuck in an endless cycle of creating one user interface design after another, for which they will provide the design by guesswork without having done the proper research.

When this happens, you can refer to the story that I mentioned in the preceding section–in the end, he failed because he didn't have a product strategy and didn't do research to check whether his idea was worth his time.

So, the question now is, how do we align the UX design with our company's or client's company's business strategy?

Well first we will need to have some kind of information, or, better, documents that will help us to have a clear understanding of the company business strategy:

- Annual operating plan
- Marketing plan
- New product plans
- Strategic-gap analysis
- Sales projections
- Supply-management plan and value-management plan
- Competitive analysis and strategies
- Industry analysis

The hardest part is getting access to all these documents. The owners of these documents will complain or may resist giving you or any UX team access to them, and they will have more questions regarding the use of these documents for the UX of the product. However, these are good resources for a problem that is worth solving. We, as UX professionals, have to explain to them that having access to these kinds of document will help us to improve our UX process and in producing the final product.

Usually, this part is hard at the beginning, but once the owner gets involved with us by meeting several times, they start to understand the value that they are providing and later may start inviting you to participate with them as a collaborator rather than just a consumer of the information. When you arrive at this stage, you can be sure that you have arrived really close to the goal of aligning the UX design with the business strategy.

After achieving the alignment of the UX design with the business strategy, for us as a UX team, the company vision will be really clear. The next step for us is to convert the resources that we collected and that company vision that we understood into a reality.

Now that we have made the connection between the business strategy and our UX road map, it will be easy for us to get people's attention and our UX strategy plan will be clearer.

Understanding our competitors

Analyzing our competitors gives us a better perspective on the UX strategy and what kinds of resources we will need to compete with that specific category of the market.

Creating a competition analysis is not easy because it is really hard to know their financial budget, financial results, features and, in some cases, it is even hard to know who our competitors are.

However, in any case, it is important for the UX team to understand the competition and get as much information as we can that is related to this:

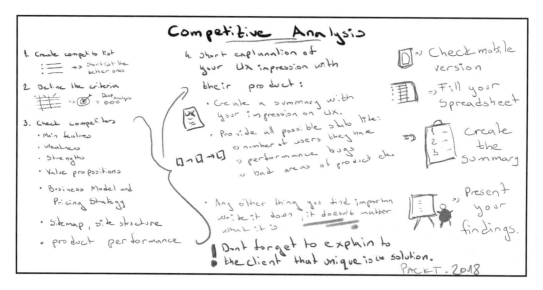

Understanding our customers

From the previous image the *Understanding our competitors* section, we have already got the basic information about who our users are from the discovery and planning stage. Don't get confused, it may seem like we are repeating the steps, but each UX process step is connected with another one, and, in some cases, you cannot prevent jumping back and forth through UX process stages, until you gather all the needed information to finalize a specific phase of the process.

All the UX process phases are connected with each other, almost for every step you will need to do some kind of analysis and research; it just depends on the level that you will need it for and the extent of your focus on it. To connect all the dots and have a clear understanding, analysis and research are required.

It is true that, nowadays, one of the biggest problems is that customers are losing interest in products quickly; this is because the business or corporation itself is losing sight of their customers. This usually happens because of the way they are organized, and that is the part that makes it hard for them to understand the customers' needs and expectations.

It is obvious that a lot of companies today try to do in-depth research about their users as much as they can. However, one thing that we cannot predict or know is how our customers' behavior with our digital product will change in the future. That is why we not only have to do research and take a look at the usability side, we also we need to try to understand how our digital world can change in the future.

In the UX strategy stage, you will need to keep in mind the following key components, because these are general things that you need to provide during this phase:

- Collect as much customer data as you can so that you will be able to guide the design team with those pieces of information
- Ensure that your UX team is aligned with the company's business strategy
- Understand your competitors, the market need, and the size of the target market
- Establish a road map that includes a prioritization schema and proposed schedule to introduce new features and capabilities
- Develop relationships with business leads across the company and explain to senior executives why user experience capabilities are a strategic asset to the organization
- Try to discover your UX strategy framework

Discovering your own UX strategy framework

Each UX team or UX professional has their own way of doing a UX strategy. As long as you can understand the needs of your client, organization and user by keeping in mind related parts that can be connected with them, you will be able to create your own UX strategy framework.

The best example of this topic is *The four tenets of UX strategy,* which was created by *Jaime Levy* in 2015:

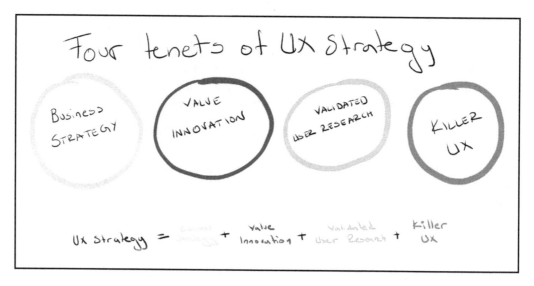

Her formula for the UX strategy is based on the following four tenets:

- Business strategy
- Value-innovation
- Validated user research
- Killer UX design

Business strategy is the top-line vision of the company; this is why the company exists in the first place. It's a way of defining the strategy for creating company profit or generating profit by a specific product that they have. We discussed this topic in more detail in the previous pages, where we explained different ways of understanding the business and its importance to the UX strategy.

Value-innovation is the part where the difference for a digital product is happening. After a lot of research and data collection, you will bring to the market an amazing product that people will enjoy using since it provides something that your competitors don't, or some features that were missing in products already available in the market. Value-innovation can usually happen on existing products.

Validated user research confirms the assumptions that you have made about the design. You try to track whether your product is on the right path and validate every time that you are providing value to the users. Drawing from experience, when dealing with senior management with outlandish product/feature recommendations, validating user research is key to focusing on the right problems and making decisions. A useful way to do this is to bring the various stakeholders to user research and testing sessions. This way, everyone involved can see for themselves how a product/feature performs in front of real users. This collaboration will help organically build agreement on the value innovation and any changes that follow.

In the **Killer UX** design tenet, the designers try to provide value by taking the following actions:

- Working collaboratively with stakeholders and teammates during the idea's inception
- Determining the key features that are critical to your product
- Learning everything about the existing market space to identify UX opportunities that can be exploited
- Speaking directly with potential and existing power users to discover and validate the product's primary utility
- Weaving the UX through all touch points–online and offline–to enable an experience that is frictionless

As I was saying at the beginning of this section, everyone has their own way or process for doing the UX strategy right. In this section, I tried to help you understand it better through the example of the four tenets of UX strategy by Jaime Levy, which shows us how to create our own UX strategy framework.

I usually go with the first approach, by trying to understand the three components mentioned at the beginning of UX strategy: understanding the business, the competitors, and the users. Through this strategy, I am able to define my own framework for doing a proper UX strategy.

Before moving to the next phase of the UX process, keep in mind that the UX strategy is a way of thinking. It doesn't mean creating a perfect plan, it is more about researching what is out there in our market category, analyzing opportunities, running different test cases or case studies, failing, and then learning. The best way to learn something is by failing smartly, learning from the mistakes, and moving your team in the right direction.

UX research

In the user research stage, we focus on understanding the product itself first, the user's behavior with the product, their needs, their pains, and their motivations for using our products.

Research is the key part of UX process because it prevents us from designing the wrong product. Also, research is considered as one of the key areas of UX itself because it is involved in all the stages of the UX process, so depending on the need for informations on a specific stage, we have to conduct research as many time as required.
Imagine that we design a product that nobody wants to use just because we didn't do the research; all our hard work, time, and money will be wasted.

There are tons of reasons why UX research is important; the following are some:

- It removes assumptions from the design process
- We will have a lot of data to back up our design process and work
- It will save our company and clients valuable time and money if it is done properly
- We don't have to go back and forth fixing the mistakes that could have been avoided from the beginning, because the later in the product design process we discover that our assumptions are wrong, the more time, money, and resources it will cost us to fix it

When our research is done correctly, we will quickly discover the right requirements for the right people at the right time, because research affects our entire UX process from the conception of an idea up to the product's delivery.

In the UX research stage, we have to provide reliable data insights that will help our product teams to make decisions. A comprehensive insight into the data can help us to build better, more useful, and resilient products for our customers.

The UX research phase is a proven and correct way to get more insight, pieces of information, and correct measurements to create a successful design solution.

There are a lot of different methods and techniques that can be used during the UX research process, but we can separate these methods based into two groups:

- Quantitative research
- Qualitative research

Consider the following diagram:

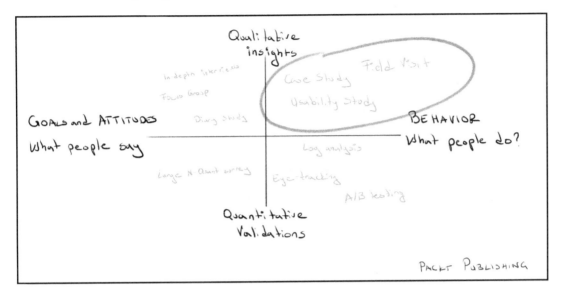

Quantitative research is research that can be measured numerically. Usually, here we are talking about the data that we understand and is valuable to us.

We have it on a statistical manner, because we gathered this data from people's actions when using our product.

This data includes how many times they clicked on a specific button, how many times they interacted with our call to the action button, and which part of our product they were using more.

We can get this kind of information by including third-party software or even analytics tools, such as Google Analytics, and in the end, we can see the complete statistics on what users have been doing when using our product.

Qualitative research—often referred to as *soft* research—helps us to understand why people are doing the things they do. Usually, this kind of research happens via interviews or conversations with the users. For example, why they are switching our product on or off that way, why they cannot find that specific thing that they were looking for, and how they interact with our product.

The key to performing better qualitative research is observation–always observe the user's actions in relation to your product.

As per the Nielsen Norman Group, the UX research process can also be separated into four different stages, as follows:

- Discover
- Explore
- Test
- Listen

Each different research methodology falls into one of the preceding stages:

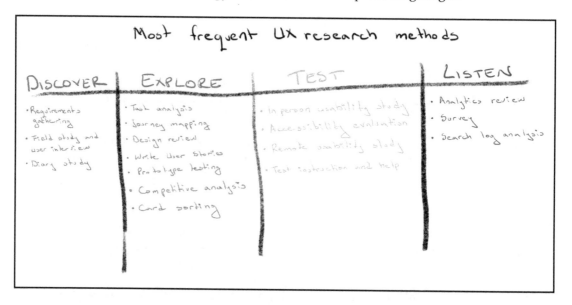

A good guide for selecting a specific UX research method is by knowing at the initial stage what you want to achieve by the end of the research, otherwise you will be gathering all that data without a specific goal.

The discover stage

In the discover stage, we, as a team, will try to figure out what pieces of the product we are going to build are missing, what information we need to get started, and what people actually want our product to solve for them.

In this stage, it is important that we validate and remove the assumptions, and then present correct and accurate data to our team.

Do not make the wrong conclusion. This stage is not the same as the first stage where we were just doing discovery and planning. In the first stage, we were trying to get an initial idea about the product from the client before we start planning for it; here, we are doing deeper research about the product itself, involving real users.

Usually, things to do during this stage are: conduct field studies, meet our users, have conversations with them, note their troubles with our product, watch how they solve the problem, ask what they need, and, most importantly, observe and listen to them.

Also, it is a good idea during this stage to perform interviews with our category of users and run diary studies to understand our user's information needs and behaviors.

It is also good to interview the stakeholders to understand their business requirements, and interview other department teams as well by getting some answers from them, such as what is their most frequent problem, their worst problem, and what makes them angry or upset during the process of solving that specific problem.

Earlier, I mentioned that there are different methodologies that fall under each of these steps. In the discover phase, the top UX research methods most frequently used are as follows:

- Field study
- Diary study
- User interview
- Stakeholder interview

Field study

We conduct interviews with a real user in their space environment. By doing this, we are not only observing their actions, but also getting a better understanding of what kinds of user we are creating the product for. Here, we usually ask open-ended questions and extend them with additional questions to get to know the user's behavior better:

Diary study

A diary study, often referred to as Camera study, is a method where users log their daily activities to give us better insight into their behavior and needs. This method can be performed both by recording user behavior using a camera or by users writing their daily activities on paper:

User interviews

User interviews are a great way to extract information from users to understand the user experience, the product's usability, and ideation. Interviewing users requires a lot of effort and planning. Depending on how extensive the research is, you might spend several weeks preparing for the sessions, several days talking to your users, and several hours capturing and organizing your notes.

Always give proper instructions to your tester, answer their question with a question when you run a test, and observe them as much as you can:

Stakeholder interviews

Usually, we need to interview the stakeholders to gather more information about the business strategy and understand the business requirements and constraints.

Stakeholder interviews can be considered as a really strong and powerful tool that can give us a lot of insights, data, and information about the category of the business that we will be working with. Also, it will help us to understand the business goals and stakeholder objectives.

You need to know that a stakeholder can be a person, group, or organization that has an interest in or concern with an organization or company that we are working with.

Understanding the value of our business and the business market is an essential component for any product if we want to succeed. Stakeholder interviews allow us, as product designers, to learn more about the business and market that we are working on.

In order to conduct a successful interview, we need to plan, prepare our field guide, conduct our interviews, and, finally, document our findings.

The explore stage

In the explore stage, we use exploration methods to understand the problem we want to solve, design the scope, and address user needs properly. In this stage, we compare our product and its features with that of our competitors, do the design review, create user personas, and write user stories.

The following UX research methods fall into this stage:

- Competitive analysis
- Design review
- Persona-building
- Task analysis
- Journey-mapping
- Prototype feedback and testing
- Writing user stories
- Card-sorting

Competitive analysis

This method is used to determine how our product is performing as compared to our competitor's product. The comparison can be on different aspects, for example, based on the ranking standing of products, their features, their content, or even the design elements across the product itself. We compare in-depth with a few competitors who are in the same market as us by looking at their strengths and weaknesses, the trends that they are following, and the patterns and other things that they are providing differently from us. Take a look at the following diagram:

Simple Competitor review table					
Competitors	Chat feature	Free or Paid	Direct Messaging	Extra features	Ux Impression
TRELLO	NO	FREE	NO	Drag n' drop	... %
ASANA	YES	BOTH	YES	Multi teams	... %
JIRA	YES	PAID	Yes using plugin like: HIPCHAT	Advance API	... %

Packt ...

Design review

We mentioned in the preceding UX research method that we will check our competitor's strengths and weaknesses. This is common across all markets–so, while doing this, we have to understand that even our product has its strengths and weaknesses, but using the UX review method, we can help the team identify the weak spots in their product. The goal of any UI/UX review is to study goals, objectives, and behaviors to check whether they align with the company's intended goals. User experience pertains to user behaviors and how people interface with a website or web application.

Persona-building

The purpose of personas is to create reliable and realistic representations of your key audience segments for reference. These representations should be based on qualitative and quantitative user research and web analytics. Remember, your personas are only as good as the research behind them. We will go deeper into creating a user persona in Chapter 5, *User Profiles/User Personas*. Take a look at the following diagram:

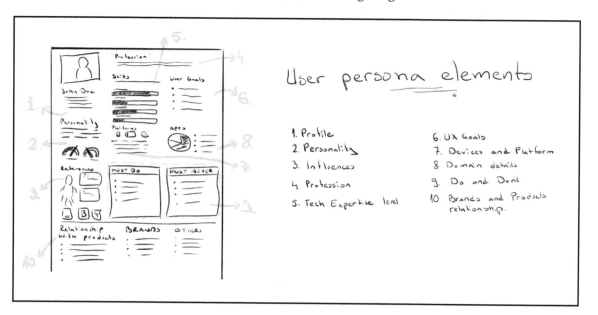

Task analysis

Task analysis is the process of learning about ordinary users by observing them in action to understand in detail how they perform their tasks and achieve their intended goals. To put it simply, task analysis is a step-by-step analysis of the user's task, from their perspective.

Journey-mapping

The journey-mapping UX research method is a visualization of the process by which how people go through a number of steps to accomplish a specific goal. Usually, here, we try to understand their needs and pain points during the process when our user tries to finish that specific task.

In other words, journey-mapping starts by compiling a series of user goals and actions into a timeline skeleton. To begin, a journey map has two essential components when visualizing a user experience:

- **Touchpoints**: Also called actions, this is what our customer is doing and/or what is needed to get to the next step.
- **Categories**: This encompasses touch points and breaks up an experience into simple steps, as shown in the following diagram:

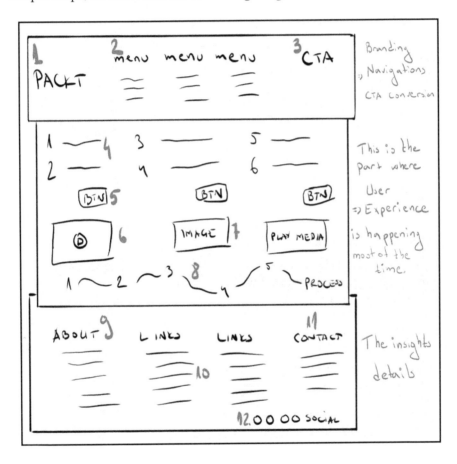

Prototype feedback and testing

Once you've built your prototypes based on the ideas you and your team generated, it's time to gather feedback from the people you are testing these with. Optimizing how you gather feedback–and therefore learning from your prototypes and users–is essential to help you save time and resources in the prototype and test stages of the UX design process.

When we finish the prototype, it is always important to review it first, then, if needed, we can redefine the missing or incorrect parts and redo the prototype. A simple example is provided in the following diagram:

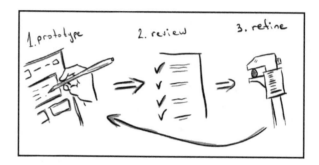

Writing user stories

At its core, a user story describes something that the user wants to accomplish using the software product. User stories originated as a part of the Agile and Scrum development strategies, but, for designers, they mainly serve as reminders of user goals and a way to organize and prioritize how each screen is designed.

For Agile product teams, a user story is the gold standard for communicating product requirements to all team members. They're brief, specific, and quickly understood. The following are some ways to test the user story:

- Is it something a real user would say?
- Does it help you to design and prioritize?
- Does it unnecessarily constrain possible solutions?

Take a look at the following diagram:

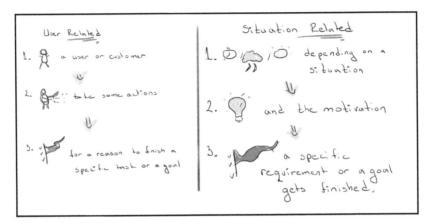

Card-sorting

Card-sorting is a method used to help design or evaluate the information architecture of a site. In a card-sorting session, participants organize topics into categories that make sense to them, and they may also help you label these groups. To conduct a card sort, you can use actual cards, pieces of paper, or one of the many online card-sorting software tools.

Card-sorting is a great way to become familiar with information architecture and user-centered design. It's cheap, reliable, and easy to set up. This is a technique where people take a bunch of stuff and organize it into groups that make sense to them. You analyze the grouping to create an information architecture.

Card-sorting is typically done in three groups of five to six people. You can do it independently, but it is better to do it in groups, especially where there is a large amount of data:

The test stage

We use testing and validation methods to check the design during development and beyond to ensure that our product works well.

UX research methods usually involved in this stage are as follows:

- Qualitative usability testing (in-person or remote)
- Benchmark testing
- Accessibility evaluation

Qualitative usability testing

Usability testing is a widely used research method used to collect detailed and direct qualitative user feedback about our product.

It's as simple as inviting a user (or a potential user) from your target audience and showing them our product, giving them specific tasks, and monitoring what they are doing.

If you do it right, you will get a bunch of useful and actionable insights. You will be surprised by how often the feature you consider to be one of the most straightforward things on your site turns out to be the most confusing for your target audience. That's the point here–to see and feel the actual troubles of your users.

Benchmark testing

Benchmarking is the process of testing a product's progress over time. This testing method is not cheap, but it's efficient when you need to polish your product on all stages. This can be progress through different iterations of a prototype, across different versions of an application, and even across different sites–yours and your competitors. A lot of companies like to run benchmarking studies because they show actual data as it changes over time. It adds a quantitative dimension to the qualitative research you have already been doing, which can drive home your findings and add weight to your suggestions.

Accessibility evaluation

Accessibility is an important facet of the user experience and the searcher experience is one of its subsets.

Web accessibility refers to the inclusive practice of removing barriers that prevent interaction with, or access to, websites by people with disabilities. When sites are correctly designed, developed, and edited, all users have equal access to information and functionality.

The listening stage

The listening stage during the complete UX design process will help us to understand existing problems and look for new issues, because we will be gathering data and monitoring the incoming information related to our product or market trends all the time.

To execute the listening stage, we need to perform the following:

- Surveys
- Search-log analysis
- Usability-bug review
- **Frequently Asked Questions (FAQ)** review

Surveys

Online surveys are commonly used by marketers, product managers, strategists, and others to gather feedback. There is a big chance that you have already been involved in one of them yourself before, but, most of the time, they are poorly executed.
Surveys are increasingly becoming a more accepted tool for UX practitioners. And for using this type of method, the cost is really low, even free in most cases, because we have Google Forms and other software that is free to use and no effort to learn them is required.

Creating a great survey is like designing a great user experience. They can be a waste of time and money if the audience, or the user, is not at the center of the process. Designing for your user leads to the gathering of more useful and reliable information.

Search-log analysis

The analysis of site-search logs is one of the biggest missed opportunities in UX research. Much emphasis is placed on external search optimization (getting the visit), but less attention is paid to on-site-search optimization (serving the visitor).
Web-wide search engines can provide a website's search statistics–that's the outside view of your search traffic and shows which terms and websites drive traffic to your site.

Usability-bug review

Recruit people for future research and testing and actively encourage people to join your pool of volunteer testers. Offer incentives for participation and make signing up easy to do via your website, your newsletter, and other points of contact.

UX analysis

UX analysis is another stage of the UX process. It helps us to measure the interaction between a user and user interface; often, in this case, it can be an application, a digital product, or even the design itself.

You can do UX analysis in different ways and using different approaches. We covered some of them, such as competitor analysis and task analysis.

When we are creating a UX analysis, it is always important to keep in mind all the aspects that are connected with the product we want to build, such as:

- User perspective
- Business perspective
- Expert team's perspective
- Technical perspective

Refer to the following diagram:

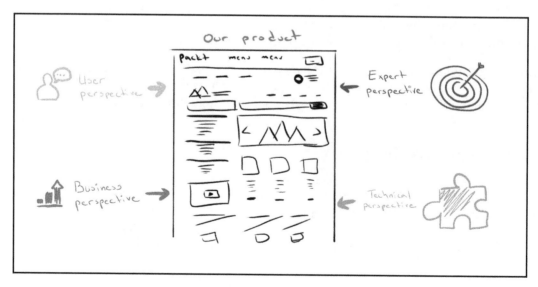

The UX analysis includes different methods that vary in terms of formality and user participation. Then, by combining the results of these different tests, we will be able to create an overview of who our community is, as follows:

- Who our customers are
- Where our user category is
- What information they need and seek
- How they prefer to access that information

Often, during the UX analysis phase, when we analyze users, it leads us to change the product design or its features, especially on the interface side.
The part where we improve our product design or mobile and web-user interface to have better user engagement and make the product work for them is called the UI design; we will discuss this more in the next stage of the UX process, which is the design part.
Analyzing the user experience leads us to new design changes, but those changes help us to engage customers with our product, make them use our product often, and also lead us to other new customers.

The following are some of the methods used for measuring the UX analysis:

- A/B testing
- Heat-mapping
- Research group

If we have to deal with a digital product, such as a mobile or web application, we can use external tools or services, such as Google Analytics, Hubspot, Moz, or CrazeyEgg, and tons of other tools available on the market.

Using A/B testing, heat-mapping, or other analytical tools, we can measure how users are interacting with our product through the statistical information that will be provided by that specific method.

We have to display the things that are important to interact with in our product. The key here is not to add tons of buttons, features, and possibilities, but to provide the elements that make sense for users; take a look at the following remarkable quote from Steve Jobs:

> *I know you have a thousand ideas for all the cool features iTunes could have. So do we. But we don't want a thousand features. That would be ugly. Innovation is not about saying "YES" to everything. It's about saying "NO" to all but the most crucial features.*

If we don't focus on our main goal of why we started the product in the first place, by adding too many features, we will create too much noise for our users. We have to avoid saying yes to every feature, focus on the main one, and work hard on it. If we add many features, we will reduce the flexibility and increase the complexity, and it will take more time for the user to understand it, and, in other words, the product will be complicated.

Research is a key value in the UX process, but in order to use the data that we found during the research phase in a proper way, we have to analyze and prepare it for the team. Analysis is the process where we, as researchers, identify the patterns in research, propose other possible solutions, and make new recommendations.

Sometimes, during analysis, we will need to include techniques for creating different personas and different scenarios, and describe the user's behaviors in detail by providing different graphs or chart statistics to our team. Conducting research is an important part, but we have to understand that the research itself has value only if we share it; if we keep it for ourselves, no analysis can be done related to that research and no help can be provided to the team.

User analysis

To create a great user experience, we have to start by understanding our users. However, only knowing who they are is not enough. We need to dive deeper into their motivations, fears, mentality, and behavior.

User analysis will guide us in finding the answers to our questions about end users' tasks and goals so that these findings can help us make decisions about creating and designing a better product.

By analysis, we will be able to identify roles and define characteristics that aren't always possible through market research, such as knowledge, state of mind, comfort with similar products, use cases and environments, and frequency of use. With this data, it will be much easier for us to do feature changes and improve the user's experience with our product.

By doing a proper user analysis, we will have the following benefits:

- **Better product:** We will have a better product because we also involved the user by understanding the business objectives, which will always result in a product that will work better for their specific purpose.

- **Cheaper to fix the problem:** It will help us to face the reality of our product and change things that won't work while we still have the product only on paper. Making changes to wireframes or prototypes is much cheaper than trying to fix something technical on a live product.
- **Easy to use is a common requirement:** Customers often use the terms *usability* and *user experience* when describing qualities they seek in products. Therefore, user analysis drives our product to have better selling points.

User analysis will allow us to create a better product that will work for them; if we ignore user analysis, then the product wasn't created for the users–it means that we lost time and resources creating the product that we wanted and not the one the users did. Users don't care if our product has tons of features, or if it can do a thousand things; they just need a product that works for them.

To clarify this process, and to not get you more confused, I'll try to keep it clear: UX analysis is the phase where you start to analyze all the data and insights that you got from the previous stages, especially from the research phase, and convert them into a clear document or specification to have an understandable meaning for the whole team.

I hope that it is now clear and that you understand the difference between all the stages that we've explained so far about UX research methods and the UX process itself, and how to analyze data so that you can start implementing it right away in your design process. Use it as early as possible and as often as possible in your process of product design to provide the benefits of a better user experience to your users.

Design

Here comes the exciting part of our product development. After a lot of research and collecting valuable data for our team, now we can start thinking about designing the product itself.

In the design phase, we conduct a meeting with all the other teams in our company, including managers, the marketing team, the design team, developers, sales people, user support, and any other team inside our organization. During this meeting, we unpack all the knowledge and research data that we have collected during the previous UX process stages and show them to the team.

We show to the team all the information that we have collected so far, with no exceptions, as follows:

- We start the meeting with a general presentation from the project manager and UX leader by explaining to the other teams the idea of the business and the opportunities within it.
- Then, we start showing them all the competitive research that we have done so far and explain how and what our competitors are doing differently and what our approach will be.
- We explain the problem that users have in carrying out the specific task, and how we will try to solve that problem with our product by showing to them the user research that we have done.
- A detailed overview, approach, and a walk-through for our proposed solution will be presented to them.
- We will provide the created user personas to the team members so that they can also try to understand what kinds of user we have to deal with and for whom we are solving the problem with our product.
- All other related analytical data from the UX research phase, such as surveys, field study, and user interviews, will be shown and everyone will be given access to it.
- The measure of success is the business metrics that we will try to achieve during this process and by creating this product.

This meeting is really important because every team needs to be on the same page with the UX team and with the product that we will create. This will make the process easier because, at a later stage if any team needs help from other team, everything will be easier because every team has a general idea of the product that we are going to build.

In the correct order, the stages of Design phase from UX process will be like this:

- Concept, sketching, and flows
- Wireframes and prototyping
- Visual design and interactions
- Documentation
- Development

Concept, sketching, and flows

At the beginning of this phase, you need to check whether you have enough data to start the design to achieve your main goal for the product or whether there is still something missing. The goal is to have enough data to make it easier for you to take any decision to start the design of the product.

When it comes to the concept, you can use different methods, such as storyboards, project briefs, or project outlines, to start sketching your product design ideas.

Sketching is one of the easiest ways to visualize your concept ideas, which will allow you to see different design solutions before you decide on the concept you want to go with.

As UX professionals, you will probably sketch every day, no matter which phase of the UX process you are in. Some other professionals who work in UX fields like to start immediately by creating a prototype on the computer because they think it is easier, but you need to avoid doing this because it is not the best way to visually solve the problem. As I mentioned, the stage of the UX process doesn't matter; if it is needed to provide a visual idea of the new digital product through storyboard workflows or user flows, the more efficient way would be doing it through sketching.

You don't need to have perfect sketching skills; as long as they are understandable and clear, everything is fine, because the more often you do it, the better you will get. By sketching, we try to express our way of thinking to solve a specific problem.

Think of sketching as a form of visual communication that will help others understand the visualization that you have put down on the paper.

Depending on your needs, you can involve other things during sketching as well, such as sticky notes for more explanation on a specific area of your sketch if more information is needed. You can use a ruler if you have to deal with more advanced problems or for small details that you need to involve in your sketch.

The technique of sketching is not used only by UX designers, but also by other team members, such as project managers, developers, or business analyst, who explore their ideas for their own needs in their area by doing different sketches.

Creating good sketches will make your life easier by having a better understanding of the design problem that you are trying to solve, and you will also save time. But also it is important to be aware that this type of method is helpful for basic prototyping and brainstorming on early stages of product development mostly, because in later stages, the product gets bigger and more complicated, so to re-do prototypes we need to use prototyping tools instead of paper. Whenever you start creating the sketches, don't force yourself to immediately come up with a final result; draw some flows first, brainstorm your idea, and then put all of those things together, similar to the following:

Another good thing that you can do during the sketching phase is to brainstorm at the same time since sketching is a key element when you have to deal with design brainstorming as well.

Feel free to use any kind of sketching technique, as long as your goal is to provide a design with a great user experience in the end, because you can get as many idea as you want when you sketch, and, in the end, you can choose the best one to start the wireframe process.

Wireframes and prototyping

Wireframes are usually referred to as a visual guideline that explains our digital product structure, such as its hierarchy and its key elements. Usually, wireframes are mostly used when we are creating a web or mobile application; the UI designer will take them as a reference for creating prototypes and visual design.

During the process of creating wireframes, we also start connecting the dots, or in our case the screens, by creating the product flow.

By flow, we mean what will happen on each screen when our user interacts with it, what their next step will be, and where the user will land after any action they take on that specific screen.

Most of the time, we start creating wireframes by sketching them on paper. So, during that phase, we will also try to figure out the flow of each screen so that we have a better understanding of the steps and actions that can be taken when using it.

Design flow describes the processes and graphical assets needed to make a working product.

There are different tools available today, which allow you to convert your paper wireframes into digital ones, such as SketchApp and Balsamiq, or even more advanced design tools such as Adobe Illustrator.

It is obviously clear that we need to start the wireframing process at the beginning stage of design, where our product didn't have a proper structure and the design ideas were only on paper.

Also, another benefit of wireframes is that they can give the client an overview of what their product will eventually look like. This way, we are also removing an issue that could happen later with a client arguing about our design elements and why they were created or placed that way. The following screenshot is an example that presents wireframes screens, how they are connected together, and their flow; usually this process is known as screen-flows:

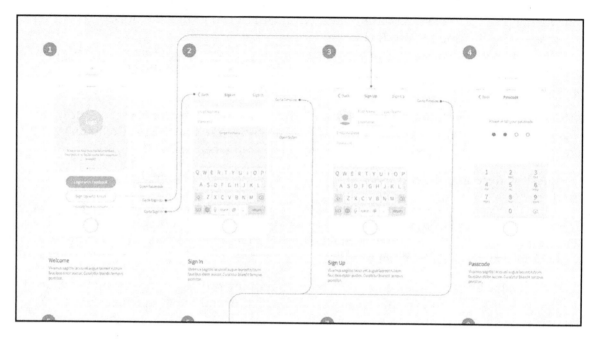

Wireframes stand mostly on low-fidelity groups of prototyping, which generally have a limited function and limited interaction compared to high-fidelity ones where prototypes take place. After wireframes and interactive wireframes, a higher requirement stands for prototype. The prototype stands on high-fidelity groups because they are more interactive and fit better on the final user interface.

We create wireframes mostly to get a clear idea of structure and the visual hierarchy and also to experience interacting with them to get a better understanding of both areas, that is, how the product looks and feels when using it. The prototype is usually referred to as a simulation of the product and is commonly created using clickable wireframes.

For creating wireframes and prototypes, we can use different kinds of tool, such as Adobe Experience Design, InVision, Balsamiq, UXPin, Sketch, or Figma.

Here, it's important for you to understand only the general meaning of wireframes and prototypes because we will go into them in detail later in `Chapter 8`, *Wireframes and Prototyping*, which will focus only on creating wireframes and prototypes.

Never move to the next step until you finish all the wireframes, product screens, and their flow. You need to have a clear idea of how many screens you have inside your product, how they are connected with each other, and how the user can navigate through them.

Visual design and interactions

Here's where a design comes to life: how the screen looks, how it behaves or interacts, and more.

We create a visual design by combining both sides, UI design and graphic design, using different elements of design itself, such as colors, types, images, and form, to create and improve our product's user experience.

This part is mostly done by a UI designer. Unlike a UX designer, who is involved in the overall process of the product, a UI designer is a person who creates the visible part of our product and how the product is laid out. The UI designer is responsible for designing each screen or element of our product based on the data that we provide to them.
Besides this, another side that UI designers are responsible for is creating a cohesive style guide for our product and ensuring that a consistent design language is applied across the product.

Tools that can be used to create a UI design include Photoshop, Sketch, Illustrator, Fireworks, and Figma. It all depends on the UI designer's preference. But what's important is to achieve high-fidelity mockup results, as shown in the following:

One general responsibility of the UI designer is to produce high-quality visual designs, from the concept, sketching, and wireframe stage up to its execution. It depends on what kind of digital product we are building; if it is an application, the UI designer has to provide various solutions for visual design, including all different devices, such as desktop, web, or mobile, by providing the assets as well, such as icons, graphics, and other needed graphical materials.

Another key part during the creation of UI design or visual design is interaction. You experience interaction every day on your mobile devices, for example, when you pull down your mail to refresh it to check whether you have any new emails, or when you swipe left or right to access a specific action or menu. That is the work of an UI interaction designer. Compared to a visual designer, who usually creates static visual assets for us, an UI interaction designer creates animation inside our product.

The interaction designer has to deal with what an interface does after a user performs an action on it, such as touch, swipe, and shake. A properly-done interaction becomes an integral part of the user interface by providing a static visual design with a better understanding of how to use the product.

Tools that interaction designers use to create animations include Adobe After Effects, Core Composer, Principle, Framer Js, and Flinto.

Similar to wireframes and prototypes, we will go deeper into visual design and interactions in Chapter 7, *Visual Design Principles and Processes*, where I will guide you through which tools to use and how to create a visual design from scratch. Here, these are explained so that you can understand the basics and the design stage, so bear with me.

Documentation

The documentation stage is the part where you realize that after all these long processes, it is time to create the full documentation to finally start developing our product.
In this part, we will create all the style guidelines to help our development team, especially the frontend one, to have a clear idea of our design elements, the colors that we should use, the design layout, fonts, assets, and other elements that we create during all those phases, especially on the visual design part.

This documentation will include other assets as well, for example, what animation will happen on a specific area of our product when the user interacts with it and what should or should not be visible to a specific range of users.

Having all these things documented in a very clear way will help the developers to clearly understand the product we are going to build. Also, then they can decide on the different frontend frameworks that they will use during the development stage.
For example, for CSS frameworks, they may choose bootstrap, foundation, skeleton, material design, or even create their own from scratch.
Based on the complexity of the project, they can also decide which JavaScript framework to choose, such as Angular, ReactJS, and VueJS, or even–if the product is really simple–the jQuery library.

Designers nowadays upload their complete work via tools such as Zeplin, Sympli, or InVision Appare after finishing their design.

By uploading your final design in these kinds of tools developers will have a much easier life, because they can access all the main things in one place. It doesn't matter what it is as long it is related to that visual design. They will be able to access all the different colors, even customize whether they want HEX colors, RGB, or RGBA, download all the images or other assets, have specific measurements that they need, CSS styles, and tons of other features.

Refer to the following screenshot to have a better understanding of what a developer will be able to get from designing with the Zeplin tool:

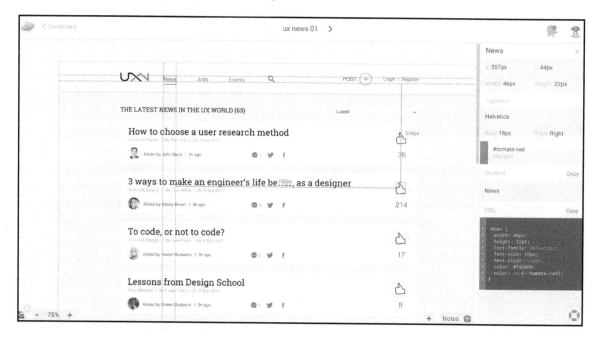

After this phase, we are ready to go on to the development of the product. You have come a long way, but things are just getting more exciting here, so let's dig deeper into all those product-design creation parts.

Development

Finally, after all the research, documentation, workflows, design, and interactions, the time has come to bring our product to life.

By starting the development process, we have to improve our communication skills with all teams around our company, because communication is the key skill for creating a great user experience.

The development team is now responsible for creating a functional implementation of our product interface. During the previous phases of our design process, we created all the required information for this team; now, we hand over static visual design and the other documentation to them so that they can translate the designs into working and interactive experiences.

All these assets are provided to the frontend development team, and they start coding the visual interaction that the interaction designer has come up with.

The tools or skills used during the frontend development stage are HTML, CSS, and JavaScript. The development team will share their work with us and other departments on each screen implementation.

Also, they will gather feedback for each part of the product that they have developed, and if it is necessary, they will implement the required changes to their code.

During the development stage, the product designer plays a really important role. Their job is to be generally involved in the process and provide any answers about the look and feel of the product that is being created.

During the process of development, various design roles can be very fluid; for example, some designers will be expected to do interaction design, the UI designer will create new visual designs needed by the development team, someone will be involved in updating the documentation on every new change that we make, and even, in some cases, they will be involved in small amounts of coding if we have a full stack designer in-house.

By having all these different teams and tools involved in the development stage, it will be easier to think harder and come up with better ideas for how to delight our users.

The trend on the part of UX teams to involve different areas inside of it, such as providing colorful designs, better product performance, a lot of motion UIs, and different coding approaches, is increasing rapidly; that is why, in the upcoming years, we will have even more delightful products for our users and give them a better experience when they are using the products.

Whether we are using light tools and a light process during our development stage, the goal of each UX design is to come up with a great product for our users. During development, we can evolve our UX process because even the product itself will evolve over time.

So far, the goal of this chapter was to clearly explain all the dots in the UX process to you; now, we will touch on each part in a more comprehensive way and give you a bigger picture of the complete product design and development, and the required tools and skills.

Production

This is the last phase of the UX process and will continue till the product's UX process lifecycle exists.

The production phase actually can start with the design of the UX process, especially when we start developing our product, since that is the phase where we start giving feedback for a product which we can visually see, touch, and feel.

From my own experience, usually I like to separate the production phase into two parts:

- Beta release
- Live product

By doing this, it makes it easier for me to leverage the design and do quality assurance and usability testing before the live release of the product.

When the product goes live, the UX team and other teams involved start generating different documents and statistics about the product by measuring the performance that our product is offering.

We can collect data in different ways, as follows:

- **Collecting performance reports**: Usually, here, we will have data on how our product is responding on the performance side–whether it is slow, whether the users had any problem finishing a specific task, and more.
- **Collecting of analytical reports**: Sometimes, I call them demographic reports–who is using our product, their profiles, or how they are accessing it. It is good to create some kind of dashboard to put all these pieces of information in one place and provide different options for filtering so that we can have a clear idea of what is going on.
- **Issue-reporting**: Issue-reporting inside our product is another important area when we go to production. Usually, we listen to the users here, understand their issues, and then analyze what was developed wrongly and how much time we need to fix it.
- **Help support**: By having this place in our product, we can easily collect data from our user feedback, what they want, what hassle they have when they use the product, which features they are suggesting, and more. By having all these pieces of data, it is easier for us to predict the next step, which is what to provide to our users or the customer category based on the requirements noted in our support center.

When our product is live, the ongoing measurement and monitoring of the data created by different users or our customers helps us to take the next decisions to improve and ensure the life cycle of the product. This kind of information is key for keeping our product live and usable for a long period of time.

So, as you can see, the main thing we do after our product is live is delve more deeply into the analytics of the product.

Keep supporting your product when it is live and try to improve the parts where your product is lacking to provide the best experience to its user base.

Summary

In this chapter, you learned different areas of the UX process. You need design documentation, which will be complementary rather than supplementary to our process. You learned that you should try to adapt all these techniques to your own needs, and try to understand that it's all about giving to a better design result for your product. So, adapt to the process, methods, and techniques explained here based on your own needs because you do not need to follow them exactly in the order that we covered them.

In the next chapter, we are going to talk more about user behavior and how to conduct proper user research.

3
User Behavior Basics and User Research

As UX designers, or as a UX design team, we will need to think about more than just how our product looks. We will need to encourage users to take specific actions with our product or service to engage with it. So, to do this properly, we have to watch how users behave with our product, and, for this, fortunately, we can use some psychological principles to analyze how our users think about, behave with, and react to our product.

In this chapter, we will cover the following topics:

- User behavior basics
- Psychological principles and theories used for design
- The Gestalt theory
- Things you should know about psychology in UX
- Understanding the user's motivation
- Understanding the user's ability
- Understanding what triggers our users
- User research
- The benefits of user research

User behavior basics

To become an expert in the field of UX, it is essential for us, as UX professionals, to understand the behaviors and needs of our users. To create a better product for our users and to understand their needs, we have to learn some basic principles of psychology. Otherwise, we will always keep wondering why users are not taking specific steps when they use our products and why they are not interacting with it in the way we expected.

As human beings, we do not like to think too much; for example, when we see a product that has tons of features, as much as it excites us at the beginning, we tend to lose interest in it later. It's not that users don't want to make an effort to look at the features, it's because most of the time we are too lazy to check the things that we are not interested in at that moment. However, in some cases, too many features or too many options inside the product can confuse users; take a look at the following example, which distinguishes old TV controllers from new ones:

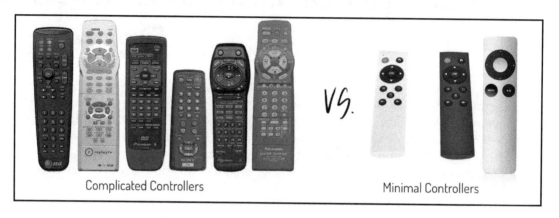

Complicated Controllers   Minimal Controllers

More choices need more cognitive load.

> *"The cognitive load is describing how much time it can take for a person to decide or make a decision as a result of possibilities that they have, the bigger number of choices that he or she will have, the longer it will take them to take a decision."*

—Hick's law

Another thing that will drive the users to move their attention away from our product might be multitasking. If the user's attention is drawn toward other tasks when they are already working on the main task, they might end up not finishing any of them. The more we focus the user's attention on one task at a time, the better our results.

It is understandable that human beings make mistakes, but they get a second chance to rectify them; therefore, when a user makes a mistake while using our product, we must provide them a way to undo their moves or provide with way to fix that mistake. Actually, a user experience is good when users are not able to make a mistake; so, every time the user makes a mistake while using our product, it's our fault, not theirs. We will need to avoid designs that drive users to make mistakes.

Sometimes, we think that users will not make the same mistake twice because they will remember it, but that's untrue because human memory is too complicated and unreliable. Most people will not waste their time learning how to use our product; they just want to use it without thinking about anything else other than finishing a specific task. Our habits reconstruct our memories, which leads to memory change, so it is a must for us as UX professionals to avoid forcing people to remember the actions that they should take while using our product.

Then, how do we guide users to take actions that will prevent them from making mistakes? Well, we can get their attention by providing different or unique options inside our product. For example, take a look at the following screenshot:

Psychologically, human beings give their attention to things that are different/unique. So, as a UX designer, we will need to provide steps or actions with great usability to be able to grab our user's attention.

However, how do we know whether the user will like that specific thing? Well, as we know, the human brain is complicated and very difficult to understand. Often, users are unaware of what they want until they experience it; so that's why it's really important for us to understand the user's psychology.

If you come to UX with a background in psychology, then all the theories, rules, analyses, and experiments that you know or learned before are really important and useful for a career in UX.

So, to better understand the psychology aspect of UX, let's start by introducing the Gestalt theory.

The Gestalt theory

The Gestalt theory was created by the famous psychologist Max Wertheimer along with other psychologists, such as Kurt Koffka and Wolfgang Köhler. This theory came about in the early 20th century, and addresses perceptual experiences and other related patterns of stimulation.

Another type of Gestalt theory is known as the law of simplicity.

"The whole is other than the sum of its parts."

— Kurt Koffka

The following are some really important Gestalt laws to learn as UX professionals:

- The proximity law
- The similarity law
- The closure law
- The figure-ground law
- The common region law

Before we go deeper into each of these laws, if you want to learn more about UX laws besides Gestalt ones, check out this website, https://lawsofux.com/, which contains amazing information related to UX laws.

The Proximity law

Based on the Proximity law, when we perceive or have a collection of objects, we will immediately be able to separate or differentiate the objects that are close to each other by forming different groups. Take a look at the following example:

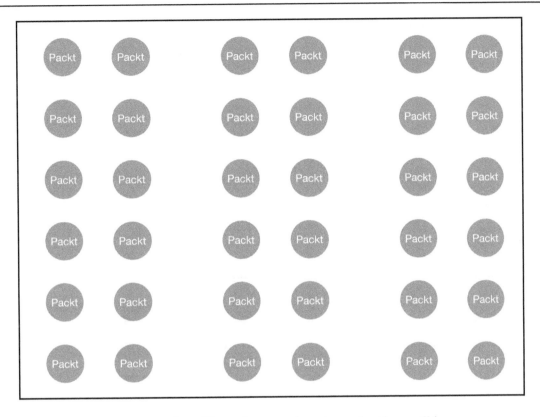

The principle of proximity is that things that are close to each other will be seen as a group. Basically, proximity means closeness. If we use a clear structure and visual hierarchy, we will be less charged by the limited cognitive resources of users, so they will be able to quickly recognize and react to them.

Let's take an example of how the proper usage of the proximity law can help us design better interfaces, and how using it in a bad way can create a bad design.

So, if we use it properly, we can achieve something such as this:

Do

Separate in two rows clearly the boxes, and give space between each others, so the users can read and understand easily the points that we are showing.

 JOHN DOE
At half-past eight the door opened, the policeman appeared, and, requesting them to follow him.

 JOHN DOE
At half-past eight the door opened, the policeman appeared, and, requesting them to follow him.

 JOHN DOE
At half-past eight the door opened, the policeman appeared, and, requesting them to follow him.

 JOHN DOE
At half-past eight the door opened, the policeman appeared, and, requesting them to follow him.

However, if we ignore the law of Proximity, then we will have something confusing for our users, such as this:

Don't

If we order all the boxes in a way that they don't look separated between each other, and we do not give them spaces between rows, than the human minds groups this boxes in the different way, and most of the time it represent not what we wanted to show.

 JOHN DOE
At half-past eight the door opened, the policeman appeared, and, requesting them to follow him.

 JOHN DOE
At half-past eight the door opened, the policeman appeared, and, requesting them to follow him.

 JOHN DOE
At half-past eight the door opened, the policeman appeared, and, requesting them to follow him.

 JOHN DOE
At half-past eight the door opened, the policeman appeared, and, requesting them to follow him.

The Similarity law

This law states that viewers will group elements that share consistent visual characteristics, such as a similarity in terms of colors and shapes:

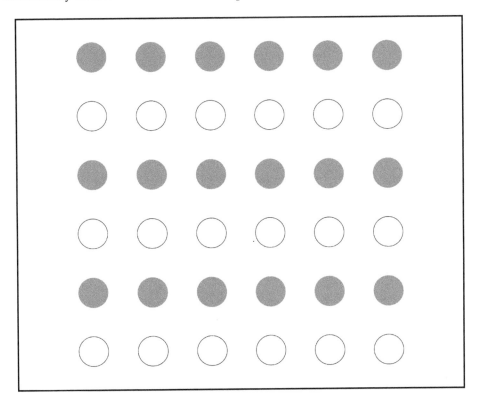

The law of similarity is based on the idea that if elements are similar to or the same as each other, we will perceptually group those objects or elements together.

> *"Consistent sequences of actions should be required in similar situations; identical terminology should be used in prompts, menus, and help screens; and consistent color, layout, capitalization, fonts, and so on, should be employed throughout."*
>
> — *Ben Shneiderman*

We will do what we did for the Proximity law for the law of Similarity. Let's design a user interface that has the law of Similarity in mind and one that ignores it.

We will have a similar result, such as this:

Do

The goal on this part of design is to create three groups which represent the same size, color or visibility.

JOHN DOE   **JOHN DOE**   **JOHN DOE**
Professional   Professional   Professional

At half-past eight the door opened,   At half-past eight the door opened,   At half-past eight the door opened,
the policeman appeared, and,   the policeman appeared, and,   the policeman appeared, and,
requesting them to follow him.   requesting them to follow him.   requesting them to follow him.

Alternatively, if we ignore the law of Similarity, our design will be as follows:

Don't

To have a proper order and visibility, we cannot display groups with different opacity, colors or text and font order.

JOHN DOE   **JOHN DOE**   JOHN DOE
Professional   Professional   Professional

At half-past eight the door opened,   At half-past eight the door opened,   At half-past eight the door opened,
the policeman appeared, and,   the policeman appeared, and,   the policeman appeared, and,
requesting them to follow him.   requesting them to follow him.   requesting them to follow him.

The Closure law

Based on the principle of good continuation, there will be a tendency to group simple elements or objects, independent of continuity or similarity. This will give results based on the effect of filling the missing piece with a different shape or color to make it a whole; we can even play with positive or negative space to give a complete meaning to the objects that we are trying to display.

The closure law can be easily seen in the first diagram in the following graphic, but it's a little complicated to understand how it works. The second diagram can be read as an overlap of two different objects, in our case, two rectangles; the same thing can be read with three objects, as shown in example number 3. In example 3, we can see the final shape where a curve joins three uneven shapes or squares touching each other:

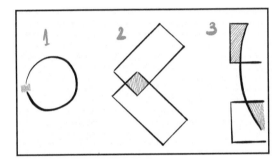

Closure can be explained differently when we fill in the gaps–for example, when we encounter a complex element with a missing part or break, we look for a continous and smooth pattern.

Now, let's create an interface that has the Closure law in mind. The example that I created shows the user that the boxes displayed on the user interface can be more than just what they see. The following example shows a user interface that has the Closure law in mind:

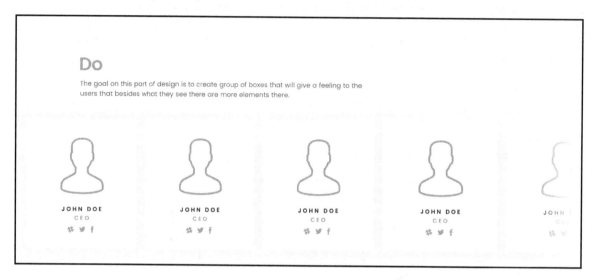

So, as you can see in the preceding user interface example, it gives users the feeling that they can swipe or scroll the boxes to see more. However, if we totally ignore the law of Closure, then we will have something such as this:

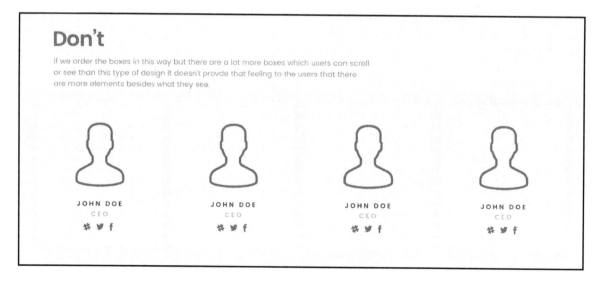

The Figure-Ground law

Using the Figure-Ground law, we can differentiate between an object or element based on its surrounding form or area, where its shape is naturally perceived as an object or figure while the surrounding area is read or seen as a background.

If we balance the object and background, we can perceive a clear image. Using the figure/ground relationship, we can create a clear view of the image and add interest to it.

The law of Figure-Ground refers to the relationship between positive and negative space. The idea here is that our eyes will separate whole elements or objects from their background so that we can better see and understand the whole image, which is usually one of the first things we do when we look at any composition. Take a look at the following example:

This law is very useful when we want to influence the focal point of the screen.

To give you a better understanding of this law relating to are designing user interfaces, let's take the same example that we used for the previous laws.

The following is the result of a user interface design with the Figure-Ground law in mind:

In the preceding example, we try to make the subscribe field and button our focal point so that users can easily find a way to subscribe to our product. This case can be used on modals or specific areas of our user interfaces, but let's see what happens when we ignore the Figure-Ground law:

As you can see in the preceding example, users do not have a focal point, so they may be distracted by other parts of our user interface design and not finish the main task that we want them to do.

The Common Region law

Using the law of Common Region, we show a connection between two elements or groups by enclosing them with each other. Whatever is included inside the enclosure is seen as related, and everything outside the enclosure is seen as a separation. Take a look at the following example:

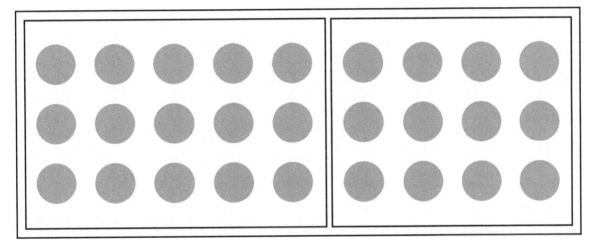

The usual way to see a Common Region example is by drawing one box around related elements, as has been done in the preceding diagram. Placing those elements or objects on a different background color will make the view clear so users understand that those objects are separated from each other. Also, instead of adding the difference on the background color, we can just add borders or strokes around the group of objects and separate them.

In design, we often use cards or borders to group coherent elements.

Let's move on to the interesting part by creating a user interface example with the Common Region law in mind:

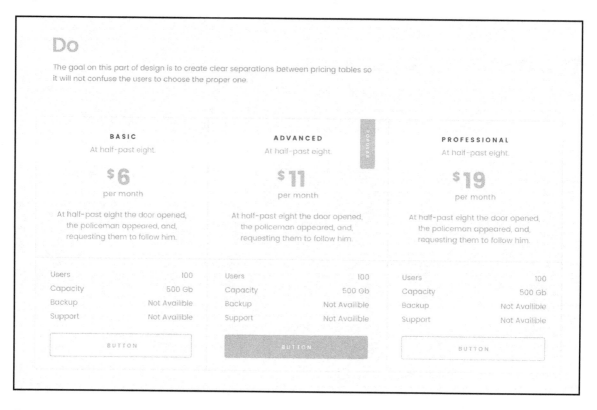

So, as you can see in the preceding example, I show three different pricing tables on our interface design, properly separated and clear so users to take action.

This user interface is designed with the Common Region law in mind, but look what happens when we ignore this law, and just remove the borders and touch nothing else:

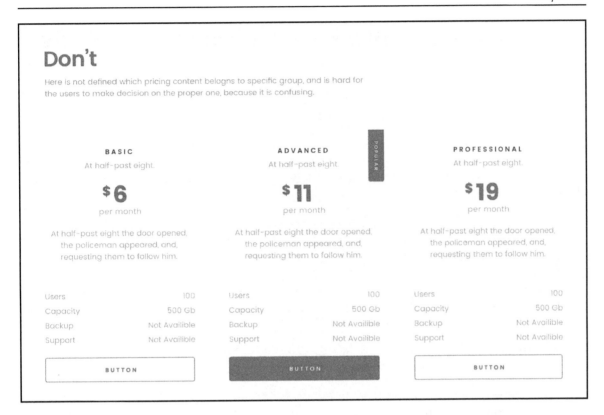

The preceding example totally confuses the users since there is no proper separation between table boxes, and users are not sure of the action that they should take.

This section was included with the intention of emphasizing the importance of psychology in UX design. Besides the Gestalt principle, there are many other different aspects of psychology that are used in the UX discipline.

Things you should know about psychology in UX

Let's say that we launched a product and people are starting to use it. However, we soon note that, instead of an increase in the use of our products, users are rejecting our product.

Based on recent research and studies, it is noted that around 35% of the users abandon the app after their first use. As time goes by, this number increases. Based on the studies performed by companies such as Localytics, Google, and Marketingland, it is reported that only roughly 40% of the users return to use the app more than 10 times.

 Check out the detailed report generated at Localytics for the study they did on how many users return and how many stop using applications after they download them for the first time. For more information, check out:

http://info.localytics.com/blog/24-of-users-abandon-an-app-after-one-use

So, what do we need to do on the UX side to avoid this? Well, there are tons of things that we can do, but the most important one is to connect our product with the users.

A lot of great products and ideas have failed or didn't find a path to success because they were missing one thing, that is, the users couldn't connect to their products. That is why the simplicity of a product design is not always the main thing that matters to our users–this is the part where psychology gets involved.

As much as other aspects of the product (such as visual design, being easy to use, being a good idea, market research, product marketing, and design research) have their importance to our users product design, what is going on inside the mind of our users, also ultimately determines whether they have a good experience when using our product.

We will need to look at the psychology to understand the reasons behind our users taking specific actions or carrying out certain behaviors when they are using a product. Once we start to understand the broader mechanisms of our users' behaviors, we will be able to create a better experience and design better interfaces.

The following are three things from the psychology side that are really important for our product user experience:

- Motivation
- Ability
- Triggers

Understanding the user's motivation

Let's say, for example, we want to create a product or an app that will help people lose weight, but the hard part here will be motivating people to lose weight, with or without using our app.

On the psychology side, we will distinguish between two different motivations:

- Extrinsic motivation
- Intrinsic motivation

By this, we mean that users can be driven to take actions or do something either by external factors, such as receiving a monetary reward, or by internal factors, such as the enjoyment of doing a specific activity using our product.

So, when we create our app, we will need to encourage people to start losing weight by providing them with a reward whenever they take actions, until this becomes a habit for them.

To understand why people do what they do, and how to influence what they do, you have to look at the motivation behind their behavior.

In simple words, we can explain that motivation is a term that comes from psychology and deals with behavior. This concept describes something that makes people take specific actions and it specifies the reason for those actions or needs.

However, motivation alone isn't always enough to enable or change a person's behavior. This is something that's presented in the BJ Fogg behavior model, which states that three elements have to be present at the same time for a behavior to occur–motivation, ability, and triggers:

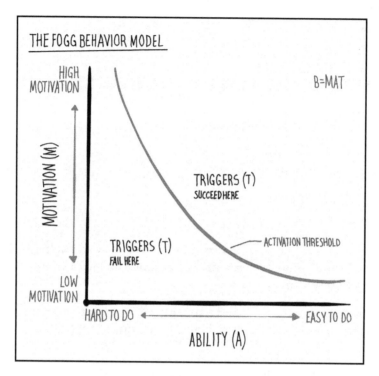

The Fogg behavior grid was created to help people think clearly about behavior changes; it describes 15 different ways a behavior can be changed.

Each type, for 15 behaviors, uses a different psychological approach and persuasive techniques. For example, using the method, we can note using the difference between how people buy a book online compared to how people try to quit smoking:

	GREEN Initiate new behavior	BLUE Reinitiate familiar behavior	PURPLE Increase behavior intensity	GREY Decrease behavior intensity	BLACK Stop existing behavior
DOT One time behavior	**GREEN DOT** *Do a new behavior one time*	**BLUE DOT** *Do familiar behavior one time*	**PURPLE DOT** *Increase behavior one time*	**GREY DOT** *Decrease behavior one time*	**BLACK DOT** *Stop behavior one time*
SPAN Has a duration	**GREEN SPAN** *Do behavior for a period of time*	**BLUE SPAN** *Maintain behavior for a period of time*	**PURPLE SPAN** *Increase behavior for a period of time*	**GREY SPAN** *Decrease behavior for a period of time*	**BLACK SPAN** *Stop behavior for a period of time*
PATH Lasting change	**GREEN PATH** *Do new behavior from now on*	**BLUE PATH** *Maintain behavior from now on*	**PURPLE PATH** *Increase behavior from now on*	**GREY PATH** *Decrease behavior from now on*	**BLACK PATH** *Stop behavior from now on*

As mentioned in the preceding example, there are two types of motivation, external and internal, differently known as follows:

- Extrinsic motivation
- Intrinsic motivation

Extrinsic motivation

Extrinsic motivation, which is also known as external motivation, groups together factors that come from external or external sources, such as motivation from relationships, friendships, families, competitors, and different environments.

External motivations usually encourage the users to deal with their outside world. This also includes motivations that are generated by other people that they are surrounded with because there is no other way to achieve their specific goal. Also, the cultural background, including things such as age, gender, education, country of residence, religion, and family, can create and correct reasons coming from those outside factors and motivate users to communicate and behave in a specific way.

Competition itself presents the situation of a strong external motive. For example, some users do not care too much for the reward that they can get by using a product but they want to compete with what others are doing, and this competitiveness can become even stronger when they compete with others, especially with their friends or followers.

These are really important factors that we can use during our research as UX professionals, because they present the possibility of showing our product to the outside world and show us how we can influence these kinds of people.

Intrinsic motivation

Intrinsic motivation, which is also called internal motivation, is the set of factors that comes from the person themselves, from their inner world. Usually, these motivations are formed by their needs, wants, and wishes. Also, the user's intelligence and personality are counted as factors here.

Understanding the user's ability

When we want to launch the product, we will need to answer the following questions:

- In which place or environment will our users be when they use our product?
- What is the main task that our users will be performing?
- What issues or frustrations might they face when they use our product?
- Is our product straightforward and user-friendly?

In answering these questions, we will develop a clear idea of what we should improve in the product user interface so that it can meet user requirements.

During the research phase, we observe our users as much as we can and collect that information to create a better understanding of our user's ability to interact with the product interface. We have to be sure that our users will be able to finish the most common tasks quickly and that the steps for finishing this task have great usability and accessibility.

Also, the important thing is for us to be prepared and use some tests and research to determine the possible errors that users can make and try to prevent them.

Understanding what triggers our users

Understanding what motivates our users, and how to adapt our product to their level of knowledge, comfort, and ability, are two really important steps.

We will need to convert their good intentions into actions by trying to trigger them to behave in a certain way.

Usually, in the mobile world, we trigger users to take actions by sending them phone notifications, and if we send those notifications at the right time, our product receives more attention than ever from our users.

This part can be tricky, because if we count the number of notifications users get daily on their mobile devices, we will note that we need to avoid sending them too often; we should send them wisely so that we can avoid the possibility of users turning off our notifications.

If you've learned about Fogg's behavior model, you know that it gives us a good idea of where to place to triggers for the users to take actions. The model shows that triggers are the best and most effective way when the level of user motivation and ability is sufficiently high.

For triggers to happen, timing is a crucial factor; for example, a notification about performing a daily exercise routine during working hours probably will not trigger the users to take actions or they may find it annoying because they are currently dealing with something else that is more important.

We will need to work with our users to find the right time to motivate or trigger them to take actions; in the end, we share the same goal, which is to create a behavior change.

A quick summary of this section

In short, we can conclude the following points:

- **Motivated:** Does the user need our product? Will it add value to their life?
- **Ability**: How can they access our product, where will they get it from, and how do we present it to them?

- **Triggered**: Have we triggered them to perform the behavior? Do we have steps for them to take actions? Are we reminding them why they picked our product in the first place?

Also, before moving on to the next part of the book, I would like to mention the psychologist and cognitive scientist Dr. Susan Weinschenk and her 10 points, explaining how she views psychology from the UX side:

- People don't want to work or think more than they have to
- People have limitations
- People make mistakes
- Human memory is complicated
- People are social
- Attention, because people are easily distracted
- People crave information
- Unconscious processing
- People create mental models
- People understand visual systems

These are only a few tips and examples of how UX and psychology can be combined to encourage behavior change. Having a formal model such as Fogg's model can help you structure research and design processes to ensure that the user's needs are considered. Also, these 10 points from Dr. Susan Weinschenk can be a great guide to better understanding UX psychology.

The bottom line here is simple: if you want users to like and use your product, give them a reason to love it.

User research

User research is a key component of UX design itself, never let anyone tell you otherwise. We have already covered the topic in Chapter 2, *UX Design Process*, but, in this section, I will explain how to do it in practice.

There are a lot of different opinions on where and how to perform user research, for example, doing it before you start the product development phase, after you start the development of the product, or after you launch your product.

Actually, all of them are right, but the best solution would be to do it really early and as often as you can in each stage.

So, in this section, we will go more into how to prepare and conduct user research, and I will try to explain the steps that I take when I do user research.

So, the following are the eight steps that we will follow to perform user research properly:

1. Setting objectives and a brief
2. Defining the audience
3. Selecting the research method
4. Designing and validating your research
5. Organizing interview
6. Conducting the research
7. Analyzing and validating the results
8. Defining the problems

In the following diagram, you can see what a simple user research roadmap looks like:

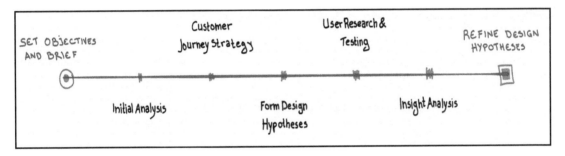

Setting objectives and a brief

In the first step mentioned in the list in the preceding section, we set up a meeting with all our team members, and start receiving the brief and setting objectives for starting product development.

We ensure that all team members fully understand the requirements and opportunities of the product.

We carefully prepare the timing and deliverables and any other relevant communication tools and methods that will be used during the user research phase.

This is the stage where before knowing who to test or what method to use, we have to know what to test. So, for that, we create questions, which is the base of any structured research. The questions created need to be as specific as possible and focus on critical points or on a new concept that we will create. Our research questions will define the focus of our research.

Defining the audience

We will need to clearly define our target audience. We should be focused on relevant people who will be our possible users in the future. There can surely be exceptions in some cases, that is, testing the product with random users, but the main focus should be on relevant people who can be our users.

This will be easy to define once we get the proper questions for them, so once we define critical points that we want to test and to whom it will be critical, it will be much easier to know which people we should test.

Selecting our research method

When we arrive at this stage, we need to choose the research method that will be the best fit best for us. Then, we should have a clear idea of research steps, and why and how we will conduct them. Also, we will know what to test and with whom to test it.

The challenging part during this step can be the research method, because we have tons of different research methods in UX that we can choose from; so, to choose the proper one, first, ask some questions:

- Will we conduct the research remotely or in-person?
- Do we want to have more quality research by doing the interview with selected people, or do we just want to have quantitative data and do the research with random people?
- Will we automate the process using available tools, or will we work in moderated sessions and collect the data manually?

The decision when choosing the research method will also depend on the stage of the design process that we're in, so, for example, if we are at the beginning of product development, we will use a different method compared to, for example, when we are testing the usability of our UI design.

If you find anything unclear in this part, you can always refer to the research methods that we explained in Chapter 2, *UX Design Process*, of this book.

Designing and validating your research

In the preceding section, we decided on a specific research method that we will use. Now it is time for us to design the process of how we will perform the research in detail.

We will analyze every step that we will take during the start of research phase, and how we will proceed with the method that we have chosen.

By this, I mean that we will think about the questions that we will ask during our interview, because to have a good interview we need to be prepared to ask users what we want to know and to be sure that we will know what to ask them and gather the answers that we need.

Also, a good practice is to not only ask a direct question but to ask a masked questions, which will activate their unconscious processing.

After we design the process for user interview, we move on to validating our process. We can do it by testing the research using some users from our targeted audience, or we can find someone from our network circle to test the process by interviewing them before we start the real interview.

This may look like a waste of time, but it will really help us to identify flaws or the gaps that we have in our interview-design process.

Sometimes, during this test phase, we will find that we need some extra questions to be added or to be reformulated so that we can get to the heart of our problem.

Organizing interview

We have now arrived at the final stage before we start performing our user research (in our case, using the user interview research method). So, here, we check whether everything is organized and whether we are ready to perform the research. We should plan the time in detail so that it can give us and the UX team an estimate of when we can expect the results and what kind of results we should expect.

When we have to deal with tight schedules, we have to do the planning from the beginning.

We also need to organize all the questions and prepare for our research; by doing this, we avoid missing any useful organizational questions.

We should know exactly how many participants we will involve in this research and how we will recruit them. For example, if we are going to have an in-person interview, we will need to prepare the environment to suit the candidates; or if we are going to do it remotely, we need to prepare the screen-recording tools and equipment that we will need during the interview.

Here, we also need to be really careful about legal issues, especially for sensitive data that we want to collect during the interview. We have to inform the candidate, provide a proper agreement letter for them to sign, and explain what kind of data we will get from them and for what purpose.

Conducting the research

Finally, we have arrived at the most interesting part; the stage where we wanted to be at the beginning of this process.

The product study, which we created, will be sent to our participants. It doesn't matter if we are doing it remotely or in-person, what is important is that our research design has been put out to the people who can test it, and we can get feedback from it.

To have better results, we make sure that our timing is planned properly and the resources are reliable and consistent. For example, if we are doing in-person interviews, we should do as many sessions per day as we can handle, without losing focus and disturbing the candidates.

During this time, we will need the whole UX team so we separate the teams in groups and start interviewing one or two people; by doing this we create equal research conditions for all the tests that we will perform.

Analyzing and validating the results

In this phase, we start to analyze the results that we gathered from the preceding stage, and it is really important to start this phase immediately after we conduct the research because the fresher our impressions, the more detailed the documentation we can create.

We will start sorting and summarizing our results, depending on the method that we have used during the research phase. We group our findings and add comments to them, so this will help us to get a good overview of the overall results.

Positive comments are always nice to have, but we will try to be focused more on negative comments during this phase because we want to improve the product. Once we group similar results in the same groups, we will define their common issues and prepare to take action. Last but not least, we can add a severity rating for each issue and the estimated effort it takes to fix it. This will help us decide in which order to address these issues in the design iteration.

During the research phase, some critical issues may be revealed; if this happens, our primary goal will be to tackle those critical issues first and then move on to the others.

There will be some issues that are not clear or not applicable to most of the users, for example. If this kind of issue came from the research that we did remotely, we can conduct in-person research to validate it, or vice versa.

Defining the problems

Once we validate all the issues and have a clear picture of which of them are a high priority, we can start improving the product by fixing them. However, this doesn't mean that we stop the research process. As I mentioned early on this chapter, good research is research that is conducted early and often on every phase of the product development, as needed.

A user-centered design is an iterative process in which we do the following steps:

1. Analyze the context of use
2. Specify requirements
3. Come up with a design solution
4. Evaluate this solution with our users

If our design doesn't satisfy the specified requirements, we go back and change it. This will be an on-going process till we get the results that we want for our users.

Market research is not user research

Sometimes, there is a lot of confusion between market research and user research, even though they have few things in common, but they are two different things.

Market research is a process where we collect and analyze data from our targeted customers, our competition, and the target market environment to aid in making marketing, branding, messaging, positioning, and pricing decisions. Our main goal during the market research process is to understand what people will buy and how to incite them to buy our product.

The main focus of market research is monetization; on the other hand, user research's main focus is to develop a great user experience.

Usually, market research is not conducted by the UX team. Most companies have different teams, or groups of teams, to do marketing research and user research. Not only that, they are separate departments; they also use different methods, and have different mindsets.

The two functions are often delineated in something like the following way:

- Marketing research team usually does the quantitative research, whereas UX focuses more on qualitative research
- Marketing research measures branding and satisfaction, user research observes behavior
- Marketing research does segmentation, user research manages personas
- Marketing concerns itself with what customers will say, user research is concerned more with what customers do

When the team is doing the market research, they simply rely more on subjective and self-reported data, which has its own limitations. It is good for market research to get user feedback for an existing product, but that data won't be useful in identifying innovation opportunities.

Market research is primarily about understanding what people will buy. It uses both qualitative and quantitative methods, but the ultimate goal is always to understand what people want to buy.

In general, we can say that market research only uncovers the incremental improvements of an existing solution. However, the data collected from the market research department is really useful to the UX team department not just for user research but in the overall stages of UX.

The differences between market research and user research are as follows:

- Wants versus needs
- Reactive versus proactive
- Statistical significance versus good enough
- Incremental versus innovation

- Time-consuming versus quick
- Infrequent versus iterative
- Subjective versus objective
- Direction versus design

When you see a product or even a website design, you can easily tell what kind of research was done by the team who developed it. If it looks pretty much the same as other websites or products available online, it is likely that they have done only market research, but if there is a specific product with a unique design and it solves a specific problem, it is more likely that the development team has conducted user research.

Both methods have their own importance, but we, as UX professionals, must avoid relying on market research for driving our UX design efforts since UX design as a discipline requires different pieces of information compared to what we will get from market research.

User research is not like other types of research. User research is different from competitive, market, and marketing research, user research; methods are used to uncover issues related to use and usability of a product, not whether there is a market for a product, how to sell that product, or how competitors are positioning themselves.

An important thing for us as UX professionals is to know when market research is needed, and when user research is needed. If you understand how these two methodologies work together through a product's life cycle, you will be able to work effectively with marketing departments. You can demonstrate the value of including user experience research in their projects since you will be able to explain how it complements the market research they have been already conducting.

The benefits of user research

User research ensures customer validation, clarity, and a process when producing the products of tomorrow. Conducting user research has certain benefits.

The following are some of the benefits that we gain when we do user research:

- Helping to create the right product from the beginning
- Increasing conversions and revenues
- Avoiding surprises saves time and money
- Improving SEO and marketing

- Customer retention and loyalty
- Providing competitor insights
- Development resources
- Early design guide

Helping to create the right product from the beginning

Let's take an example. Let's assume that we have an idea and we want to create a product for it. Our product will target a specific market, but if we design something that does not meet the expectations of that market, all our effort will have been wasted.

That is why it is really important to conduct user research from the first stage.

Having interviews with our potential users at the beginning of our product design can be a really good way of understanding specific user needs, and then we can validate our concept designs and give our product the shape that it needs to have.

We've mentioned that this will save us money and time because having the right information from the beginning helps us to avoid mistakes in the early stages.

Increasing conversions and revenues

The data that we collect during the user research phase gives us real insights on improving our conversion rates, such as online purchases, subscriptions, user registrations, and bookings. We can find out from the user research data why users are frustrated when using our product, information on our competitor's products, and why the users are dropping out and not understanding our product's offering. So, we solve those points for them and try to provide a better product presentation to our users.

This ensures that we not only improve conversion today but gain the knowledge to design more effective solutions for tomorrow. The insights gained from research and the data allow us to pinpoint changes required to impact conversion.

Avoiding surprises saves time and money

It is far less expensive to prevent a problem or a usability issue from occurring in the first place than to fix it later. Getting early feedback from our target users and performing a deeper research into our users will help us avoid those expensive errors, saving hundreds of engineering hours and thousands of dollars.

Improving SEO and marketing

Yes, you read it right. Search engines love great user experiences. Google gives you a rating to improve results in both organic search results and with Google AdWords. The user experience of your site is a big part of their calculation for your rating. Have a poor user experience, and Google will penalize you; you will either fall off the top page of results or be inefficient in your Google AdWords campaign.

Customer retention and loyalty

By conducting user research and analyzing data,you can gain customer loyalty if it's done properly. Customers who have a positive user experience are going to be more likely to stick with your products and become your brand advocates. Investing time and resources into the customer experience will help you reduce churn and guarantee customer loyalty.

Providing competitor insights

User research is a great spy tool for our competition. We can easily analyze and run different user tests on our competitor's product and find out what the users are doing right with their product, and where they are suffering, and more importantly, you can find out whether the users trust them more than you, or vice versa. You can also find out which other companies in your industry your users already have been doing business with and why they like working with those companies.

So, do not fall behind by not investing the time and budget on user research because more companies than ever before are investing in user research, and chances are, your competitors are, too. Customers are growing to expect good user experiences and becoming increasingly intolerant of bad ones.

Let's be brutally honest. If our customers have an easier time doing business with our competitors, then that's exactly what they'll do.

Development resources

Upfront user research can hone developmental goals and help prevent scope creep. Understanding who your users are, what your users need, and how your users interact with your product can help refine your understanding of the problem space and allow you and your team to focus developmental resources on the area(s) that will make the most impact.

Early design guide

Upfront user research can influence the look and feel of your preliminary design work, which, in turn, can heavily influence the final user experience. Lacking a solid understanding of your users' characteristics can set your UX designers on a stray path. Having early design guidance can help positively influence the outcomes of subsequent design work.

There are a lot of other things that user research helps us uncover by conducting it. User research is an essential step on the way to validating our thinking. So, it doesn't matter much whether we use a combination of traditional UX research methods or new methods, as long as we gather qualitative insights from our users.

Any kind of user research is beneficial in creating a compelling product or service. When we have sufficient information for the product that we are building, the results will be much better. That is why we need to do user research from the early stages and as often as it is needed.

So, if you find yourself wondering why you should do user research, keep in mind that at least you'll validate the assumptions that you made about your audience at the beginning of your product idea, and avoid costly mistakes that would have led you in the wrong direction.

Summary

In this chapter, we covered the focus of user research on understanding user behavior, needs, and motivations.

We started the chapter by explaining the importance of psychology in the UX field, then we explained BJ Fogg's behavior model, and how behavior is impacted using motivation, ability, and triggers.

We explained the difference between market research and user research; also, we created a list of the benefits of performing user research.

The next big thing will not be the new Facebook or Google, which will try to solve the same problem that these companies are already solving for their users, it will come from people who will build simple and elegant solutions for user needs and wants.

When we shift our focus from what people do to why it matters, we will be on the right path to creating an outstanding and powerful user experience.

4

Getting to Know Your Users

To deeply and clearly understand why people use specific products and how they use them, we first need to get to know users. In this chapter, we will explain the importance of knowing the users during the process of UX design and how, by knowing more about our users, we can easily create successful products.

In this chapter, we will cover the following topics:

- Getting to know your users
- Grouping customer information
- How to conduct user interviews
- Preparing for the interview session and more

User Research

To clearly understand why the users of our product behave in a specific way, we first need to know them. We can make assumptions on who they are and what they need, but it's important to support those assumptions with facts. The more we know about our users, the more informed we will be about the actions and decisions that we should take for our product design and development. It is no accident that the majority of successful products out there were devised using extensive user research.

We can use different methods of user research, specified in Chapter 2, *UX Design Process*, and Chapter 3, *User Behavior Basics and User Research*, to collect data about the users. It doesn't matter which method we use, what matters is having the necessary data required to use as a starting or reference point for different kinds of research.

> "Successful products are created by designers that know their users. Everyone else is designing in the dark."
> – Jerry Cao, UXPin

There is no exact process or model that we should follow for conducting user research; each company or UX professional has their own way of performing user research. Most of the time, this depends on the kind of product they are developing.

The following example shows some of the different forms of user research that I mostly use myself :

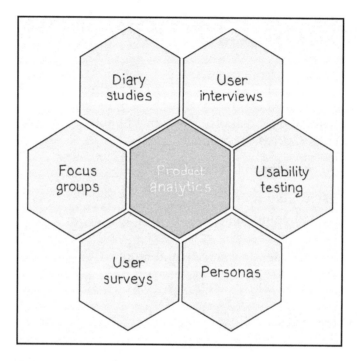

As I mentioned several times in this book, everyone has their own process of UX research and user research. For you, as a UX professional, you should understand every method clearly; you need to know what it does and where it can be used. Later, during the process of user research, you will get a better understanding of which approach you will need to follow for a specific phase or product that you are designing and developing.

The following questions can be answered by our user research data:

- Where do our users come from?
- How did they find out about our product?
- Which language do they speak?
- Which devices do they use?
- What is their age?
- What is their gender?

- How frequently do they use our product?
- What problems are they are solving by using our product?
- In which parts of our product are they are more interested?

It doesn't matter what digital or physical product we are creating, the product's lifetime depends on the users who are using it. So, getting to know our users better is critical not only when designing our product features and user interface, but also for the many other activities that go into making the product successful, such as promotion, business models, and community.

Grouping customer information

Des Traynor, the cofounder and Chief Strategy Officer of INTERCOM, explained that we can group customer information data into four categories:

- Profile data
- Business data
- Activity data
- Communication data

Refer to the following diagram:

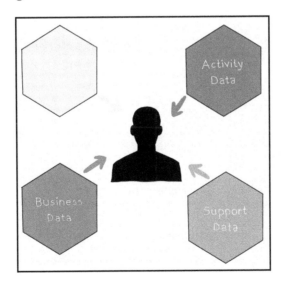

So, we should obtain the following kinds of data from the users when they are using our product:

- **Profile Data**: We include pieces of information about our user's category, that is, about our users and their background.
- **Business Data**: We include data that the financial department cares most about. Here, we have business information, such as our user's account status, whether it is a free or paid one, and their membership or subscription status.
- **Activity Data**: In this part, we collect our user statistics. For example, the amount of time that they spend using our product, the kind of activities they perform during the usage of our product, and other analytical-related data.
- **Communication Data**: We include information that we get from the users, their feedback, and what kind of help they usually need from us.

If we do not have data for these four categories, we will be in a weak position, since we can end up losing time, money, and effort trying to provide something that our customers might not be interested in using; even worse, they might not be the customers that we wanted to target in the first place.

None of this is desirable, and all of this is preventable. We simply need to stop thinking in silos. Silo data costs us customers and leaves us clueless as to why we're losing them. Refer to the following diagram:

Very often, we aren't particularly interested in learning more about our users, and avoid interviews with them, claiming that we don't have enough time; sometimes, we neglect to create focus groups for research saying that we do not have the budget. However, honestly, this is not true. If we think about how many days and hours we spend on different meetings, where a few people discuss and debate a new feature or new product design services, we can compare how many resources or hours we waste during these debates and meetings. It is always cheaper and much easier to spend our time speaking with and getting feedback from our real customers.

In the end, it doesn't matter how many meetings we had; if we build a product that the users do not want, the money and time spent in building the product will have been wasted. So, it's always better to do some user research or run some interviews with our possible customers to better understand their mental models.

You can get more information about your users not just from the UX research methods described in this chapter, but also by doing your own research online–since we have customers telling us about themselves all the time. For example, think about how much information we can get from people's social accounts, such as Facebook, Twitter, and Instagram. A lot of people post different kinds of information daily using social media. So, here, we can get different support queries for our customers–the point is just to start collecting them, listen to what they say, and analyze their data.

There is a good chance that we probably have a lot of valuable customer information from the people who work in the same office or company with us, such as people, research reports, and testimonials. We can collect all this data together and start categorizing it to better understand our users.

We do not have to just speak with our users or interview them, we will also need to observe them, and obtain as much information as we can from them. A lot of the time, users will say one thing and do another, so instead of just speaking with them, observe what they are doing.

It is really easy to build a product based on something that you need as a person, a product only for our own use. You do not need to talk to anyone else in this case, because you know the problem that you are facing and you clearly know what you want. But when it comes to building a product that will be used by other people, it is essential to talk to them and discover their needs, expectations, and experiences. The best way to do that is by using the UX research method of interviewing users in-person.

"You cannot understand good design if you do not understand people; design is made for people" — *Dieter Rams*

That is why we are going to explain how to conduct user interviews in the next section.

How to conduct user interviews

Interviews help us gain a deeper understanding of our users, so I will present detailed steps to help you get the most out of user interviews.

However, before proceeding with individual interview steps, I would like to mention three distinct roles on every design-thinking team:

- **The Facilitator:** This is a person or thing that makes an action or process easier. In one word, a facilitator is a *leader*. They will provide all the materials, outline the project, and provide an objective. They will create the session plan and schedule. The facilitator enters after the UX process is finished and the interviews are done. Then, they lead the team with a new mind and then during the way he must not get upset or angry with the process. A good facilitator has to adapt easily, even when there are a lot of challenges.
- **The Interviewer:** Each team needs a primary interviewer who schedules user interviews and breaks the interview down to stakeholders and users identified by stakeholders. The purpose of the interview is to get the user to open up, which is the job of the interviewer. This is empathy at work, and it's crucial for the successful completion of your application project. A natural interviewer will be friendly, curious, warm-hearted, empathetic, and a guider.
- **The Partners:** The partners take notes during the interview blueprint while the primary interviewer is working and asks follow-up questions to clarify important points. After the interview process, they will receive all the answers. They will consolidate it down to a master blueprint for that user. Partners shouldn't ask questions during the primary interview–they should wait until the interview is done–to avoid losing the direction of where the interview is going. Later, they can add their input.

Now, it is time for the steps that we usually take when we have to conduct an individual interview with a possible customer.

So, the four steps we will follow for conducting the interview are as follows:

1. Preparing for the interview session
2. Identifying who we want to talk to
3. Setting up screener surveys for filtering the participants
4. Conducting the interview

I usually choose the individual interview method because of the following reasons:

- We can talk to one specific person at a time
- We have more time available to talk about different topics in detail
- We don't need to worry about the group dynamics of a focus group
- We can give our full attention to our interviewee and adapt the interview style based on their needs

So, let's start with the process of conducting a proper interview.

Preparing for the interview session

This is the step where we take actions before we perform the interview. We define a clear goal and what we want to get out of people during the interview with them.

When we start conducting an individual interview, we will need to consider the following things:

- We need to have a clear goal and idea as to what we want to get from those individuals.
- We write the interview protocol, which the interviewer will follow. The protocol itself includes different questions and tasks for the interviewer to follow up with.
- We need to have a skilled interviewer, who knows how to deal with interviewees, makes them feel more comfortable, and asks questions in a neutral manner. This type of person usually listens well to the user and also knows when and how to push the users to provide more details.
- We need to take permission from the interviewer that we can record them.
- Have one or more notetakers during the interview.

We need to ask ourselves the following questions:

- What do I need to know about our users?
- How will that knowledge improve our product and inform our design process?

Identifying who we want to talk to

After we identify what information we want to get from the users, we can identify the people who will be able to provide that information. We have to identify whether our product's customers are existing ones or new ones.

For individual interviews, we usually will need 6-10 participants, because we want to get as much insight as we can from different people.

Compared to the user-test method, during the individual interview it is suggested that you look for people who can be your potential customers and not those who are already using your product.

To find these kinds of participant, we can search inside our network to try find someone similar. There are other ways as well, such as paying a third-party recruitment company to find participants for us. If all else fails, we can try contacting people on social media and conduct a meeting with them.

Setting up screener surveys for filtering the participants

So, when we find potential participants, we prepare and send screener questions to these participants for them to answer. The whole purpose of this screener process is to filter out participants who do not match our criteria.
Even if we have criteria for choosing the participants, there can be different things that we couldn't have known. For example, we can filter by participants who work on software and design firms, or we can choose candidates who their members of the family, or their friends are working on those related areas that we are interested in for research. These kinds of participant may know a lot and can provide detailed information to help us during the interview process.

We can prepare screener surveys really easily using Google Forms or any other similar tool that you are familiar with.

After participants start to sign up for our screener survey, we will need to schedule and book a time for them to speak with us in person or remotely.

Since, in this case, I am talking about individual interviews, it is always better to talk to them in person, because the natural emotions that you will see when conducting the interview in person will give you a much better filling and key answers to your questions in your UI/UX.

Conducting the interview

Finally, we've arrived at the point where we wanted to be. Now, we start the interview by introducing ourselves, the company that we work for, and the main purpose of conducting this interview.

So, before we start, we will explain the reason why we are conducting this interview to the participant, what we need their information for, and what it will be used for.

After we explain this, we need to ask them whether they have any questions before we begin. This is how we start to create trust with our interviewee and make them more comfortable.

We mentioned that it is important to record the conversation in case we need to refer or return to it later. However, whether we record it or not, it is always recommended to take notes and get key observations and statements from the interviewee. We try to take as many notes as we can because this kind of data will be useful later in the persona-creation process.

The four things to always remember when we are conducting an individual interview are as follows:

- During the interview, give complete attention to the user.
- We have to listen without providing answers or opinions. However, if needed, repeat and rephrase the question.
- Never talk down to the user.
- Users speak, and we have to understand.

At the end of interview, allow the participant to contribute any thoughts or feelings that they felt were not covered during the interview.

The following are a few points to keep in mind during the interview process:

- Refer to the challenges as defined in the interview
- Show the prototype and explain it to them
- Listen again without judgment, by asking the user again, "What do you think?"
- Stay positive when listening to negative or new ideas
- Reframe and realign questions and suggestions
- Remember that this is an interactive process
- Agree with the users, start the redesign process, and return to them

Conducting the interviews is key for us to get an in-depth understanding of our customers and develop empathy for them. The data will lay the foundations for us to create user personas, which we will use and refer to throughout the product's design and development.

The key part in our complete user-research process is being played by the user personas that we create. That is why, in the next chapter, we will go more deeply into creating personas; how and where to use them, and what they can provide to our research process.

Summary

The best way to create a great user experience is to communicate with our users and customers directly. We need to be in their shoes to understand their pains, needs, and wants. If we don't communicate with them, our designs will not make sense, so we covered how to prevent this from happening.

We need to give a lot of attention to user research during our product's design and development processes. By doing this, we will understand our users' different habits, problems, needs, attitudes, and their frustrations in how they are dealing with challenges in their life. Understanding and getting to know our users is the only way to deliver the right solution for the product that we are building.

5
User Personas

To help us achieve our goal of creating a great user experience for our targeted users, we need to create user personas. Personas are fictional characters, based on the user research that we have done in the previous chapters, that represent different user types that we think will be using our product.

User personas are important to us because we can easily know who our user is during the product design process.

In this chapter, we will cover the following topics:

- User personas, and why we need them
- What kind of information we include inside user personas
- The proper structure that user personas should have
- Different perspectives in personas
- The benefits of creating and using user personas during our UX design process

What are user personas?

User personas, or just personas, in UX, are fictional characters created to represent a type of user that might use a site, brand, or product in a similar way. The purpose of personas is to create realistic representations of the users who will use our product.

We create these fictional characters based on the previous steps of UX research that we discussed in the three previous chapters. The idea of personas is to create different types of users that might use our product, which will help us to understand the user's needs, experiences, behaviors, and goals.

We can think of user personas as detailed representations of the different segments of our target audience.

With personas, we create a representation of a group of users who exhibit very similar patterns in terms of their behavior in using a particular application or product regardless of age, gender, location, education, or profession. These behaviors are typically specific to a particular technology/product, decisions, preferences, usage style, and so on.

In the marketing field, personas were introduced in the mid-1990s, but since that time, personas have become a really important part for the process of UX research and other processes of product design and development.

The person credited for the invention of user personas is a software designer and programmer, Alan Cooper. He invented them in the 1980s when he was working as a software engineer.

User personas are the key and the most important document that we will create for analyzing the users. They will be the foundation for the rest of the user documentation, which will expand on personas for deeper insights. It is not a good idea to skip the creation of user personas during the UX process.

Personas are the most important people in the room when making design decisions. The psychology, behaviors, and demographics of our target users feed into these fictional identities.

So, how do we create them? Well, this depends on our product design needs. They can be large in some cases and small in others. What's important is not how much information they contain, but that every piece of information is relevant and supported by product-usage data.

The following are some of the points that most of the personas should have:

- **The profile section**: Here, we include basic demographic and geographic information, such as the person's age, country of origin and residency, gender, social class, and psychographic information.
- **The personality section**: In this part, usually, we have to get answers by asking questions, such as which statement describes this user better? For example, whether this person likes to pay attention to facts and details or is just not too focused on taking any actions.
So, we check the personality and the user character type, because it helps us to have a realistic scenario and mental model for our persona creation and it also helps us to determine what this user type needs.

- **The expertise section**: In this section, we will describe the person's expertise in the platform on which we're building our product; for example, their level of expertise with computers, mobile phones, and technology. So, this section will mainly be about our product.
- **Must do and must never section**: One of the most actionable areas is included in this section. Here, we try to figure out what our user expects and wants to do, and which things frustrate and annoy them.
- **The referents and influences section**: Here, we represent the user's favorite people, brands, and products – what is influencing them when they use a specific product and how they interact with different devices, such as computers, mobile phones, software, and mobile apps. Just like in the preceding point, this can change based on our product-development area; for example, a digital or physical product.
- **The devices and platforms section**: Which kind of devices or platform is this user using? What are their favorites apps, and what kind of technology are they familiar with?
- **The product section**: Here, we write down their current product lists, those that they are dependent on a daily basis, and those they use rarely.
- **The archetype section**: Here, we will refer to the user personality and characteristics stuff to define their relationship with different products or services that they are using.
- **The key quotes section**: Here, we describe the user, add comments for them, and reflect on their behavior and attitude.
- **The experience goals section**: What does this person like or expect when they use and interact with specific services or products? For example, it can be the speed of finishing a task or it can be a funny service.
- **The brand-relationship section**: Here, we mention the relationship between the person that we are describing and specific products or brands.
- **The picture section**: After we finalize most of the points for creating the persona profile, we add a picture that illustrates the personality, attitude, and lifestyle of our person.
- **The user type section**: Here, we can describe our person type; for example, what kind of personality they have, how patient they are, how fast their mood can change, and so on.

So, by keeping the preceding points in mind, we can visualize the user personas as something similar to this:

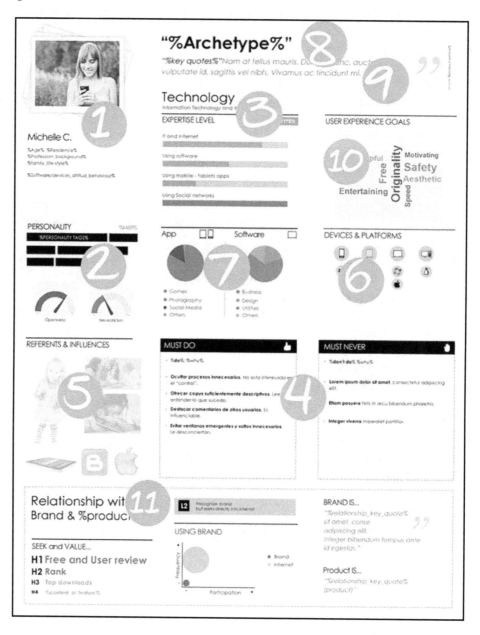

Creating a persona

We have to ask a lot of questions during the process of creating the user personas, so keeping in mind the points about personas, we can separate them into a few groups that will help us to organize the user's data.

Personal information:

- What is our user's name?
- How old are they?
- What is their professional job or occupation?
- What is their level of education?
- What do they do in their free time?

The professional side of the user, their needs, and their goals:

- What do they target or want to achieve?
- Why do they want to achieve that goal in the first place?
- What are their needs to achieve that goal?

Technical expertise and workplace:

- Where are our users working and how much time per day do they spend there?
- How many hours do they spend using computers or mobile phones?
- What are their favorite mobile apps or websites?
- What devices do they prefer to use and why?

Personal quote:

It can be anything that can identify them as a person, or a phrase that they often use. Also, as we create the user personas based all the things we know so far, we have to keep the following points in mind:

- Think about a different group of users that we spotted in our research
- Think about the product and problem that we are solving for this specific user or group
- Separate them, and define how each group is different

So, now, let's use some real data to take a look at examples of final personas. Let's take the example of different users who are brand managers:

Name:	TJ Thyne
Occupation:	Co-founder and Chief of Marketing
Company Size:	Startup (Team of 5)
Education:	MA in Communication
Age:	31

Goals

1. Spreading the message about his new startup,
2. monitoring the web for any mention about his new startup and competitors' actions
3. providing great tutorials
4. increasing new sign ups

Needs

1. Fast and easy tool to manage Social Media
2. Mobile device support and app
3. Collaborative tool
4. Metrics on the go

Technical background and workplace

TJ lives and breathes the Web. It's easier to mention the websites he doesn't visit every day. Thinking about it, he's interested in everything from growth hacking to copywriting. He's a one man marketing machine for his startup. He works from his home office, Starbucks and even from a beer joint. He's permanently connected and working. He loves to travel and runs to relax. He is active on Twitter and Quora, a Facebook addict and Instagram junkie followed by over three thousand people. He uses iPad mini, iPhone 5 and MacBook Air (retina). He loves products that are usable and well designed.

Experience	★★★★☆
Business value	★★★★☆
Frequency of use	★★★★★
Cooperation	★★★★☆
Cost efficiency	★★★★★

That's going on Twitter right now!

Consider another example:

Name: Margaret Atkins
Occupation: VP of Branding
Company Size: Fortune 500 Company
Education: MBA Degree
Age: 47

Goals

1. Maximizing Brand Presence in order to achieve the highest possible ROI
2. Reducing churn by 50% in the next 2 years
3. Mitigating possible losses from bad PR strategies
4. Improving inter-departmental

Needs

1. A collaborative tool
2. Extended analytics report
3. 24/7 media monitoring
4. professional advice

Technical background and workplace

Margaret is a person connected to the internet 24/7. She uses MacBook pro, ipad, iphone and kindle. She spends her entire day working at the office. She travels on business a lot, meeting new people and attending conferences. Her favorite business website is MarketingProfs.com. She is a PRO member of their network and has a special deal with them for all her Branding Department employees.

Experience	★★★★☆
Business value	★★★★☆
Frequency of use	★★★★☆
Cooperation	★★★★★
Cost efficiency	★★★★☆

 Let's assume we're in. How will we benefit from this?

A persona does not, however, represent every potential user. Personas are designed to create stronger relationships with the most important (and largest) part of that base.

Four different perspectives on personas

A Ph.D and specialist in personas, Lene Nielsen, in her article on *Interaction Design Foundation*, describes four different perspectives on personas, as follows:

- Goal-directed personas
- Role-based personas
- Engaging personas
- Fictional personas

Goal-directed personas

In goal-directed personas, Lene Nielsen describes the main focus of what our typical user wants to do with our product. The objective of this kind of persona is to examine the process and workflow that our user would prefer to utilize to achieve their objectives when interacting with our product or service. This kind of persona is based on the perspectives of Alan Cooper, which we described in more detail in the preceding content. To get a better picture of a persona, check out the following diagram, which illustrates the relationship between users, personas and the goal:

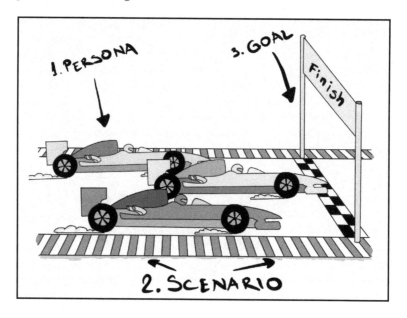

Role-based personas

This kind of persona is also a goal-directed persona, but they focus on behavior. Role-based personas are hugely data-driven and incorporate qualitative and quantitative information, and they are mainly focused on the role of the user inside the organization.

We can try to examine the roles based on what our users do in their real life to help us get information for a better product design and development decisions.

With role-based personas, we need to obtain answers to the following questions:

- Where will users use our product?
- What is the purpose of the product?
- What business objectives are required and what can be achieved with them?
- Which people will be impacted by its role?
- What kind of functions are being served by this role?

Engaging personas

This kind of persona includes both the goal-directed and role-based ones, but they also cover the more traditional rounded persona, which includes only basic information about the users, such as their geographic data and their basic needs and wants.

We usually create this kind of persona so that we can be more engaged with them.

Involving and engaging users with personas, and creating a type of persona so that we can consider them as real users, will help us during the design process and enable us to create a better product by having the persona in mind.

Since personas can examine the emotions of the users, their behavior, and psychology, they will give us more relevant solutions for the tasks that we are working on.

Personas are described as follows:

> *"The engaging perspective is rooted in the ability of stories to produce involvement and insight. Through an understanding of characters and stories, it is possible to create a vivid and realistic description of fictitious people. The purpose of the engaging perspective is to move from designers seeing the user as a stereotype with whom they are unable to identify and whose life they cannot envision, to designers actively involving themselves in the lives of the personas. The other persona perspectives are criticized for causing a risk of stereotypical descriptions by not looking at the whole person, but instead focusing only on attribution."*

—*Lene Nielsen*

The following are Dr. Nielsen's 10 steps to create engaging personas and scenarios:

1. Collect data
2. Form a hypothesis
3. Everyone accepts the hypothesis
4. Establish a number
5. Describe the personas
6. Prepare situations or scenarios for our personas
7. Obtain acceptance from the organization
8. Disseminate knowledge
9. Everyone prepares scenarios
10. Make ongoing adjustments

We can do it on a piece of paper if we want. We just display the characteristics of a persona in a few columns and add key details about them, similar to the following image:

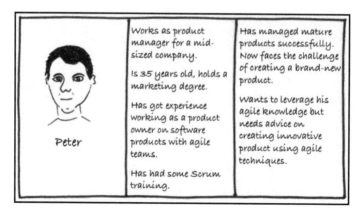

Fictional personas

Unlike the other personas, this kind of persona does not emerge from the user research but from our experience during the UX process or from the UX team itself. We, as UX professionals, and together with our UX team, are required to make assumptions based on our past interactions with the user base and products to deliver a picture of what, perhaps, typical users look like.

This kind of persona allows us to involve the users on our UX design process in the early phase, but, of course, we do not consider them as final personas, or as a well-defined user base – we just use them as a guide for the development of our product's early stage.

Benefits of personas

User personas help us to focus on our decisions for the product design, because having a real user problem in mind will make it easier for us to provide an adequate solution. Personas can offer us a quick and cheap way to test and prioritize different features and ideas during the design process.

They can help us in different areas, as follows:

- Stakeholders and leaders can evaluate new product-feature ideas
- Information can architects develop informed wireframes, interface behaviors, and labeling
- Designers can create the overall look and feel of the product
- System engineers/developers can decide which approaches to take based on user behaviors
- Copywriters can ensure that the site content is written for the appropriate audiences

I'm really glad that you made it all this way. Now, since we clearly understand the UX process itself and its benefits, it's time to move on to the more interesting part of product creation: the design and development stages.

Summary

In this chapter, we explained that personas are fictional characters, which we create based on our user research process. We create them with the intention of using them to help us understand our potential users' needs, experiences, behaviors, and main goals.
Creating and using user personas make our tasks less complex and will guide us during the design process by having some specific potential users in mind. We explained how engaging personas can help us ideate our users' behaviors and provide the best product design for them.

6
Designing Behavior

In this chapter, we will explain what drives users to behave in a certain way or take certain actions. Besides the BJ Fogg model, which we explained earlier, we will cover a few other behavior models that are worth knowing and understanding in the UX world.

After this, we will move on to explain the five factors for users to take action.

We already know that designing for a behavioral change is really hard, which is why we will go through what kind of behavioral approach we need to take when we designing our product.

So, we will focus on the following areas in this chapter:

- What and how to design for a behavior change
- Behavioral design models
- The five factors for users to take action
- What behavioral approach should we take during our product design

Designing behavior

First, let's not confuse user behavior with design behavior. User behavior, which we explained in detail in Chapter 3, *User Behavior Basics and User Research*, is more about how users are using our product, that is, their behavior when they use our product; design behavior is how we design the product, which will affect our users' behavior.

When we design behavior for our product, we are more concerned with how our design can shape or influence our users' behavior.

We have already learned that a product is only as good as its ability to influence behavior. There are tons of wonderful products that are available to us nowadays that are executed to perfection, but that failed to get any true user adoptions.

A simple example can be taken from a lot of websites that use fancy 3D animations and different effects; unfortunately, these kinds of product are fancy to look at but not to use, and they are less efficient, because the UX quality is lower than in normal products. They fail to fit into or change the behavior patterns of their users.

In Chapter 3, *User Behavior Basics and User Research,* we discussed three aspects from psychology that are really important for our users' product experience; when a behavior doesn't occur between the user and the product we created, it is because one of these three elements is missing or insufficient:

- Motivation
- Ability
- Trigger

We will not describe these three elements again here, but if they are still not clear to you, you should return to Chapter 3, *User Behavior Basics and User Research,* and read this part again. We have to understand that to look at a behavior, first, we have to ask ourselves what the problem is and where it lies.

In most products or situations, not only can one of these elements be missing, but all the three elements may be insufficient. However, to improve the product, we should always start with the first element – analyze it, identify the issue, and solve it.

To design a good behavior, we have to match our own goal with the user's goal. Since often we want the user to do something specific when using our product, but they do something else, these two goals are not the same; however, it is our job as UX professionals to match them.

How do we match these goals? Well, we need to design interfaces with intention, not just some fancy artwork. When we design with intention, we should always keep in mind that when the users complete their own goal, they should complete ours as well.

What kinds of action users take to achieve their goal using a product or service can depend on different factors, such as:

- The environment that they are living in
- Their needs and desires
- Their experience

There is no specific thing or magic formula that says if we do the preceding steps, users will take the actions we want them to. Since all users, as individuals, are unique, they are have different environments and their decision-making process is really complex and can be full of surprises.

Despite the complexity of understanding people's decision-making processes, there is always a better chance of designing a better product by keeping these factors in mind.

To design for a behavior change, it requires a lot of effort to understand how the user's mind works, how they will interact in the environment where we are now, and how the product we are creating can help us change their behavior for good.

When we're better able to understand these kinds of thing, we start designing better products. Often, these kinds of product change our users' daily routines and behaviors.

Our focus as UX professionals is to follow UI and UX best practices, which will allow users to take towards actions r their goals by removing their current frustrations and pains, making their decisions less complex and the product easy to use.

So, when we know how our mind makes decision, it's easier for us to create more engaging products for our users, and this will be like a new tool for us, which will support us in creating products that our users will interact with.

Five factors/preconditions for users to take actions

Let's imagine we are creating an application that will help people organize their morning routine. Our app will allow them to organize important tasks, tasks that they should finish first, their next steps, and much more. In the app, we will also include healthy tips, such as short morning exercises, meditation, and even breakfast suggestions.

Also, let's say that hundreds of users have downloaded our app. However, often, we expect our users to open the app, organize their tasks, their morning routine, and we expect that, the next morning, they will wake up and follow our app instructions, right?

Well, that barely happens, because we make the wrong assumptions about our users. We think that they found us on the internet, or heard about us in an advertisement and loved what we were doing, and that is why they started using our product. However, research results tell a different story. Having hundreds of users who take action immediately by using our app takes a lot of time and effort, and it is done not just by having an amazing product design.

We need to use a simple model of when and why we act. A lot of times, at different moments, we take different actions, or, sometimes, we do not take any action at all, which is why we need to know why we undertake one action and not another one.

There are several factors that need to happen for people to use our app, and to make this happen and help us in that direction, we will follow the five preconditions for users to take actions.

These are five preconditions for actions that must occur at the same time before our users act. When designing products for a behavior change, encourage users to take action by influencing one or more of these five preconditions for action:

- Cue
- Reaction
- Evaluation
- Ability
- Timing

So, to explain these five precondition better, let's return to our example of the morning routine app. Let's imagine we were watching television when suddenly we remembered that we wanted to wake up early tomorrow and create a morning routine, such as eating breakfast, exercising, meditating, and finishing simple tasks.

Also, we have already downloaded the morning routine app on our mobile phone. So, the question is when and why would we suddenly get up from our couch, search for our mobile phone, and start using that application to organize our morning routine?

It is a bit weird to think about, I know, because we usually do not perceive user behavior in this way. We usually go with the wrong assumption that our users love the app and that they are using our app whenever they want to once it is downloaded.

So, back to our example, the following things need to happen for users to take action on using the morning routine app:

1. **Cue**: Something must signal our mind to start thinking about our morning routine or about the app itself. It can be anything, a commercial on TV, phone notifications, a message, or a friend's invitation.
2. **Reaction**: After the cue, we will immediately react to the idea of a morning routine, and in seconds we will think about the app on our phone. We will start thinking about whether the app is any good and about the experience we had the last time we used it. Will the app's features help us toward our morning routine goal?

3. **Evaluation**: Here, we might start thinking about it consciously and start to evaluate the costs and benefits of using the app. For example, what will we get out of using that app? What value will the app provide towards our achieving our goal? Is it worth the time and effort of getting up every morning and organizing our routine using the app?

4. **Ability**: Then, we will start thinking whether using the morning routine app is feasible for us. Are we sure that we still have that app on our phone? Do we remember the email and password for using that app? Here, we will need to be able to act and to know why we are taking certain actions. We need to have these resources before we start using the app.

5. **Timing**: After the previous four factors, here we need to have a clear reason for why we are going to act right now and not continue watching TV. Here, we will start having questions such as, is it worth doing it now or can it wait until we finish this TV show? Is it urgent? Is there a better time when we can do it? This may occur before or after checking for the ability to act; both have to happen though.

If all of these five actions happen positively, then we actually execute the action. These five factors are preconditions for our users to take actions. All these factors must be completed successfully in order for our users to consciously engage in taking action.

We can think of the preceding five preconditions as a leaky funnel that has two holes on each stage. Either our users do not take action because they do not value it enough or they don't think it's urgent for them, or they get distracted by external factors, such as a phone call from a friend or a new notification:

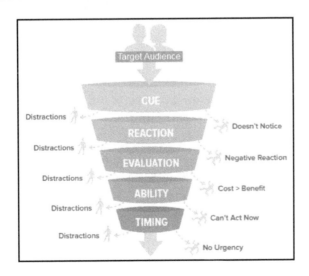

To make our users happy with our product, they have to use our app over and over again till it becomes a habit for them.

So, to support our users in taking action, we need to take the following two actions:

- We need to be sure that the five preconditions for actions are met while designing our product. Providing a clear call to action inside our product, ranking the urgency of tasks, and building the user's self-confidence will entail strategic thinking about how our users will interact with our product.
- As UX professionals, we have to find the big holes in the funnel and try to plug them; in other words, we have to figure out whether users are thinking about taking actions and why they are not doing so. For example, it can either be a painful task or there may be a lack of urgency for them to take action.

Models of behavior change

For centuries, different researchers and philosophers have been studying how and why we take the actions we do. Usually, this kind of research was mostly focused on people's minds to understand what makes them act and why they are taking those specific actions.

We discussed Fogg's behavior model in Chapter 3, *User Behavior Basics and User Research*, so we will not repeat it here, but here I will cover another model of behavior change, which is **Ajzen's theory of planned behavior**.

This theory dates back to 1991 and was founded by Ajzen, a professor of psychology at the University of Massachusetts at Amherst.

In this theory, Ajzen focuses on how our intentions to act are formed as a product of attitudes, norms, and perceived control over behavior.

Ajzen here explains that intentions and behaviors are influenced by our user's attitude toward that specific behavior; this attitude is affected by both subjective norms and perceives behavioral control.

In other words, we can say that our user's decision to take action is based on whether they gain anything from doing that behavior, how much pressure they feel to do it, and whether they are in control of the actions in question:

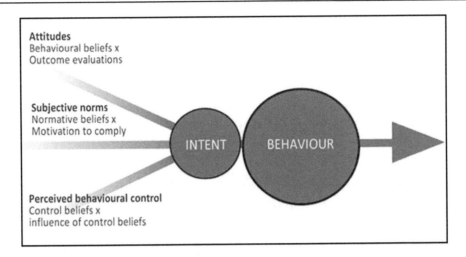

The preceding theory is interesting because it correlates intent and behavior and shows designers how they can increase or decrease user activity by changing the user's attitude.

There was another behavior model proposed by Prochaska and Velicer's in 1997, called the **Transtheoretical Model**.

This model looks at the stages of change that a person goes through from starting to contemplate an action to changing their behavior and maintaining it.

The following are some of the other models:

- Social Cognitive Theory/Self-Efficacy from Bandura
- **Heuristic-Systematic Model** (HSM) from Chaiken, Liberman, and Eagly
- **Elaboraton Likelihood Model** (ELM) from Petty and Cacciopo

However, if we compare other models with the Fogg model, we can see that the Fogg model is focused only on a behavior change, whereas the other ones are focused on information-processing or attitude change.

Behavioral approach for product design

Designing for behavioral change is really hard. We can see this happening daily, not just for our users or other people, but also for ourselves. Just think about how many product subscriptions we have currently that we are not using, how many to-do tasks we have for weeks that we do not finish, or how many times in a year we have been to the gym even though we paid a yearly membership for it.

All these things – unused product subscriptions, a gym membership, financial plans to save more, and our decision to eat healthily – never come to fruition. Even though we have a number of great services or products available to help us in that direction, most of the time it is not enough for us to take action.

That is why for us as UX designers, creating a good product that successfully can accomplish those specific objectives for users is immensely difficult. However, we also realize that the traditional design methods aren't enough for us to tackle these complex behavior challenges effectively.

We will need to have a process for designing behavior changes and a framework that will guide us during our design process and will evaluate the behavioral effectiveness of our products.

The framework needs to include something that will grab the user's attentions and will influence them to use our product. The users need to be able to see the benefits and goals that they can achieve by using the product. More importantly, we need to design our product in such a way that users can get into the habit of using it.

Some points that we can approach when we are designing a product are as follows:

- Grab user attention, make the product inviting and provide a clear message about the benefits of using the product.
- Provide a UI design that stands out and can be easily memorized by the users.
- Show more personalized content, which is more specific to one user base or category, and show more of what they are interested in and provide values that they want.
- Make the language of your product warm and inviting.
- Notify users about any unusual activity that is going on with the product; this way they receive surprising messages that are both personal and emotional, and that is how we grab their attention.
- Remove the use of jargon and provide clear and simple content that they can understand.
- Offer recommendations for their issues or for specific goals that they want to achieve; this way, the users become more engaged with the app.
- We need to describe the benefits of using our app, whether financial, lifestyle, or comfort-related; we have to provide them with information on what value they are getting from our product.
- Send them messages that will encourage them to take action.

- Guide them about the next steps. After the users make a decision to take action, it is time to help them with the next steps, following through, and guiding them to their next actions.
- Break down actions into small and achievable steps.
- Help them to create a plan so they can follow up and progress through that plan over time.
- Ensure that you ask for them to take action at the right time. Timing is critical, so we need to be sure that we trigger them at the right moment.
- After they take action and achieve small tasks, we will need to reward them with positive feedback and also show them their progress over time.
- It is important to build a long-term relationship with our users; so, instead of just one-time communications, we need to get feedback from them, in such a way that we can help them improve their experience.

These are just a few points that we can follow during our behavior-design process. There are tons of other things that can help our users get the best product experience.

As a UX designer, we have to consider different experiences that people go through when they are using our product. We have to understand what bothers them about our product, what makes them take action, and what motivates them to engage with our product over time.

Designing with behavior change in mind will help us identify what part of our application is hard to adopt on the part of our users, what is not triggering them, and what makes them not want to take action.

Summary

Behavior change is considered a relatively new field for UX research, but it is becoming more popular each day, and UX professionals are becoming aware of its importance.

We covered how changing or preventing long-term behavior is much cheaper and much more effective than treating the problem. Also, the really interesting and important topic covered in this chapter was five ways to help users to change or take actions.

As UX designers, we should have a solid understanding of the human mindset and how it works—what motivates people to use our product, their triggers, and how and what we need to design for them so that they can get the best experience.

In the next chapter, we will move on to one of the most important parts when it comes to creating a UI design: design principles and their processes.

7
Visual Design Principles and Processes

When we want to speak about the language of design, we need to provide a proper visual design to the users so that they can understand what we are trying to tell them. So, in this chapter, we will go through the basic elements of visual design, what they are, and how to use them.

We will explain visual design elements in detail and move on to design principles; using these principles, we will create a better language of communication through visual design.

In this chapter, we will cover the following topics:

- Basic elements of visual design
- Using lines, shapes, and colors
- Designing effectively through alignment, hierarchy, space, and textures
- Creating a visual design that will direct the user's attention to specific areas using the relationships of design elements, sizes, colors, and typography in the right way
- The meaning of colors
- Design principles such as repetition, balance, contrast, hierarchy, and spaces
- Designing with color and types
- Placing all those visual design elements and design principles together

Introducing visual design principles and processes

I am really happy that you have made it this far in this book, and you have just arrived at one of the most important and interesting parts of the book when it comes to product design.

This chapter is added before wireframing and prototypes deliberately, because to create good wireframes, we first have to understand how the design itself works and not just how it looks.

We will start this chapter by covering the basic principles, such as the influence of size, color, and layout of our design on the users and product directly, and then it will be easier for us to see the pros and cons of creating wireframes, visual designs, and prototypes.

To help you understand this chapter better, we will divide it into two important parts: first, we will talk about the basic elements of visual design, and then we will move on to explain the design principles.

Basics of visual design

To create a good user experience and a great visual design for the product, we will need to combine different elements that will give a better shape to the product that we are designing.

Visual design covers both sides of the design categories, the graphic-design side and the user-interface side. It focuses more on the design aesthetics of our product and other related elements, such as colors, images, typography, and shapes.

Let's take a look at an example. Consider that we are traveling to a new country, which has a different culture and language. Usually, the first thing that we try to do is learn some basic words of their language, because, we want to be able to communicate with the people there.

Communication is an essential part of our life; when we cannot speak words of an unknown language, we start using body language to ask or answer questions. We can make signs for showing direction, danger, and much more.

We use the same principle for visual design. We communicate visually there. For directions, we use arrows created by lines; for important areas or danger, we use colors; and we design different blocks to help users understand our design and other elements. So, here, we will explain the basic elements that we use during design so that we can communicate visually.

When we pay attention to those small details during product design, we create a significant change to the user's experience of our product.

The basic elements of visual design that we will cover in this chapter are as follows:

- Lines
- Shapes
- Colors
- Font/typography
- Textures
- Form

Using lines

Everyone knows that one of the most basic elements of design is a line. It is an essential element for creating visual designs. A line can be solid, broken, thick, or thin.

Lines are used to connect two different points. We can separate specific parts of our design or even direct someone's attention to a specific area using them:

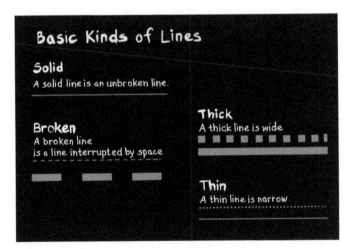

We can draw lines horizontally, vertically, or diagonally. Lines can lead our eyes across the composition and can provide information to us through their design and direction:

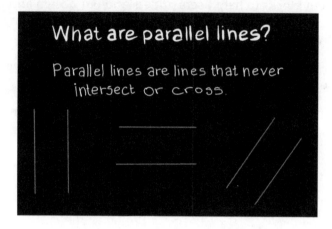

Also, we can have the following lines:

- **Straight lines**: They are not angled or curved
- **Angled lines**: Usually, they are two straight lines that join together from a different direction, and if we combine more than two straight lines, then we can create shapes such as rectangles, triangles, or squares
- **Curved lines**: They are created when a straight or solid line bends or curves in the shape of letters, for example, S, C, or U:

As you can see in the preceding diagram, all the lines have length, width, and direction. So, by the preceding characteristics, we can use lines to create different shapes, or even if we repeat them, we can create different patterns:

It is very simple to create lines by just connecting points using a moving point, and there is an endless variety of shapes that we can create by just connecting different points by lines:

So, the question that we now have is how to use lines during our product design? Well, usually, we use them to organize, categorize, connect, or separate different information in our visual design.

Connecting the dots by drawing the lines can take our product design as far as our creativity and imagination can go.

Let's summarize this here. We use lines during our designs for the following purposes:

- Organizing our design elements by separating or grouping them
- Creating different patterns that we use during our visual-design phase
- Guiding the human eye using arrows created by lines, and making it easier for them to see the parts of design that we want them to see
- Using different sizes of lines and different contrasts, we can use designs to make a statement

Lines are an essential part of creating different blocks inside our visual design. When we combine the lines with different shapes, form, colors, and textures, we can create a visual design that can communicate with the users.

Using shapes

In the *Using lines* section, we have already mentioned that shapes can be created by a combination of one or more lines; also, they can be created using differences in colors or textures.

Shapes can be represented visually by natural elements, or can be man-made. They can be regular or irregular, organic or inorganic, angular or round, big or small, open or closed, and even two-dimensional or three-dimensional.

Icons, symbols, textures, and colored spaces are examples of shapes.

Shapes can be categorized in different ways, for example, polygons can be classified based on the number of angles or edges. Other common shapes are points, lines, planes, and conic sections such as ellipses and circles:

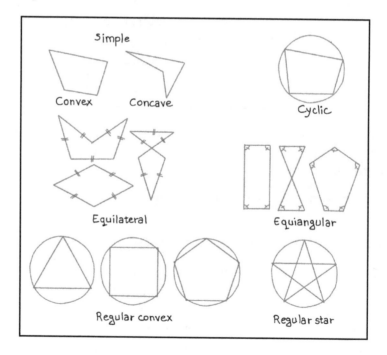

Shapes have an endless representation of visual communication; each shape can represent its own unique message to our users.

Now, the question is where and how can we use the shapes during our visual design phase?

Well, we use shapes during the process of designing our product for the following benefits:

- We can organize the information in our product design to connect or separate specific components or elements of the product
- We can differentiate the ideas using symbols
- We can create movement, depth, and textures
- We emphasize and create entry points for the areas we want our users to see
- Same as lines, we can give direction to people as to what elements they should look for using shapes

Types of shapes

As I mentioned in the previous section, we can have different kinds of shapes, and we can create endless different shapes and communication visually with them.

Here, we will cover a few types, as follows:

- Geometric, organic, and abstract shapes
- Positive and negative shapes

The two main categories of shapes that are well-known are the geometric shapes and organic ones, which are also known as freeform shapes.

In the group of geometric shapes, we have circles, squares, rectangles, and spiral shapes. Also, other shapes included in geometric shapes are stars, polygons, arrows, and ellipses.

So, let's use some of the basic geometry shapes and combine them together so that we can produce some kind of message or meaning visual design, which can be used to communicate with users.

For example, using circles, we can represent daily elements or things such as the sun, moon, universe, earth, and anything else that can be considered a celestial object. Usually, circles have no start or end, and they represent a well-rounded and complete shape. We can use circles to represent the infinite, unity, and harmony:

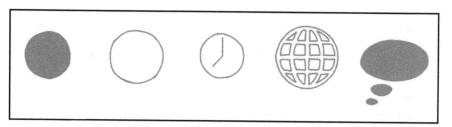

We usually represent honesty using geometric shapes such as squares or rectangles. These types of shapes are the most commonly used ones, and they represent mostly everything inside our product design, starting from the text we read to the shape of the product itself.

Usually, it is said that this kind of geometry shape represents conformity, solidity, security, and equality:

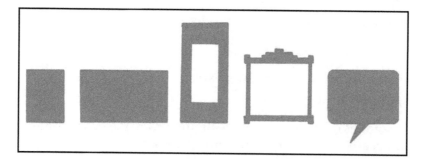

Spirals represent the expression of creativity. Most of the time, we find them in a natural growth pattern, and it is said that they represent the process of growth and evolution.

We can use spiral shapes to convey the ideas of fertility, birth, death, transformation, or expansion:

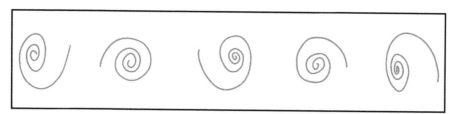

On the other hand, organic or freeform shapes have a free-flowing nature that represents a sense of informality and spontaneity. Usually, we use them in a visual design to show the outline of a human gesture, organic things, or products:

Positive and negative shapes are another type of shape. A shape can be represented either in a positive or negative way.

A positive shape usually represents the focus of some specific elements, figures, or shape of the picture, whereas the negative one will usually represent the empty space of that specific object or figure.

Let's take a look at the following example:

Shape usage in visual design

Shapes are used to add and sustain specific interest inside our product design. Using the shape properly, we can create specific focal points inside our design and direct the user's flow inside the design.

We have already mentioned that shapes organize the elements and parts of our product design by separating or grouping specific objects or elements.

We can play around with shape sizes, colors, depth, and so on. For example, the larger the shape size, the nearer it will be to access; the smaller the shape, the farther away it will look.

Note the following examples:

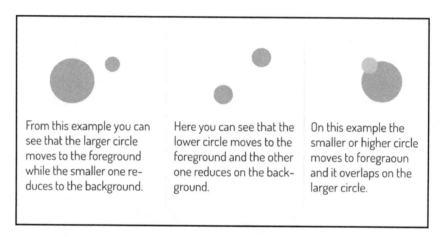

From this example you can see that the larger circle moves to the foreground while the smaller one reduces to the background.

Here you can see that the lower circle moves to the foreground and the other one reduces on the background.

On this example the smaller or higher circle moves to foregraoun and it overlaps on the larger circle.

So, we can see in the preceding diagram that similar to lines, shapes are also an essential part for creating proper visual design and providing proper communication through visual elements to our users.

Even if we want to ignore the usage of shapes during our visual-design process, it will be impossible to do so if we leave the page empty or blank.

There is an infinite number of shapes that we can create, but for creating visual communication, we will mostly use geometric shapes or specific symbols or icons created by shapes.

Let's conclude this section on shapes by just keeping in mind that everything around us is created by different kinds of shapes—not just physical things, but also the visual ones that we often use as directions for taking specific actions.

Using colors

Every day, we are surrounded by different kinds of colors. So, I don't think that it is necessary to explain how important color is to visual design, but I will give you a brief overview of it.

Using colors in our visual design, we present the mood and the atmosphere, generate emotions, and guide our users to their next actions based on the colors that we use inside our product.

Consider traffic lights. We have only three colors, but we are used to them, because each of them communicates something to us.

Red tells us to stop and the green one tells us to go, and sometimes we do not even think about them anymore because we got habituated to them, so we just take the appropriate action.

So, when we are designing a product, we always need to choose the colors carefully, and when we use them, we need to be sure that each color will represent the same meaning to the users.

Be mindful when choosing colors; as I mentioned at the beginning of this section, colors can really affect and dictate the mood of a design since each color has its own meaning and communicates something different to the users.

Another reason why colors are so important to design is because they have a bigger percentage of accent, and can be easily remembered.

For example, green represents nature, energy, life, and other related things, whereas red represents something stormy, danger, and anger. Blue represents calmness and more passion, whereas yellow represents warm feelings and happiness.

What is more important to know about colors is that people perceive and see lights and colors a bit differently. For example, how I see the color blue can vary and be different from how you see it, but in the end we both call it blue.

We may also be differently affected by colors; I may react a certain way to specific colors, whereas you may react differently to the same ones, because colors are relative.

Let's take a look at the preceding example in the following diagram, which for each of us can have different depth and light:

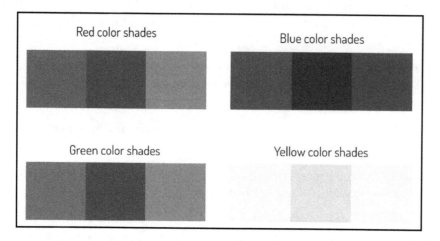

If you want to become better in the UX and UI design field, it is important to keep in mind when designing a product that the product first should look good and work well in grayscale (an absence of color) before it looks amazing in color.

So, our design should look good first in grayscale because colors should enhance the product design to make the product look good, but it should not be the design itself.

Color is usually one of the first things that our users will notice when they start using our product, and with that, they can determine whether the user interface design is aesthetically fulfilling or pleasing.

To go deeply and explain every part of colors, we will need an entire book solely for this purpose, but, in this chapter, I will explain the important parts of colors, which you need to know as a UX professional, so we will cover the following topics:

- Color theory
- Color systems
- Color wheel
- The meaning of each color

So, let's start talking more about the first topic, color theory.

Color theory

We already know that color is light; the range of the wavelength that we receive in our eye creates the visual spectrum.

For example, when the light shines on a specific object, some of this light's wavelength can be observed by our eyes and the others are reflected. So, the reflected wavelengths can be seen as colors.

When all the wavelengths lights are absorbed, then we see dark, which is the color black, whereas when all the wavelengths lights are reflected, we see the color white.

This can be better explained by the Munsell color system. This system was created by a Professor Albert Munsell in the early part of the 20th century.

With this system, as Munsell explained, the colors are specified by color spaces based on three color dimensions or components, as follows:

- Hue
- Value (the light range)
- Chroma (the purity of color)

Even before this system, there were other systems as well, but this one was the first one that separated these three color dimensions into independent components, and it was also the first system that illustrated the colors in a three-dimensional space.

The United States Department of Agriculture was the first to adopt this system in 1930 as their official color system for their soil research, and, since then, it has became widely used by everyone else.

Let's explain this system using the following image as an example:

In the preceding image, we showed a circle of hues, which has a value of 5 and a chroma of 6. Also, the pipe shows neutral values, which can go from 0 up to 10.

As you can see in the preceding diagram, there are three ways of describing these colors:

- By their names
- By their purity
- By their value (also known as lightness)

Let's explain each component that we displayed on the image so that you can better understand it:

- **Hue**: Every time we mention hue, we are actually talking about the object's current color. For example, the blue is hue as it is other color like green or red.
- **Chroma**: When we talk about chroma, we refer to the purity of the hue, which depends on the shades of gray. From the pipe in the image, we can see that the gray color can vary from 0 to 10.
  For example, the fewer shades we will have, the better and higher the chroma we receive will be; the more shade that we add to the gray color, the more the hue will reduce its own chroma.

- **Saturation**: This indicates the level of purity of a hue. The concept is similar to the chroma, but it is not the same thing; for example, pure hues are more clearly visible when they are highly saturated, but when we add more gray shades, the overall color becomes desaturated.

- **Intensity**: Intensity means that we are clearing the brightness of a color to make it seen better, or we remove the brightness thus removing the shines of the color, making its visibility harder to perceive as a specific color. We can remove the brightness of a color by adding or removing the white or black color. When the color has the right amount of intensity and it is highly saturated, that color can have a high chroma as well.

- **Value**: Using value or luminance, we measure the amount of light that is reflected from the color and check how dark or light the hue of that color is. Adding more black to a hue will make the color darker and decrease or lower the value (luminance), but adding white will make it lighter and will increase the value or luminance.

- **Shade**: The shades are the result of adding black to the hue for producing the darker hue.

- **Tint**: Tint is the opposite of shade, which is the result of adding white to a hue to produce or create a lighter hue.

- **Tone**: Tone, sometimes called the color tones, is the result of adding gray to a hue, which we usually refer to as the gray that is in between the white and black one. It is also good to know that we can create color tones using shades and tints.

So, now that you have the basic understanding of color theory, we can move to the next section for understanding colors better by explaining the color systems.

Color systems

How do we create colors? Well, that is done using the color systems.

We already mentioned that colors are seen differently by different people. For example, how I see colors on my mobile devices or computer can be different from how you are seeing them; the same thing also applies to physical objects.

For example, how we see colors on the computer can be totally different from how we will see them after we print our design on physical objects or paper. To help us achieve the same thing on both sides, we need to have proper color systems; I will explain the two most important ones:

- **CMYK**: Subtractive Colors
- **RGB**: Additive Colors

Subtractive color: Subtractive color is created by not pushing light in or out but by the reflected light.

This color system has three main colors, which are Cyan, Magenta, and Yellow. The color black is created by combining all these three colors. The color black is referred to as Key, hence the name **Cyan, Magenta, Yellow, and Black (CMYK)**:

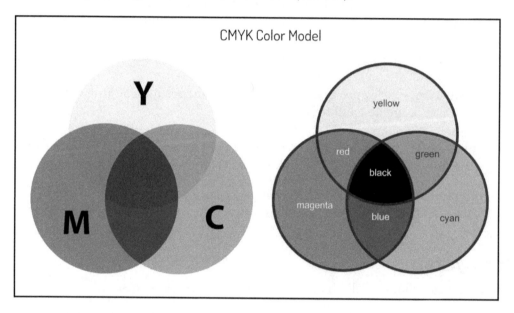

Let's understand why this is called subtractive colors. When we want to see blue or red, we absorb all other light wavelengths till only red or blue is reflected.

So, to produce the color that we want to see, we remove all other light wavelengths that we do not need or want to see.

By adding more colors to the system, the lights get absorbed more, which makes us see the darker color.

Subtractive systems start with white, and we achieve black by combining or adding all the other colors together.

The CMYK system is mostly used for prints.

Additive colors: The additive system is the opposite of the subtractive system, because compared to subtractive, where colors are reflected and the light is absorbed, in the additive system, the color is created by adding the light, where the light source itself comes from the outside system:

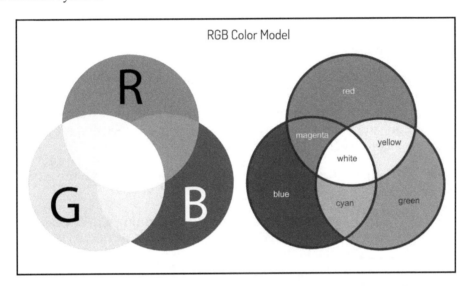

So, to keep it simple, always keep in mind that subtractive colors get darker if we add more colors or light to it, whereas additive colors get lighter when we add more colors or lights to it.

The best example I can provide to others when it comes to explaining the additive colors is through the example of sunlight. For example, the stronger the sunlight, the brighter or lighter the colors we see, and the weaker the sunlight, the darker the colors we see.

Additive, or RGB, colors are created from three primary colors: Red, Green, and Blue, that's why it's called RGB.

So, by combining these three colors, we see all other colors that are represented on our digital devices or computer. By adding more colors, we will go toward white colors, whereas the black will be created in the absence of those colors.

RGB, which is an additive system to create colors, is mostly used in digital media, whereas the CMYK system of colors is used mostly for printing.

It's amazing that you've made it this far. Now that you understand color theory and the color system, let's dive into understanding the meaning of each color.

Using the color wheel to understand the meaning of colors

When it comes to combining different colors, it is hard sometimes to find a match to make our visual design stand out.

For example, we ask questions such as why the blue and yellow combination is good but orange and yellow doesn't work, or why the green and orange combination is better than green and yellow. Well, this has everything to do with color theory, which we explained in the preceding section, and the best way to understand this combination is by understanding the color wheel and how it works.

The color wheel will help us to create color palettes, which will contain mixed colors based on contrasting degrees.

It was first introduced by Isaac Newton when he was performing a prism experiment in 1666. He concluded that the pure white color in the light contains the full spectrum of colors, or all colors, similar to the RGB color type, which was explained in the preceding section, but, in our case, instead of green, the primary color is yellow:

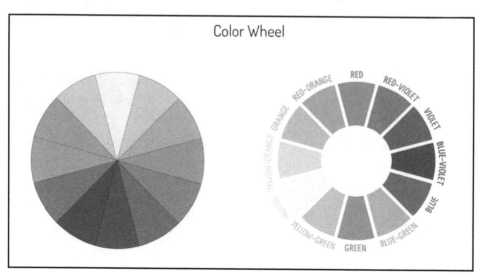

After this experiment, Newton created a wheel that contained 12 colors and classified them in three categories of colors:

- Primary colors (red, yellow, and blue)
- Secondary colors (orange, green, and violet)
- Tertiary colors (red-orange, yellow-orange, yellow-green, blue-green, blue-violet, and red-violet)

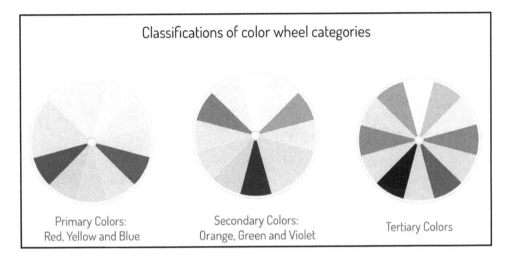

Secondary colors on the color wheel are created by mixing the primary colors, whereas the tertiary colors are created by mixing primary and secondary colors.

In the tertiary category, there are colors, such as red-orange, yellow-orange, yellow-green, blue-green, blue-violet, and red-violet.

In most of the visual design applications that you will use to create different user interfaces or graphic design assets, you will use the RGB color wheel a lot, where, besides the colors, you can also choose the shades and tones of the colors.

It doesn't mean that colors near to each other are related to one another, just keep in mind that the color wheel, also known as the color circle, is just a representation of colors, and you have tons of way of representing the color relationships.

So, depending on what fits your style of design better, you will choose the style of color wheel for creating your visual designs.

In the following diagram, I provided two different examples of showing the colors in different ways on the wheel (circle):

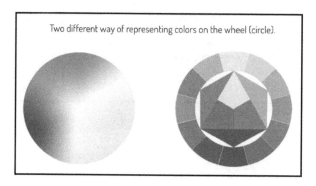

Two different way of representing colors on the wheel (circle).

The meaning of each color

As humans, we can be influenced psychologically by colors. It has been proven that colors have a connection to our health, and they can change our mood based on the designs that we see every day.

Each color has its own meaning, and it visually communicates with users through the designs. So, it's not enough for a designer to choose the colors for their design just based on whether they like a specific color:

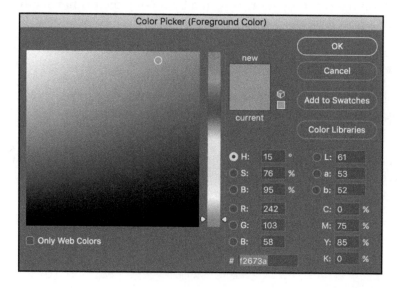

Similar to layout, lines, and shapes, colors also are considered as tools for designers, which they have in their toolbox, for creating and providing a proper design.

Before we dive into the details of each color and its meaning, it is really important to know that there is no substantive evidence that supports or stands behind one universal or general system of color meanings.

It's not that every color provided to us has to have its own meaning, but over the decades we have become used to receiving and understanding what and where specific colors are used through our life, and whatever it is surrounding us.

How we perceive color meanings can be based on our culture, where we live, or where we come from. When we are designing a specific product, we need to ensure that each color visually represents what we are trying to say through our design.

To simplify the meaning of colors, let's first separate them into the two most basic groups, which we are already familiar with:

- Warm colors
- Cool colors

Warm colors include colors that represent warmth. Those colors are usually associated with energy, happiness, passion, fire, and comfort. To make it simple, I will mention only three main colors that fall into this group: red, orange, and yellow.
The main thing that we want to draw attention to with warm colors is being more inviting and more harmonious.

For example, the following graphic represents warm colors:

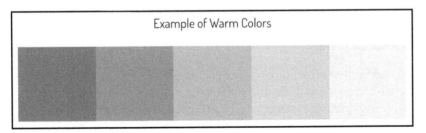

Example of Warm Colors

Cool colors can also be known as the colors of water. Often, these colors are associated with calm, cold, melancholy, trust, sadness, and professionalism. In order to keep things simple, in cool colors I will include only the three main ones: blue, green, and violet.

The following image represents some cool colors:

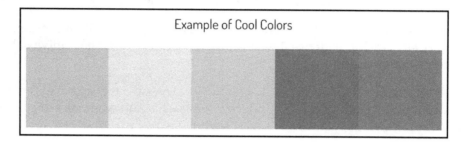

Example of Cool Colors

Let's dive deeper and explain the meaning of each color as we use them through our product design.

Red, which is really intense emotionally, is usually referred to as the color of two main things, fire and blood.
Red can be associated with things such as energy, power, danger, warning, courage, desire, passion, action, or love. Psychologically it can enhance our metabolism and also typifies our inspiration. Often, red represents increasing blood pressure, and we, as UX designers, use it in buttons to get our users to make impulsive actions in design.

Yellow, or the color of the sun as we also know it, represents attracting the user's attention, but overusing it can be distracting. This color is usually associated with warmth, happiness, wisdom, or joy. We use it when we want to mentally stimulate an activity or generate muscle energy.

Orange is usually seen as a combination of two colors, red and yellow. So, it tries to combine the energy, which comes from red, and happiness, which comes from yellow. It is neither depicted as aggressive as red nor as calm as yellow, but usually is associated with things such as sunshine, creativity, success, attraction, or even strength. It is well-known for its power to increase appetites.

Blue, which falls under the cool colors category, is referred to as the color of water and sky. This color represents the opposite of the warm colors, especially red; it shows more attention to cold things, and it is associated with calm, breathing, loyalty, confidence, expertise, and stability. All cool colors, especially blue, are used to generate a calm effect. Most of the time, during our design, we will use blue for corporate websites or a product that shows maturity, professionalism, strength, and stability.

Green represents nature. It is usually associated with optimism, growth, hope, fresh, wealth, safety, healing, and fertility. During our design process, we may use green for medical products to indicate safety.

Purple or **Violet** is a combination of two colors, red and blue. It represents the energy of red in combination with the stability provided by blue. This color is associated with things such as nobility, luxury, mystery, and ambition. For anything related to nature, purple is less frequently used, as it is considered an artificial color.

We also have the main colors, white and black. **White** is mostly associated with light, purity, or virginity, whereas **black** is associated with elegance, evil, formality, or mystery.

There are tons of other colors, which we can talk about, such as **brown**, which represents the wood or earth, or **gray**, which is connected more to security and maturity. So, in the design process, try to use a more neutral color, such as white and gray, and just highlight specific areas with accent colors.

You can find hundreds of articles online for the meaning of colors if you want to go deeper into this, but the main purpose of this book is not just to explain colors; it's important to know the basics so, at least, we can move ahead to other parts of UX, which are important to you as a designer to know and understand.

A few takeaways from this section would be for you to keep in mind that the meaning of a color can depend on the culture and other circumstances. Also, each color can have many different aspects, but the main purpose of this section was to explain simple concepts of colors so that you can have a better picture of their usage when you start designing a product.

So far, we have already explained in enough detail three basic elements of visual design, lines, shapes, and colors. Let's move on to the next element of visual design, which is font and typography.

Using the appropriate font/typography

We have come to a really important part of basic elements for visual design, which is **typography**. Typography–similar to shapes, lines, and colors–can be considered a tool for designers to create things that will be visually communicated to the users.

Typography is used to give a proper language to our product design. By using it properly, we can create a good flow for users to follow and understand our product.

Before moving deeper into this topic, I would like to clarify the main confusion that people have when we talk about typefaces and fonts.

Typeface is a visual design element in letterform, which can easily communicate to the users and they can immediately understand it, while font is how this design was delivered or presented to them.

Fonts are a part of typeface. Each typeface has its own family, and a typeface can have different fonts inside it. For example, a typeface can be a family of fonts (such as Arial or Helvetica), but when we use the term font, we refer to a single member or style of that family (such as Arial Italic or Arial Extra Bold). A lot of professionals confuse these two things, so hopefully this makes it clear for you.

Now that you understand the difference better, let's dig deeper and explain the different categories of typefaces. In this section, I will explain three basic categories of typefaces, as follows:

- Serif
- Sans-Serif
- Decorative

Serif typefaces are easily recognizable by tiny lines that are placed at the edges of their strokes, which are usually known as *Serifs*. Most of the time, this kind of typeface is used for headlines, website headings, or narratives.

Font families such as Times New Roman, Cambria, or Georgia fall into the serif typeface category.

You can take a look at an example of how serif typefaces look and their tiny serifs at the edges of font in the following image:

Example of Serif font
For this example we will use Gerogia font which is under 'SERIF' category of typefaces

Packt Publishing

The edges in the finishing lines of the fonts which are know as 'SERIF'

Sans-Serif typefaces do not have the tiny lines in their edges as shown in the preceding diagram. Even their names come with the word *Sans* before *Serif*, which, in French, means *without*. Compared to Serif fonts, which are mostly suggested to be used on elegant ways, headlines, or titles, the Sans-Serif fonts are considered more modern fonts, which can fit in a very small screen or area and mostly are used as the body text of any website:

Example of Sans-Serif font
For this example we will use Arial font which is under 'SANS-SERIF' category of typefaces

Packt Publishing

The edges in the finishing lines of the fonts
do not include the 'SERIFS' like in above example.

Font families such as Arial, Verdana, or Helvetica fall under this category of typeface.

Often, these typefaces are used in web pages or mobile content because they enhance the readability for users and are much easier to understand.

The last one, that is, the decorative typeface category, usually consists of fonts that do not really fit in any of these two categories and are mostly used to show some creative text. The decorative type is not preferred to be used for the body text or the content of the product, because, most of the time, it is really hard to read them and have a proper layout using them. They are a good fit for, and suggested to be used only for, titles.

The following is an example of a combination of these three typefaces and their advantages and disadvantages:

Example of mixing categories of typefaces inside our content

Packt

Packt Publishing is the leading UK provider of Technology eBooks, Coding eBooks, Videos and Blogs; helping IT professionals to put software to work.

Good combination and pairing. We are using here Serif for header (title) and Sans-Serif for the content.

Packt

Packt Publishing is the leading UK provider of Technology eBooks, Coding eBooks, Videos and Blogs; helping IT professionals to put software to work.

Good combination and pairing. We are using here Sans-Serif for header (title) and Serif for the content.

Packt

Packt Publishing is the leading UK provider of Technology eBooks, Coding eBooks, Videos and Blogs; helping IT professionals to put software to work.

Good combination and pairing. We are using here Decorative for header (title) and Sans-Serif for the content.

Packt

Packt Publishing is the leading UK provider of Technology eBooks, Coding eBooks, Videos and Blogs; helping IT professionals to put software to work.

Bad combination and pairing. Decorative fonts are bad approach for using them for content or body text.

When playing with typefaces we, as professionals, should know properly how to use their font families, sizes, colors, and format. Try not to use a lot of typefaces. Only if you are a professional should you do such an experiment. Using these elements properly, we can create a usable and readable hierarchy of our content that we can display in our product.

The following are a few other things to keep in mind when dealing with typography:

- **Alignment and Proximity**: This element refers to how text is displayed, for example, whether it is aligned in center, left, or right. Proximity means to consider other things, such as white space and how to arrange elements near to each other.
- **Measure**: In this element, you will need to consider the width of your content or the line of the paragraph that is being displayed on a specific column of design.
- **Leading**: This is alternatively known as a line height, so, here, you need to consider the space between two lines of paragraph or text.
- **Weight**: You need to consider the space that the font you have chosen will take, which means that you need to know the thickness of your typeface.

As a designer, you will need to be really good with typography, so, here, I just provided the basics for this topic, but you can always develop your skills on typography by being patient, vigilant, and constantly practicing it.

I am really glad that you have made it this far. Now, we move on to the next element of visual design, which is textures.

Textures

Textures are an important part of creating a proper visual design. They are associated with what they look or feel like.

Everything that we see around us has some kind of texture. For example, when we touch physical things, we can determine whether they are smooth, rough, shiny, or even silky. So, we feel their texture when we touch those physical things.

However, what about the textures that we can only see but not feel, for example, digital designs? Well, these kinds of textures, which we cannot feel but see, are known as implied or visual textures.

This kind of texture is usually created to get the attention of the users visually or for creating a focal point in a composition.

In the following figure, you can see the difference between the real and visual texture:

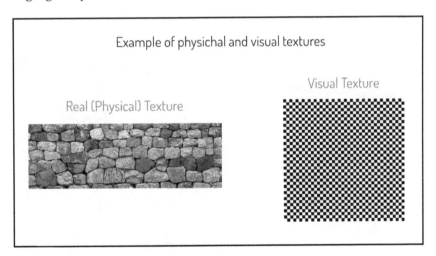

As you can see in the preceding diagram, textures can assist us in visual design to describe the details of a specific component or object that we are designing, and it helps users understand what those specific design objects are made of.

When we create textures visually, we create them to display a physical illusion that can explain what type of component that design is trying to deliver.

For example, the textures can use natural combinations so that they can bring an organizing life to our design. In the following poster, designer Dawid Sieradzki created a perfect balance between natural textures and visual ones:

A takeaway from this section is to understand that the proper use of textures can be a powerful asset or tool for creating compelling graphic designs without relying on the complexity of real-world objects. It doesn't matter whether you try to display a focal point using textures or emphasize the components, they will always have an important role in visual design for creating contemporary designs.

Now that we have arrived at the final element in basic visual design, forms, these will be explained in the next section.

Forms

This is the final element of the basics of visual design that we will discuss. When we talk about forms, we are usually referring to the elements that are of a three-dimensional nature.

For an element to be called a form, it needs to have three basic components: height, width, and depth.

Most of the things that surrounds us are created from form, starting with basic elements such as pens and pencils to the human body; all have form.

In visual design, we use form to define or describe a specific space or contrast and to add volume to a composition.

Form can be geometric or organic. Usually, since form needs to be displayed in a three-dimensional way, the illustrated or drawing element forms are designed in a 3D isometric design so that they can show the form of the object in the proper way. Consider the following figure:

Let's conclude this section. Keep in mind that a form is defined in visual design as a shape of something, and it refers to the aesthetic value of an object. The form can be created by combining two or more different shapes, which can also include other components, such as textures, tones, and colors.

This section covered six basics components of visual design, including lines, shapes, colors, typography, textures, and forms. Now, we will move on to another interesting part of how we can combine these visual elements to create a proper product design, which will be communicated visually to the humans. So, next, let's explain the design principles.

Design principles

Compared to visual design basics, design principles are more about the group of laws or guidelines that need to be followed so that we can create proper designs that can solve problems for users.

By following design principle laws, we will be able to design stuff that will have meaning for the users; for example, if we add text on our product, it should be designed properly such that users can easily read it, or if we design a user interface for a product, that user interface should be easy to use.

So, to have a successful product design, visual design elements should be combined with design principle guidelines. So, when these two are mixed together in a proper way, the final design will make sense for users.

Here, we will cover seven elements, which are known as design principles, and which we need to consider before starting our visual design process. The elements are as follows:

- Alignment
- Hierarchy
- Contrast
- Repetition
- Proximity
- Balance
- Space

If you consider yourself to be heavily involved in the visual design area, then for producing high-quality product design, these basic design principles are the key things that you have to keep in mind. It doesn't matter whether you are planing to design websites, web content, banners, mobile apps, or even physical products, design principles will be a guideline for you throughout the entire process of visual design to achieve successful results.

So, let's start with the first element of the design principle, which is alignment.

Alignment

Alignment is considered the most important and most fundamental or basic element that you should know when you will deal with visual design.

Using the alignment in the right way, we can order and balance the elements that are included in our design, and, as a result, we can achieve a sharper and clearer design.

Alignment will eliminate the distractions and messiness of our design and will align objects in the proper way so that users see a clean design. Since every element that we will include on our visual design has its own weight, not aligning them properly can result in a bad design.

When we discuss elements that should follow the alignment principle, we are not talking only about a specific one, but about all visual design elements, such as colors, sizes, fonts, and shapes. More importantly, the alignment can provide pleasing design for the users and will keep their interest positive to continue using the product, because each element will create a visual connection to each other, and it will be easier for users to follow the visual design flow.

In the following image, note the example of good and bad usage of alignment and take a look at the difference and benefits of using the alignment properly:

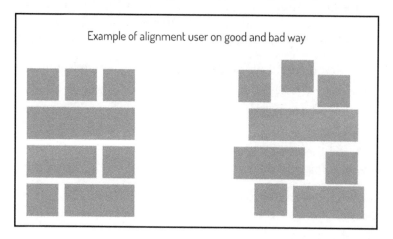

Example of alignment user on good and bad way

Hierarchy

When we do the visual design for a product, usually, we will have a lot of different elements included in the design, and we need to be sure to show more important areas better on the design and give them a better visibility so that the users of the product can receive the message correctly. The best way to do this is by following the hierarchy principle.

Using hierarchy, we can accomplish good design in different ways, for example, using the proper colors on specific areas that we want to draw the user's attention to, or by making headlines or text bolder when it's something important, or even by placing important elements higher in the design content and putting the less important ones underneath.

Hierarchy difference can be defined as a design principle that puts more important elements in the forefront and places the less-important elements in the background.

When dealing with hierarchy in our visual design, we always need to ask the following questions first:

- What will the user notice first when they look at our visual design?
- What will the user notice after they see the important content?
- What are the less-important elements for the users to be placed on our visual design?

The best way to create a proper hierarchy on our visual design is by keeping these three components in mind:

- **Size**: We can display more important elements in a bigger size
- **Shape**: We can highlight important elements inside specific shapes so that they get user attention immediately
- **Placement**: We can place important elements higher in our design

These three components, when used properly, will result in a readable visual design, which will send a visual message to the user on how to use the product.

You can understand this better from the following image, which is created as an example of having in mind the three components of hierarchy that we mentioned:

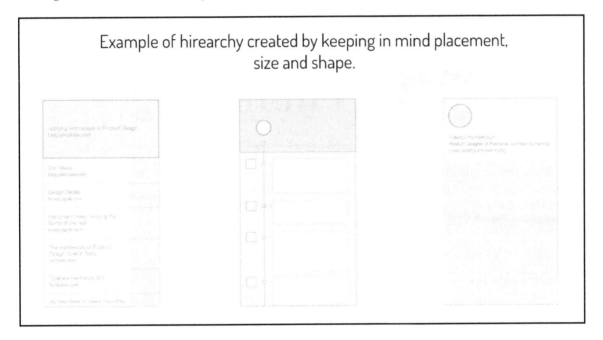

Contrast

Contrast is an important element of the design principle because we can draw out more important elements of the design and add emphasis to it using it.

Contrast often happens when we are dealing with two opposite elements in design; for example, when we are dealing with colors, contrast can happen between black and white. When we are dealing with shapes or typography, the contrast here is thick and thin.

The main reason why we use contrast in our visual design process is for grabbing the user's attention and creating a focus on a specific area of the design element that the user is looking at.

Contrast can be created on different elements of visual design, for example, using texture, typography, shapes, or colors, or even by combining all of those elements together.

Let's take an example using two different colors and typography together to create contrast between the elements that we are displaying:

The takeaway from this section is for you to keep in mind that contrast occurs when we combine two or more different visual elements, which are of different compositions. Contrast is considered a really strong principle for communicating an important part of our visual design to the user.

Repetition

When we want to create a strong and consistent visual design for our product, we use the repetition principle. Using this principle, we can even tie or connect together two different elements and make the consistency of the overall design better.

Consistency is one of the most important things when we have to deal with the branding and repetition principle. It helps us most in combining different elements of design to be tied to one another and being instantly recognizable to our users.

In the following diagram, I have taken an example of repetition used when designing different modals of websites, which are of different sizes and used for different areas of the website. However, using colors and repeating similar elements on them, we can create a proper repetition, and the design looks consistent:

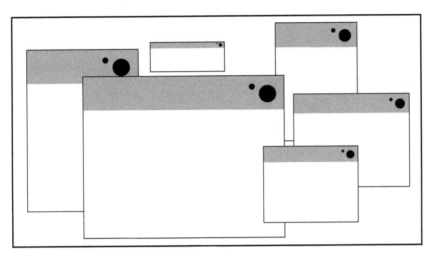

To create proper repetition, we can use similar connected points of that specific element design, for example, we can take the similar shapes or colors, as we did in the preceding example, and repeat the complete design element in other places of our visual design.

Like all the preceding three design principles, including alignment and contrast, the repetition design principle can be achieved using any of the visual design elements, such as shapes, colors, or textures.

To make it simple to understand, just keep in mind that repetition can be achieved by simply repeating the same single element of design many times throughout our entire visual design. The idea here is that using repetition properly will help us be more consistent in our design.

Proximity

We already discussed proximity in the preceding chapter, Chapter 6, *Designing Behavior*, when we explained in detail the importance of psychology on UX and, especially, the Gestalt law. Proximity is an important part of design principles because it helps us to create an organized visual design.

Proximity deals mostly with grouping similar elements of design together and creating a relationship between those elements of design. When we deal with proximity, always provide a focal point for the user so that they know where our design starts and ends.

Proximity does not always means that we place the elements of design together, but provide some visual connections between them.

Let's take an example of non-closed circles and group them together, or just provide some connection between them. You can take a look at the following diagram, which shows how it will make it easier for us to understand their connection:

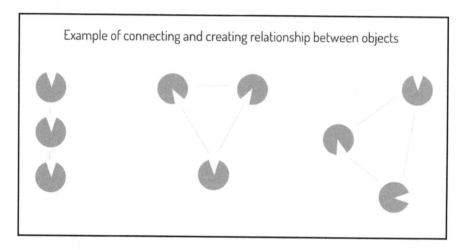

Example of connecting and creating relationship between objects

The takeaway from this section is that proximity groups similar objects together to provide meaning to design, and it is used for two main reasons:

- To provide a connection between design elements and create a visual relationship between them
- To dispel the connection; usually, we use this for separating or breaking the structure of elements that have no connection between each other

Balance

The **balance** design principle is used for giving form and stability to our visual design. It means that elements that we have on our visual design should be of the same size, color, and shape, and they need to be distributed properly and evenly across the entire visual design that we are creating.

Balance can be divided into three groups: symmetrical, asymmetrical, and radial.

Symmetrical balance means that we need to weight the elements on our visual design evenly. So, each side of the design should have the same weight of elements.

With asymmetrical balance, we can use contrast to even our design elements, for example, if we have dark elements on our design, they should be balanced by light ones.

Radial balance is created when all the elements of the design radiate from a center point, which can be another element of design. A better example of radial balance can be taken from the sun, where it is at the center of everything that it's producing.

Radial balance is a really good way to create a focus point for the user's attention. Usually, we radiate unimportant elements, that is, put them around the important one, so that the users can see it immediately.

In the following image, you would notice the difference between the symmetrical, asymmetrical, and radial balances:

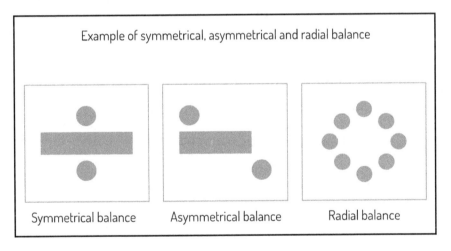

Keep in mind that balance during visual design most of the time can be found on the layout itself, and the position of design elements on the visual design that we are creating can tell us how much balance we have on our entire design.

As a designer, we should sense whether the composition on our design elements is balanced or not.

So, to create a proper balance between elements on visual design, we will need to use proper grids during our visual design process.

Using the balance principle, we can provide the proper structure to our visual design, create emphasis, and add stability to our design.

Space

Space is a really interesting and important part, which a lot of designers forget to think about at the beginning. As much as we care about what type of elements we are filling our visual design with, we should also consider its blank parts.

Negative space (also known as white space and blank space) can help us highlight important components of our visual design in the right way so that it can visually communicate with our users.

So, as a designer, we always need to consider the importance of both negative space and positive space. By positive space, I am referring to the design elements that we place on our visual design, and by negative space, I am referring to the empty space or the white space of our design.

We have already introduced this in Chapter 3, *User Behavior Basics and User Research*, where we explained the UX psychology laws, but here it is mentioned again since it is one of the principles of design and it's important for you to understand it.

Just like the balance principle, the best way to execute the space principle properly is to use grids.

We will talk about grids on UI design in Chapter 9, *UI Design and Implementation*, but it's important for you to know that the best way to organize space on design is using grids. When you learn how the grid system works, you are forced to use the space correctly.

For example, if you come from a developer background, you may already know that grids inside frameworks, such as bootstrap, force you to use specific padding or margins, which results in empty white spaces for aligning components together.

We've not explained the final element of the design principle, so let's move on and take a look at what we can achieve by combining all these visual design elements and design principles together.

Visual design tools

Now that you clearly understand the visual design elements and the design principles, you need to combine all these elements and principles together to come up with a great solution for your visual design.

Beside the concepts that we've covered so far, to create great visual designs of any kind, whether you are creating graphic assets or user interfaces, you will need to use design tools and software to produce the final design.

Before I move to the list of tools that you can use for creating visual design, let's discuss what we could to do to get inspired. For creating good-looking and usable visual design, we need to stay inspired and be creative. If it was so easy just to use tools and start doing the designs, then everyone would do it, right?

I highly suggest that if you want to focus on a visual design career path, you need to stay inspired daily, and the best way to do so is by looking at what other designers and design agencies are doing.

Two main platforms, or as I call them, design inspiration tools, which I suggest you to use, are Behance and Dribbble.

They have a big and amazing community of designers and design agencies, and you can get inspired by thousands of new works uploaded there daily. The good thing about these two platforms is that they are not focused on only one area of design–you can get inspired by graphic design work, user interface designs for web or mobile apps, and even for 3D or animation works.

Two other platforms that I recommend you follow are Awards and Inspiration Grid. These two websites also include dozens of different categories, including art, interior design, and graphic design:

Staying inspired will make your work on visual design much easier and will help you through the entire process of design, and this will result in much better visual designs and more unique ideas.

After you get your inspiration and have a better idea on what you want to design, it's time to choose the right tool for creating your design.

We will talk about tools and user interface design in detail in Chapter 9, *UI Design and Implementation*, where I will explain each tool separately and also the process of how to create outstanding user interface designs. Here I am just going to mention some of the tools so you get a better idea of which tools can be used for what.

I don't think that there is any professional designer who would not suggest the Adobe Creative Suite as one of the best toolsets or toolboxes for visual designers.

It is known as one of the best toolsets for designers because it includes various tools for different areas of design. For example, if you want to deal more with graphic design, Adobe Illustrator would be a perfect match; if you need a tool for photo-editing or photography, Adobe Photoshop would be the one to go to; if you need a tool for user interfaces, just grab Adobe XD; and even if you need a tool for creating different animation, just go for Adobe After Effect.

One of the amazing feature that Adobe Creative Suite provides is that it gets updated regularly, and it is so easy to set up through their Creative Cloud platform that you will enjoy the process of combination between the tools immediately.

Since this book is meant to be for developers who come from the web or mobile side, we will heavily use tools such as Sketch, Framer, and InVision throughout this book, especially in `Chapter 9`, *UI Design and Implementation*.

Sketch is mostly used to create user interfaces. It has tons of plugins, which allow us to interact with our design in different ways; it is also widely used and easy to integrate with other tools, such as Invision, Zeplin, and Simply, which makes the visual design process smooth and easy:

We've covered the design principles and the elements of visual design, and you got the inspiration, so is it time to grab the design tool and start doing visual designs? Well, we're almost there, but before we start doing the visual design, we need to create wireframes and prototypes of the product that we want to design and then bring it to life using the design tools, such as Sketch, Photoshop, and Framer.

So, before moving to the visual design side, especially for creating the user interface, let's move to the next chapter and explain the wireframes and prototypes so that when we move back to the visual design stage and use tools such as Sketch or Photoshop, we can create something like this:

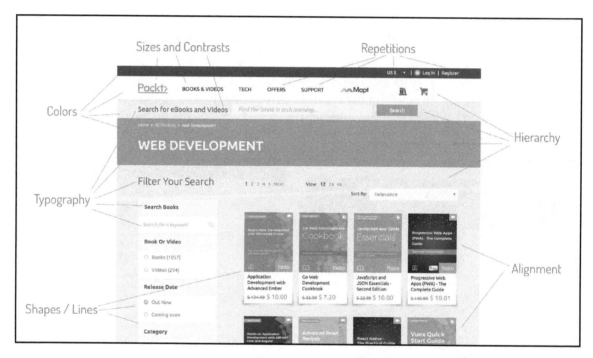

Summary

This chapter included some of the most important information that we had to cover before moving to the more interesting part of book, such as creating wireframes, prototypes, and user interfaces or visual designs, and using tools such as Framer, Sketch, and Photoshop.

Now, you should have a proper understanding of visual design elements, how to use them, and how to combine them correctly with design principles.

Keep in mind that these elements are the basics of every design that you will create. Practicing and improving your skills on combinations of those elements will make your life much easier when you start to get involved in creating visual designs. It doesn't matter what kind of design work you undertake, be it graphical, user interfaces, or 3D, this design principle will be the baseline when you start creating them.

In the next chapter, I will talk more about wireframes, how to create them, and why we need them. Then, we will move on to prototypes and the tools that we need to use for creating them, so see you in the next chapter.

Wireframes and Prototyping 8

In this chapter, you will continue to learn skills and methods for creating and designing interactive wireframes and prototypes, which will help us in the process of visual design, especially in creating better user interface designs.

I will share different examples of how wireframes can be created, what kinds of tools we can use, and what kinds of wireframes we can create to utilize better wireframes during our product design process.

Here, we will cover everything from the basics up to advanced concepts of wireframes and prototypes. Then, we will move on to explain the different types of wireframes that we can create.

By the end of this chapter, you will be able to understand the following topics better:

- Wireframes
- Types of wireframes we can create
- Prototypes
- Tools we can use to create wireframes
- Tools we can use to create prototypes
- Different types of prototypes
- Differences between low-fidelity and high-fidelity wireframes and prototypes

Wireframes and prototyping

So far, we've talked about the UX process, visual design elements, design principles, UX laws, and all the other important parts of the UX design discipline, but now it's time to talk more about the tools that are essential for us as UX professionals.

Usually, before starting the product design process, we draw some ideas on paper just to create some simple design concepts, think about the basic functionality, and see how our product will look in the end; we usually do this by creating wireframes or prototypes.

So, before we start the visual design stage for the product we want to build, we need to keep in mind that wireframes and prototypes are essential parts of our design process.

Before moving to the first section of this chapter and talking more about wireframes, I want to explain the difference between wireframes and prototypes in simple terms.

Whenever we talk about in this book, we're talking about the basic layout or structure of our product design. With wireframes, we just show the basic order of design elements inside our product—basic components that guide us to create a high-fidelity design in a later stage.

On the other hand, prototypes can be considered as advanced wireframes; they represent our product visually in a very detailed way. With prototypes, besides just showing all the design components properly, we try to give them a feeling that this is the final result of our product.

Before going deeper into the differences between wireframes and prototypes, let's first explain each of them and their use; then it will be much easier for you to get a bigger picture of their differences.

What is a wireframe?

Wireframing is one of the most essential tools that we, as UX professionals, should know about, because it is an important element when it comes to product design and development.

It doesn't matter whether we are creating a physical product, website, mobile application, or even if we are building the next start-up, wireframes are the key part for starting any of those and for keeping everyone on the same page – product designers, product owners, engineers, stakeholders, and many more.

In other words, wireframes visually represent the product's user interface before we start the visual design implementation. We use wireframes to create the hierarchy of user interface components that will be inside our product design.

To better understand wireframes, just consider building a house. For example, before you start building the house and painting and furnishing it, first you need an architect, who will draw the house plan and each floor plan for you to know where the kitchen will be, how much space you will get for the bedroom, and stuff like that.

So, the house plan or floor plan is the same as wireframes, because similar to building a house, after we get the requirements and a clear idea of what we have to build, we visually start to create the plan for it, so we start creating wireframes for our product.

We can create wireframes using only a pencil and sketch the product parts on paper, and we can even move to create more advanced ones using specific wireframes software, such as UXPin or Balsamiq.

The following are some of the reasons why wireframes are important for our product design:

- With wireframes, we can create a structure for each screen and add the needed component inside it, which will make the process much easier for visual designers
- We can create or specify different functions inside them, which will help us get an idea of how and where they will be placed in the final product design
- With wireframe, we can communicates our idea with different departments of the company, which makes it much easier to represent the product idea before presenting the design to stakeholders or clients
- We can explore different ideas of product design without too much effort by creating them immediately on advanced design software, such as Sketch or Photoshop
- We can test ideas at an early stage and use them as a basis for prototyping

Before going into more detail, don't be confused when I say that the first thing we need to do for a product design is to create wireframes, because here I am talking about only the visual design stage.

When you start the process of creating wireframes, you should have already finished the other stages of the UX process, such as research, user-persona creation, sitemaps, discovery, planning, and strategy.

We mentioned several times in this book that you are allowed to use methods from different UX stages to finish a specific one; for example, low-fidelity wireframes can be used in the early stage of the UX process when we are dealing with the discovery and planning stage, because during that part they can help us explore different possibilities for different functionalities of our product's design.

Before we start creating wireframes, we need to keep the following points in mind:

- A clear understanding of the product's goal
- A clear understanding of the user's goal
- A clear understanding of the user's motivation

If we do not have this information yet, then it is obvious we didn't do the UX process correctly. For that reason, we will need to go back to do the research and analysis, and create user personas, user journeys, a product sitemap, and other UX process stuff.

So, after we get a clear plan of what we will build, we can start with the creation of wireframes.

How to create wireframes?

Since we have collected data for our product and want to bring it to life using design, we can now start to create wireframes.

We have already mentioned that wireframes are a visual representation of our product's user interface, and we use the wireframes to guide us and make the process of visual design easier.

So, as the first step to create wireframes, we will need to have the following details so that everyone can be on the same page with us:

- **Structure**: In this part, we will think about and sketch the pieces of user interfaces components – how they will be put together, how we will structure them, and where we will place them
- **Content**: In this part, we will create a list of components, elements, or texts that will be included in our product's design
- **Informational hierarchy**: In this part, we will organize the information that we need to show to our users and display it in the best way
- **Functionality**: In this part, we will explain how the user interface will work, how elements are connected to each other, and how the users can follow the flow for finishing a specific task using this UI

- **Behavior**: In this part, we need to check how the wireframes are interacting with users, how the user interface behaves, how users can behave with the UI, and much more:

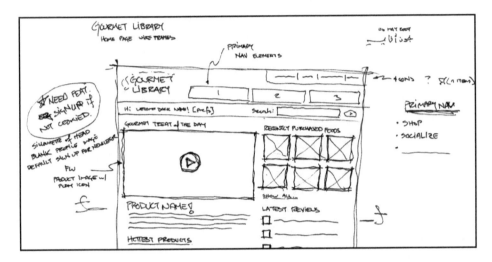

Do not confuse wireframes with visual design – they are not supposed to represent the final result of visual design or any other graphic element; they just help us to create a better visual design and guide us during the process of it.

Beside the five components mentioned in the preceding bullet points, the wireframes should also contain a number of other things, which will help other team members, especially the visual designers, to use them as a reference point, as follows:

- Each wireframe page should have a reference number, which clearly explains which page it is and where it is placed on our product's sitemap
- Each wireframe page should have a specific name or page title, and that should be linked with the sitemap as well
- Any information that will be useful to the team that will use the wireframes should be placed aside the wireframe sketch, in the form of notes or explanation text, which will help them get a better understanding of the wireframe
- Create specific components with unique reference numbers that can be repeatably used on other pages of wireframes

We have already mentioned a few components and rules that should be kept in mind before starting to create the wireframes. Now, before choosing the type and tools for creating wireframes, let's keep the following three things in mind and then start creating them.

Since the goal of wireframes is just to represent an early-stage design of our product idea, we want to keep it simple, as follows:

- **Don't use colors**: Usually, the wireframes are just black and white; the white is the background and we have black lines or shapes. So, instead of wasting time and relying on different tones of colors, we use just these two colors so that we can quickly move to creating the structure of the UI for our product.
- **Don't use images**: Most of the time, images distract us from finishing a specific task when we deal with visual design, so we just place a rectangular box with a big X inside it to show that we will place our image there when it will reach the high-fidelity design-implementation stage.
- **Don't use special fonts**: It is not worth it and has no benefits if we waste time choosing fonts during the process of our wireframes creation. We should use a generic font, something similar to Google Fonts or default ones, and care more about the structure and position of the content inside the wireframes.

In the following diagram, I've created a wireframe, keeping in mind the preceding three rules for creating a simple and straightforward wireframe:

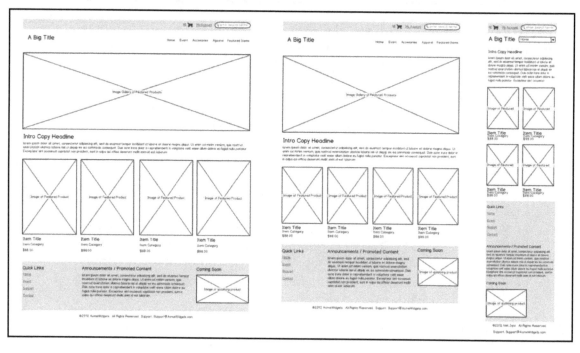

Types of wireframes

So far, I've been talking more about sketched wireframes, which are also known as low-fidelity wireframes. If we compare the tools that we use now with what we used a few years back, we will find that there is a big difference.

Often, people will confuse the types of wireframes; for example, you will hear that the wireframes are created only by pencil and paper or only by putting simple shapes on our design.

Well, again, if we compare the olden days' tools with modern software, we will note a big difference. So, these tools also improved and created different types of wireframes, in addition to the old pencil-and-paper ones.

We have three widely-used and popular types of wireframes, as follows:

- Low-fidelity wireframes
- Medium-fidelity wireframes
- High-fidelity wireframes

So, let's go forward and look at each one of them.

Low-fidelity wireframes

This type of wireframe is what I usually like to call a paper wireframe, since, most of the time we create this type of wireframes using pen and paper.

Basically, we have only two colors, white, which is the background color or paper, and black, which is the pencil. With this type of wireframe, we try to focus on our job of creating the big picture of the product, without going into detail.

The basic elements of the user interface that we can use are boxes, text, and lines, and we shouldn't add any other advanced details in our sketches. Often, this type of wireframes is quite abstract, which gives us only the basic structure of our product interface:

As you can see in the preceding photo, I sketched and created the wireframe so that I can use it as a starting point for my visual design work. Using it, I can have a simple picture or idea on how my user interface will be organized and where the block or design elements will be placed throughout my user interface.

If I were using any other wireframing tool, such as Balsamiq or UXPin, instead of pencil and paper, then for the dummy text, I would be displaying *lorem ipsum*, I could play a bit with the sizes of the fonts, and the boxes would be more consistent with one another. We will go into more detail later in this chapter and explain which tools should be used for what types of wireframes.

Each type of wireframe has its pros and cons, and I will try to cover both while I explain the types.

The pros of low-fidelity wireframes are as follows:

- It is really easy and fast to create them.
- We can easily change them to fit our needs without spending much time on them.
- It is much easier to get feedback from the client and do the changes immediately, and also to give them a better impression on how the product will look, compared to if you give the final user interface to the client. They will always hurt your feelings as designers by providing feedback for the features that you think look good but that they don't like.
- It will look simple at the beginning, showing low-fidelity wireframes to the stakeholders or client, but as time goes by, they will get used to it and will be more relaxed with the process of product design.
- Every team or department will be on the same page right from the first sketches of wireframes, and it will be easier for them to understand where the product is going.

The cons of using low-fidelity wireframes is just the simple design or ugly sketches, but you have to understand and explain to the clients or other people involved that this is just the first draft of the user interface design and they will see improvements on the way. The important thing is to create the first idea quickly and easily, and then move to the design tools.

Medium-fidelity wireframes

In contrast to low-fidelity wireframes, we use software tools for medium-fidelity, and, most of the time, instead of black and white, they are created in a monochrome palette, which usually appears visually in grayscale colors:

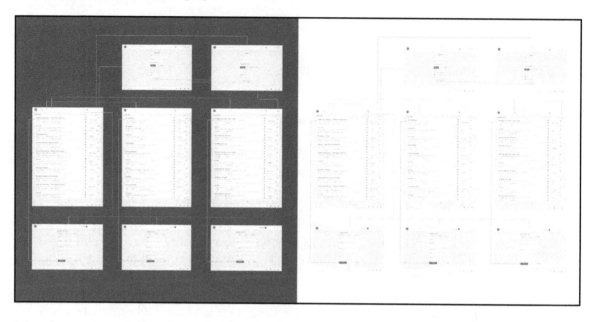

We can create medium-fidelity wireframes by either using a ready-made tool just for wireframes, or manually using Sketch or some similar tool. With this type of wireframe, we define the specific elements, which our user interface design will contain, and its visual hierarchy.

If we are creating them manually using tools such as Photoshop or Sketch, adding specific details can take a bit more time, but when we get used to it, we will be able to create them quicker.

Compared to low-fidelity wireframes, the medium-fidelity ones contain a more accurate structure of the user interface; its layout looks much better, and shows more details about specific elements or design components. For example, the difference between a link or button is much clearer and better represented; compared to the low-fidelity ones, the images or tabs are much clearer and more understandable.

Even though they are still black and white, we can use different shades of gray in this type of wireframe to separate specific components of design or make the visual designs more communicative and related to each another.

Similar to low-fidelity wireframes, here we do not care for images or font styles, so we will not put our focus there. The main focus is to provide a proper structure of UI components and a proper layout of our user interface.

The following are some of the pros of medium-fidelity wireframes:

- They show more details of UI components
- They are much easier to understand
- The design and UI layout looks much better
- It is easier to control the alignment and hierarchy of design elements

Some of the cons of medium-fidelity wireframes are as follows:

- It takes more time to create them, compared to the low-fidelity ones
- You will still need low-fidelity wireframes to create a medium-fidelity wireframe because it will be much easier to start designing the component inside design tools, such as Photoshop or Sketch, when you have the basic plan or skeleton of how your product user interface will look

High-fidelity wireframes

Compared to the other types of wireframes, especially low-fidelity ones, the high-fidelity wireframe contains a more realistic representation of the content and the UI itself.

In this type of wireframe, we can put more details into the design component and use specific typefaces, images, and proper text instead of dummy ones, as illustrated in the example of *lorem ipsum*.

Medium-fidelity wireframes are positioned more near high-fidelity wireframes than the low-fidelity ones, since both types try to represent a more complete product UI compared to low-fidelity wireframes. However, high-fidelity wireframes contain more design components, such as images, fonts, colors, and even grids:

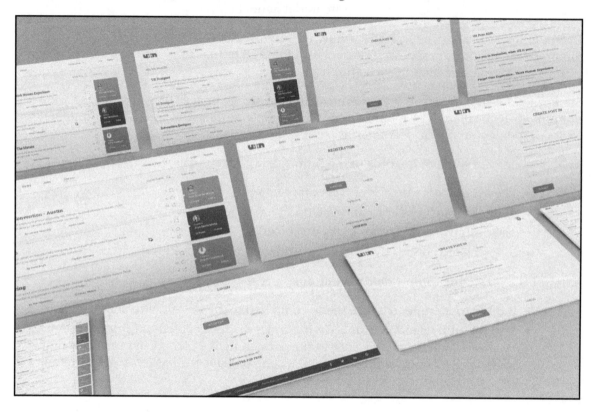

High-fidelity wireframes are usually built in the advanced stages of the product design process and intend to communicate the final look and feel of the product's design. Also, sometimes during the creation of this type of wireframes, we may include the branding colors as well.

The medium-fidelity wireframe is the most balanced wireframe type. This one should be used when we want to convince the client or another target.

Similar to medium-fidelity wireframes, we can create the high-fidelity wireframes using design tools, such as Sketch, Photoshop, Figma, and InVision Studio. So, when we are working with such advanced tools, we have more possibilities for the wireframe design and can improve the font sizes, alignment of UI components, represent colors, and so on.

In other words, this type of wireframe can be compared to the static version of our product, which can be a mobile application, website, or desktop app.

The following are some of the pros of high-fidelity wireframes:

- The user interface design looks much better than on the other wireframe types, and the amount of work that has been put in by the visual designer is visible
- If we present the high-fidelity wireframe without presenting the low-fidelity wireframes, our clients will be impressed
- With dozens of available programs nowadays, it is much easier to create high-fidelity wireframes

Before mentioning the cons of high-fidelity wireframes, I highly suggest people don't spend too much time and focus on high-fidelity wireframes since this is just the presentation stage for getting a better view of the product's design structure and layout. However, for a better and more detailed user interface design, we will go through the process of prototyping and UI design.

The following are some of the cons of creating high-fidelity prototypes:

- Despite all the advanced tools that we have, it still requires a lot of time to create them.
- To produce them is costly; you can achieve almost the same things with low-fidelity wireframes. It is not worth the price and time.
- They are complex for clients to understand immediately, and the client may confuse them with the UI design process of the product, because it will give them the feeling that this is the final design.
- The worst thing that can happen is that if the client, stakeholder, or product owner is not happy with the design, you have to start all over again, and the time you spent creating it will have been in vain.

I mentioned earlier that there is often some confusion between wireframes and prototypes, but the biggest confusion happens between high-fidelity wireframes and prototypes, and you need to keep in mind that these are two different things.

Even though high-fidelity wireframes contain similar or almost the same components as prototypes, including colors, fonts, and images, they have two different goals and are focused in two different directions.

High-fidelity wireframes are mostly focused on these structures of the UI page, whereas prototypes are mostly focused on the UI component details. The user can interact with them, and they are pretty similar to the final user interface design of the product.

People also get confused between UI design, prototype, and high-fidelity wireframes, but, again, these are three totally different things:

- UI design is the final design that we create for how our product will look and feel. It is a complete framework that contains all possible user interface components inside it.
- A prototype is the design created based on wireframes, which makes it possible for users to interact with it and get a feeling for how it looks to use it.
- High-fidelity wireframes do the same job as low-fidelity wireframes, but they are just represented better visually and try to give us an idea of how our product will look during the stage of UI design.

You will have a better understanding of their differences when you read the section about prototypes, so, for now, let's move on to the tools that we can use to create wireframes.

Wireframing tools

When it comes to the kinds of tools you should use to create wireframes, there is a lot of confusion, because some people do not suggest that specific tools are meant for wireframes, others will use simple tools, and still others will say you should use complicated and similar stuff. However, here, I will cover most of the tools that in one way or another have the options to create wireframes.

So, whatever tool can help us achieve the results of creating wireframes, even if it is not specifically designed for that, I will suggest it.

There are tools specifically for creating wireframes, such as Balsamiq, UXPin, and Wireframe.cc (https://wireframe.cc/), and there are tools that are meant more for creating graphical assets or user interfaces, but you can still use them to create wireframes, such as Illustrator, Photoshop, Sketch, and InVision Studio.

Wireframes can be created in different ways:

- Using pen and paper
- Using wireframing tools (Balsamiq, Axure RP, UXPin, or Wireframe.cc)
- Using graphical design software (Illustrator, Photoshop, or Sketch)
- Stenciling or paper cutouts

So, let's get started and explain each of the method and tools you can use to create wireframes. Keep in mind that some of them have subscription or software costs and others are free. Anyway, I will provide you with information about them, and then you can decide which one you want to use.

Sketch wireframes

This is one of the easiest and cheapest ways to create wireframes; all you need is a pen, marker, or pencil, and paper:

We have already discussed sketching in Chapter 2, *UX Design Process*, so you should already have a basic idea of it, but when it comes to wireframes, I would not recommend sketching with pen and paper as the final result for your wireframes. If you want to use sketch wireframes, buy special tools for this type.

It is always a great idea to start your wireframes with pen and paper so that you will get an idea of how your wireframes will look, and then you can move on to wireframing tools, such as Balsamiq, and present them in a better way.

When we talk about sketching, it is not just restricted to sketching wireframes on paper. You can also do it on whiteboards or even using iPad software, such as ProCreate, and do the sketches with a digital pen.

The main reason I suggested not to have the final wireframes on paper or a whiteboard is because it would be really hard to share them with the team and to organize different pages, and it would be hard to create a flow between pages. Another problem with paper is that it is not safe and can be easily lost or destroyed.

So, when it comes to wireframes, keep in mind that it is always a great idea to start the wireframes with pen and paper and then move them to wireframe tools, such as Axure, Balsamiq, or UXPing, for better presentation and ease of sharing with other members of the team.

Stenciling and paper cutouts

To create stenciling wireframes, we can easily print out or create lines and shapes based on the stenciling tool that we have. There are a few companies that sell this tool online, such as UXPin paper products or UIStencils products, where you can find dozens of different stencils. For more information, you can check out their store at `https://www.uistencils.com/collections/stencils`:

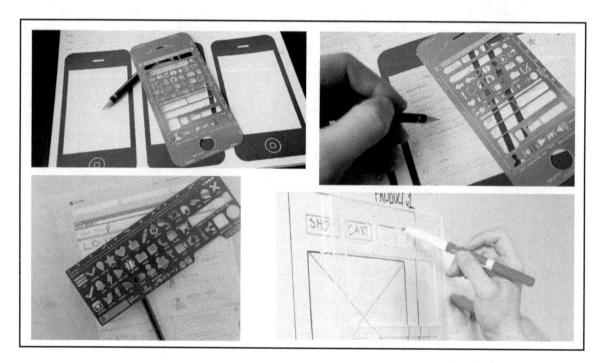

We can easily create paper cutout wireframes ourselves by cutting the paper based on the sketches we created. Then, we can use those cutouts to create different wireframes:

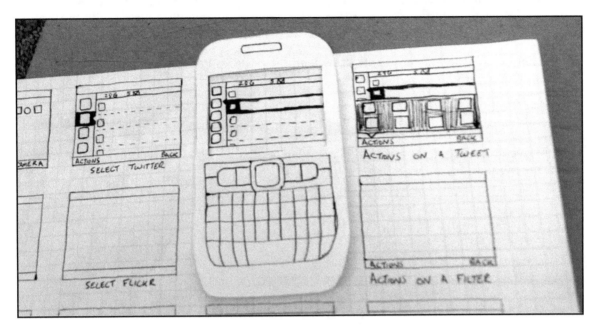

As I said for sketching wireframes, these two ways to create wireframes should not be used for the final result of wireframes. They are a great asset for creating basic wireframes, playing around with them, and testing different user interface behaviors, but they cannot be used as the final result.

Playing around with all these different methods – sketches, stenciling, and paper cutouts—of wireframes will definitely help you to create a proper wireframe using wireframing tools, such as Axure or Balsamiq, and will give you a better understanding and idea of how you should create the wireframes.

Wireframing software

Here comes the interesting part of creating wireframes—using the proper tools, which were created specifically for creating wireframes.

Let's start with the first tool that I prefer to use for my daily work when I have to deal with wireframes: Balsamiq.

Balsamiq mockups

This tool is one of my favorites when it comes to wireframes. It is really easy to use, contains a nice user interface, and contains a lot of design elements, starting with buttons, lines, boxes, headers, and inputs, which you can easily drag and drop to create wireframes.

All the design components are hand-drawn, and it gives you a feeling that you are sketching the wireframes yourself.

Balsamiq is a multi-platform tool, so you can use it on your Mac, Windows, or even the web-based version.

It is not free; it is a premium tool, but if you plan to seriously be involved in UX design, it's worth the money:

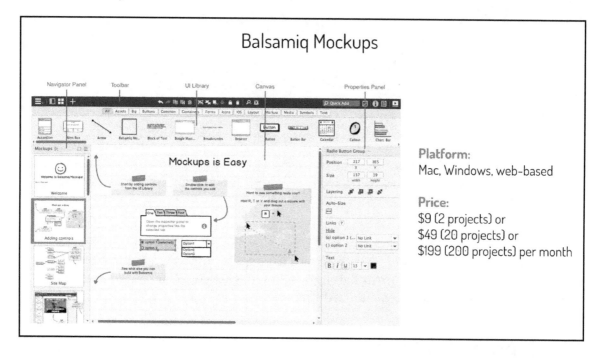

Wireframe.cc

This tool is great if you want to start building simple wireframes quickly and easily. It contains similar elements to Balsamiq, but the downside of Wireframe.cc is that it's only web-based, and you will not be able to work with it offline or have it installed on your Mac or Windows system.

It has a limited color palette, so it helps you to avoid any mistakes when you are creating the wireframes; it contains a really simple and minimal interface, and you can easily draw your own shapes to create the final design of a wireframe on the container.

It has a free subscription plan, so you can try and play around with it, but if you want more features and want to use it with a bigger team, you have to subscribe to the premium plan:

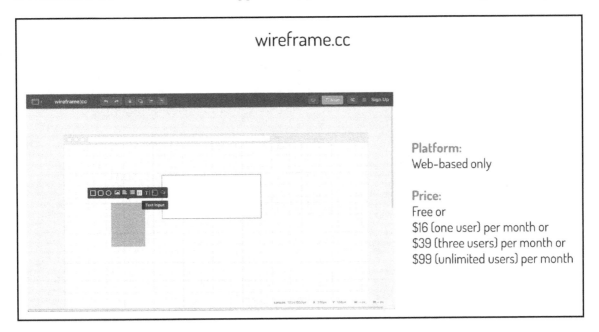

Moqups

This tool is a bit more advanced than the two previous ones, because it covers the whole process of wireframes, from the rough sketches to the final result. Also, it is a really great tool because you can collaborate with other team members.

Besides the basic features for creating wireframes, you can also create site maps, connect pages between each other, and create flowcharts, and even storyboards.

The downside of the Moqups tool is that it only comes with a web-based version, and you do not have the option of having the tool installed locally on your Mac or Windows machine.

Just like in Wireframe.cc, it comes with several subscription options, and you can use the free subscription plan to test it first before you move to the premium plan:

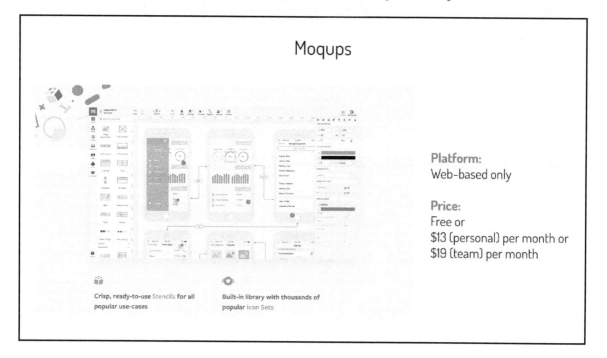

InVision

Although mostly used and known as a prototyping tool, InVision is one of the most widely-known wireframing tools in the design industry.

It is much more advanced than the three previous tools, and one of the main reasons that most businesses prefer this tool is that you can integrate it with different external services, such as Slack or Trello.

The user interface is really well-structured, and once you get familiar with it, the process of creating wireframes with it becomes really easy.

Similar to Moqups, InVision covers the entire process of wireframe design and even moves to more advanced things, such as prototyping and sharing the wireframe design with developers, where they can easily see the generated styles used inside the wireframe design.

Usually, companies that have a few different departments and many team members prefer to go with InVision because it is really easy to collaborate with each other, and it covers the different stages of the design process, such as wireframing, prototyping, and UI design.

The subscription model of InVision gives you a few choices; you can subscribe per number of projects or even per number of team members:

UXPin

Usually, I suggest this tool only when you want to create high-fidelity mockups, because it gives you the feature to create the wireframes and it gives you the options to convert your wireframes to high-fidelity mockups quickly, after which you can include interaction with UI components and convert the mockup to a prototype.

It comes with tons of UI components, which includes the UI from the CSS frameworks libraries, such as Bootstrap, or even the native iOS and Android components.

Besides the basic function for creating wireframes, UXPin comes with an option to transfer your final UI design from software design tools, such as Photoshop or Sketch, and create animations with them.

UXPin is a web-based-only platform, but its interface and speed is really great, and it is a premium tool:

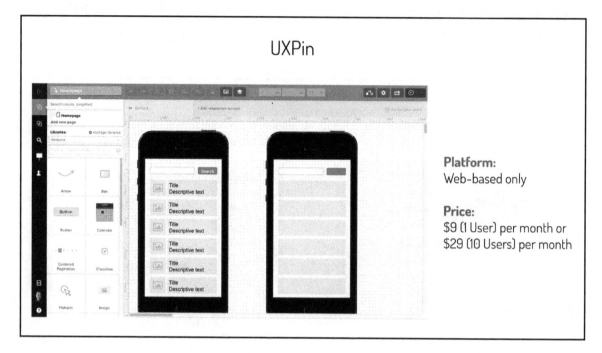

Axure

Axure is an advanced tool, mostly used for creating prototypes, but you can also create high-fidelity wireframes with it. It comes with robust features and functionalities, and it allows you to fully validate your ideas through the created wireframes before you start the design or coding implementation.

Axure provides you with the option to create different types of wireframes, screen flows, add dynamic content, and even convert your wireframe to a prototype by adding different animations to it.

Another cool feature is the wireframe-conversion-to-interactive-HTML mockup, where you can test the user interface behavior on your browser without needing to write a single line of code.

It is available only for desktop platforms, such as Mac and Windows, but considering the dozens of features that come inside this tool, it is totally understandable why they do not provide a web-based version:

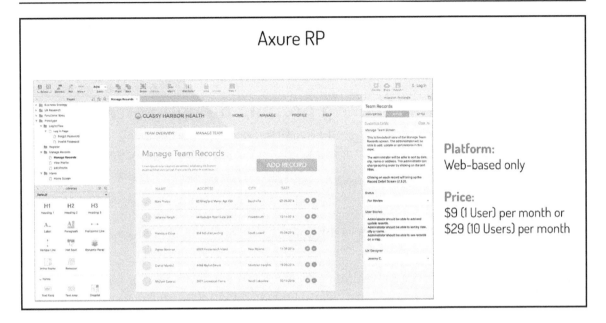

Other wireframing tools

There are dozens of other tools in the market – it all depends on your taste and budget. When you deal with wireframes, I highly suggest that you do the sketches first with pen and paper and then move on to a tool such as Balsamiq Mockups, but, as I mentioned, it all depends on your preferred choice, so you can go with the tool that fits your style of work.

Other wireframing tools that are worth checking are as follows:

- Fluid UI (https://www.fluidui.com/)
- Pidoco (http://pidoco.com/)
- Penultimate from Evernote (https://evernote.com/products/penultimate/)
- OmniGraffle (https://www.omnigroup.com/omnigraffle/)
- Mockflow (https://mockflow.com/)
- MockPlus (https://www.mockplus.com/)
- HotGloo (https://www.hotgloo.com/) and
- MockingBot (https://mockingbot.com/)

Try the tools that I have mentioned here before you make a final decision, and then use the one that best fits your style of work, and then move on to the next stages of design.

Don't get confused by the tools. A lot of them provide different features, but most of the time, using one tool, you will be able to do both wireframes and prototyping, and some tools, such as Axure or InVision, help you to build the UI design.

Creating wireframes using graphic design software

A lot of professionals in the UX design field usually create wireframes using graphic design software, such as Photoshop, Illustrator, or Sketch, so those are the clear winners if you choose to use them for wireframing too.

For many product teams, however, the better option is wireframing software because they're focused solutions for wireframing, a central medium for collaborating on wireframes, and integrating with other tools that are important in the entire product design life cycle.

This concludes our discussion on wireframes. I hope that you have a better idea and understanding of why, when, and how we use and create wireframes. So, now is the time to move on to the next section of this chapter where we'll talk more about prototyping.

What is prototyping?

While sketching and wireframing gives us a better idea of how our product's user interface will look, where specific features will be placed, and give us an overall visual design of our product, prototyping brings us to another level. It brings us closer to the functionality of our product.

Prototypes will explain and provide us with the idea of how our final product will work and how it will behave when we interact with it.

The design that we created during the wireframes stages can look really good, even on UI design stages, but we will never be sure whether its functionality works correctly or not, so this is where prototyping comes in.

With prototypes, we include interaction and functionalities in our static design. We can test all the components and get a feeling for how the final product will function.

Don't confuse the prototype with the final product; compared to sketches, mockups, and wireframes, prototypes have a higher degree of interactivity, but they will never have the final product's functionalities or interactions. To put it simply, prototypes are simulations of the final product.

Prototyping is one of the most important steps when it comes to the UX design process, because it helps us to test and work with the user interface of our product in an early stage where we can test it with real users. So, this means that it saves us from making mistakes on the final product development, because we identify the user interface mistakes in this stage and save time and money by delivering the final product properly.

With prototyping, we can easily resolve issues on the usability side before we launch the product; we can also identify the weak areas of the user interface and improve them.

There are a lot of reasons why prototypes are important and really useful during the UX design process, but here I will mention a few important ones:

- It makes it easy to communicate and collaborate with other team departments and members during the design process.
- It reduces the cost of money and time. With mockups, wireframes, or rough sketches, we can have a good idea of the product design, but with prototypes, we have the ability to test the user interface directly, interact with it, and note where we are lacking and what we need to improve in our product design interface.
- It makes the process of presenting to the client easier and increases the possibility of selling the idea. The client or stakeholders will be impressed by the presentation of the product you show them, and it will pique their interest more when they will be able to interact with it, without losing time on creating a final product for them.
- It makes it easier to set design priorities. When we interact with prototypes, we can see where we are lacking on the user interface, and what is not behaving or working correctly so that we can set priorities on what we need to improve first and what we need to avoid.

Now, the question is, when do we need to create a prototype? Well, we have to create prototypes every time that we need to show how a product design or user interface is supposed to behave and work.

The best example for prototypes can be taken from mobile apps, because on mobile devices, we can have different kinds of gestures that we use to finish a specific task, such as swiping right or left, up or down, dragging something, tapping the screen, and holding the finger on specific buttons longer.

So, these behaviors can all be created on prototypes, and we get the feedback for the design that we created from real people.

Similar to wireframes, prototypes also have three main types that we can create:

- Low-fidelity prototypes
- Medium-fidelity prototypes
- High-fidelity prototypes

The types of prototypes will not be explained again, since they have all the same specifications as the wireframes types. The only difference is that here the interaction inside the design elements is added along with other things such as animations and functionality.

There is a common misconception regarding prototypes: that we have to create them at the end of the UX design process. Well, this is not true; we should do it early and often.

However, then, the question is how to do it early when we do not have the final UI. Well, again, similar to wireframes, prototypes can be created in different ways for example, in the early stages, we can create paper prototypes and cut out parts of paper to have different kinds of interaction with them.

So, to not confuse you more with different methods on how to create prototypes, let's move to the next section and describe the most useful methods of creating prototypes in more detail.

Prototyping methods

We have already said that we have three different types of prototypes the low-fidelity, medium-fidelity, and high-fidelity ones.

Each of these types can be created using different methods or tools. So, the lower the fidelity, the less time it will take to create those prototypes, the higher the fidelity, the longer it will take to create them.

So, let's take a look at some of the methods used for different types of prototypes so that you will understand how and when to use them:

- **Low-fidelity prototypes**: Can be created using paper prototypes, stencils, or even paper cutouts.
- **Medium-fidelity prototypes**: Can be created using digital prototyping tools, which will add interaction to our design using the features of those tools. The tools that we can use here are UXPin, InVision, Proto.io (`https://proto.io/`), Webflow, and Principle.
- **High-fidelity prototypes**: Can be created either using digital prototyping tools or by coding them directly. The most widely-known tools for creating high-fidelity prototypes are Axure RP, InVision Studio, Framer, Origami, Adobe XD, and Flinto. Don't get confused when it comes to medium-fidelity and high-fidelity prototypes, because most of the tools can be used on both sides to create the prototypes. The only difference is that in the high-fidelity prototypes, we will use more design elements, such as colors, images, and real content, whereas the medium-fidelity prototypes are often visually displayed in grayscale.

Let's explain each of these methods.

Paper prototyping

This method for creating prototypes existed even before the internet did. It is preferable to use it in the early stages of product design and development, mainly to test the product idea. It is not preferred to use it in the advanced stages of product design because it will become complicated to have control over the pages that we create and to share them with our team.

It's a really easy method. We simply create the design on paper or another similar medium, cut out the repeated part, and try to interact with them by mimicking the specific design that we are trying to make.

Similar to the following figure, we create a user interface for mobile devices, in our case, for iPhone devices, so we cut out the iPhone screen and display it through different designs that we have on paper and interact with it, as follows:

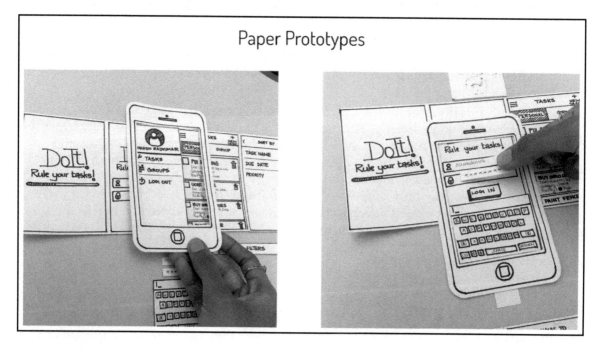

This method of prototyping falls under the low-fidelity type of prototypes, and it also has low functionalities that can be done with it.

The pros of this method are as follows:

- It's really easy and fast to create. We can create paper prototypes in 5 minutes, if needed, to test some product ideas.
- It costs almost nothing to create them, so this method is inexpensive, because we basically only need scissors, a pen, and some paper.
- They are fun to create, and it can make different groups of people interact with them using only their hands.

The cons of this kind of prototyping are as follows:

- They are unrealistic. It doesn't matter how advanced or skilled we are at creating them, they are simply poor replacements for digital systems.

- We get false feedback sometimes since people might not understand the idea of this kind of prototype and provide you feedback based on how they feel when they interact with papers, not keeping the digital devices in mind.
- It has almost zero interactivity. When you play around with them, you cannot get a proper idea of how a particular element will behave when you click, slide, touch, or drag it.

Similar prototypes can be created with paper cutouts or stenciling.

So considering both sides, the good and bad ones, paper prototypes are recommended only in the early stages of product design when you want to test your product idea, because when you start creating the real product, the gap between the product and paper prototypes will be big. These types of prototypes are good for the early stages, but avoid using them on the later stages of product design.

Digital prototypes

This is one of the most used methods for prototyping. To create digital prototypes, we will use tools such as Adobe XD, InVision, Figma, Principle, UXPin, or Origami.

This kind of prototype is much easier to produce compared to the coding ones. Also, if we compare both of them, their results will not be too different.

Some advantages of using digital prototypes are as follows:

- **Realistic design**: It depends on the fidelity level, but if we create high-fidelity prototypes, then their design will be really similar to our final product.
- **Realistic interactions**: We, or our users, can interact with them in an environment that can be compared to the final product. As per the design, the interaction will depend on the fidelity level that the prototype has been created.
- **Flexibility**: It gives you flexibility during all stages of product design. We can start testing early with low-fidelity prototypes and improve them as an ongoing process when we jump through the different stages of product design.
- **Speed**: We cannot compare the speed of digital prototypes with the paper ones, but when it comes to coding prototypes, the digital ones are in the lead. It is much faster to create prototypes with the aforementioned tools than writing the code from scratch on HTML, CSS, or JavaScript.

Beside the advantages, the two downsides of this kind of prototype are as follows:

- **Learning time** (**learning curve**): It will take a bit of time to learn how the software works. It will not be difficult since most of them have really great user interfaces, but, again, it will be a bit time-consuming at the beginning.
- **Transition to code**: This point mostly depends on the software that you choose, because when you have finished the design and it gets translated into code, mistakes can happen, for example, elements may not be compatible or the transitions may not be working; these kinds of issues can force you to recreate the prototype from scratch.

The result of the final prototype depends a lot on the tools that you use; some are better for visual design and others are better for interaction design, so it is always good to learn more than just one tool for prototyping.

It is important to know that you can create prototypes even with presentation software, such as Keynote or PowerPoints, but, for sure, there will be a lot of limitations on them.

However, when it comes to presenting the prototypes, the best choice always would be Adobe After Effect. It is a really great tool for animation and presenting how your product user interface will behave. You cannot interact with the prototype created on Adobe After Effect, but you can present how your user interface can work and what will happen when users interact with it.

Coding prototypes

This is the last method I will mention for creating prototypes. It is a really advanced one and only recommended to be used by designers who have coding skills.

It is clear that this method of creating prototypes has a lot of benefits because we can create almost-realistic products and interact with them directly, but, for a lot of companies, there is a technical cost in creating them.

When I say a technical cost, I mean that it will cost money to hire someone who knows both sides of design and coding. For this kind of work, the best fit would be a full-stack designer, as we discussed in Chapter 1, *What Is UX?*.

The downside of this method is that the person involved in creating them needs to do two things at the same time, designing and coding. This can cause you to lose your focus on designing with the users in mind, which is much easier with digital prototypes, since you have more room to explore different ideas of design and you don't have to think about the coding side since the tool that you choose will do the coding for you.

Widely-known software or tools that helps you with the coding part include Axure and Framer. Both after you finish the design and add the interactions on your prototype, they generate the code for you.

Also, another downside of this method of prototyping is the designer's coding skill level. For creating coding prototypes, a designer needs to have a pretty good knowledge of HTML and CSS and should also have some basic knowledge of JavaScript to create the animation and interaction on the design.

However, besides these two disadvantages of coding prototypes, there are the following advantages:

- It gives you the feeling that you have built the final product because of high-fidelity prototypes that can be created using them
- It is a huge timesaver when it comes to the development part, because the developers have already seen what is created on the code thus far, and it will be easier for them to avoid the same mistakes that were created during the coding of the prototypes and improve the real coding for the final product
- It is low-cost in terms of software, because you do not have to pay monthly or buy a specific tool to create the prototypes – you will only need a skilled designer who knows the coding part of HTML, CSS, and JavaScript
- You can test your prototype on different devices without any limitation on them and give the feeling to the users that this is the final product, and you will get better and clearer feedback

It doesn't matter which method you choose or which tool you pick to create the prototypes, but I would always recommend that you start creating prototypes from the low-fidelity ones and improve them, step by step, to the high-fidelity ones; if you have coding resources, it would be even better in the later stage if you can convert them to a coding prototype as well.

Before we start exploring some of the tools that you can use to create prototypes, let's explain how the process of creating prototypes works.

The process of creating prototypes

Every designer has their own process of creating prototypes. We have already discussed the methods for creating them. Some move directly to the designing and coding part, and some plan them on paper and go from low-fidelity to high-fidelity ones, but I would always suggest that you perform the following five steps when it comes to creating prototypes:

1. Planning
2. Drawing and sketching
3. Mockup and design
4. Animation and interaction
5. Exporting and testing

Planning

Similar to wireframes, when it comes to creating prototypes, we first need to create a plan for it. The plan should be clear as to what will be included inside our prototype – what kinds of screens can be used, what they contain, the flow between the screens, and the relationship among those screens.

We can create the plan using just a pen and paper, or we can use tools that will allow us to create the diagram, workflows, or mind-mapping. Many of these tools are available online, including Lucidchart, Xmind, draw.io (`draw.io`), and FreeMind, which are worth checking out.

As long as you are able to understand the steps that you described using those tools and the other team members are able to understand them, you are good to go.

I usually prefer to go with pen and paper, but sometimes it gets messy when you have to go through a lot of papers when we have to deal with too many screens.

Let's take a look at an example. Let's say that we are creating the Packt Publishing website, and we have two sides of using it—as an author or a publisher, and as a user or reader of the content that Packt is providing:

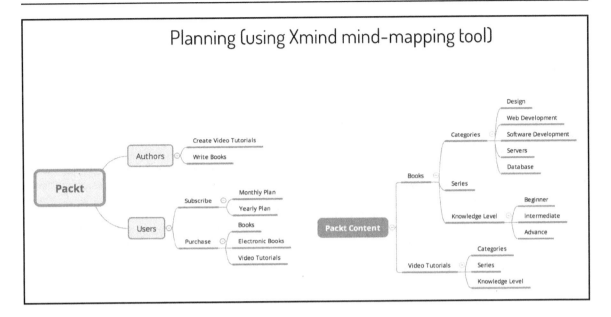

Note that I used Xmind in the preceding diagram, a mind-mapping tool used to create the diagrams that represent the content inside the Packt platform.

We can achieve the same objective using only pen and paper. In the following diagram, I am taking an example of the content of our Packt platform, the type of our pricing model, and connect the dots between them so that it will give us a better idea of what we have to design in the next stages:

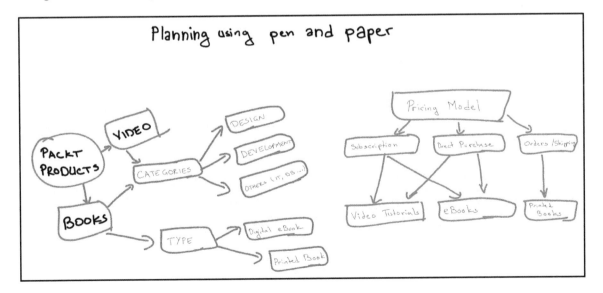

After we create in detail what our screens will contain and how they are related to each other, we move on to the next step, which is sketching the screens.

Drawing and sketching

The drawing and sketching step is really self-explanatory. All we have to do is to grab a marker, pen, or pencil and draw the sketches on paper, or you can do it on your tablet with digital pens.

We sketch the screens that we add during the planning stage and add the elements that we need to have inside our product and what we want to prototype.

Let's continue with the Packt Publishing website and create the sketches based on the preceding screen that was created during the planning stage:

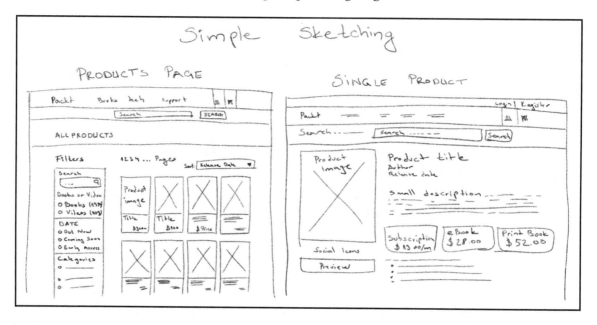

Mockup and design

In this stage, we grab a tool that we want to create the visual design with. It can be a simple one, such as Keynote or PowerPoint, or an advanced one such as Photoshop, Figma, or Sketch.

It all depends on your level of skill with those software. Whatever tool you choose for creating the designs, you will have to create the design based on your sketches from the preceding step.

Similar to creating wireframes, we align elements, create grids, and add design components. Also, here, we start by creating a color palette and the main design components that we will use inside our user interface, and add labels, buttons, text, and other necessary elements.

We continue doing this to create all the screens that we mentioned during the planning stage:

Animations and interactions

Now, the animations and interactions are the most interesting part. It's time to connect them together, to create an animation and interact with it.

During this stage, most of the time, we will have to use tools such as InVision, Framer, Principle, MarvelApp, or Atomic. If we create the design using a tool such as Sketch, this stage would be even easier. That is because almost all of the products that I mentioned now have a plugin extension, from where we can easily export all the designs from Sketch to the software and start creating the animations and interacting with them.

So, after we create all the design components, we can now add functionalities to them, for example, we link the pages with one another so that we can move between them; we add animation to modals, progress bars, forms, and much more.

Besides interacting with them, during this process, we can add different animations, such as transition between the pages when we switch, click effects, or swipe animation if we are designing for mobile, but we have to always do it in a minimal way so that it will not distract the user's mind from providing us with helpful feedback, because as we have already seen, this is just for testing purposes and not the final product design.

During this stage, we create prototypes. We can interact with them and take a look at how they behave and how the design works.

Exporting and testing

Finally, we export the created prototypes on specific devices, which our prototyping tool allows, and we start to test them with our devices and with the potential users as well.

During this stage, sometimes we will need to go back and forth between the design and animation stages, but this will only help us to improve the final product.

So, we gather all the feedback while we are testing our prototypes with our users and improve it during the course of the design process.

This is just one of the simple processes for creating prototypes; it all depends on the complexity of your project. If the project is a small one, your prototyping process will probably be much simpler with the usage of simple tools; if the project is bigger, the prototyping process can be separated into more detailed parts.

Now, let's move on to the tools that you can use for creating prototypes.

Prototyping tools

There are many prototyping tools available today for designers. They vary from static designing tools to fully-interactive design tools.

These types of tools make the process of product design faster and more effective compared to the older versions of toolsets They help us to represent our ideas more easily and to avoid mistakes in the different stages of design.

There is a long list of tools that we can use to create prototypes, and to choose one among them is a really hard task, but if we choose the right one, it will be help us to explain our ideas to the team and to our users.

In this section, as in the wireframe tool section, I will just mention the most well-known prototyping tools. It is up to you to check which one best fits for your style of work.

Don't get confused when I say that a few of them have already been mentioned in the wireframes section; most of today's tools can be used for both creating wireframes and for prototypes.

The tools that we have already covered in the wireframe section but are also heavily used for prototypes are InVision, UXPin, and Axure.

These are amazing tools that you can use for both sides, so we will not mention them here again, but it is really good for you to check them out and take a look at the results you can achieve with them.

MarvelApp

MarvelApp is a great prototyping tool; it simplifies the process in extremely effective ways when it comes to dealing with prototypes.

Its interface has an amazing user experience, and it is really easy to understand how to use it. Once you get familiar with the basic toolset provided by Marvel, you can easily start adding gestures and transitions to your design, which will result in a great prototype.

One downside of Marvel is that it is a browser-based tool, but once you get used to it, the process goes smoothly.

You will be able to upload different types of images, including GIF and PSD. Another great thing about MarvelApp is that it has an option to connect with different tools or online services, such as Dropbox, SketchApp, and Google Docs:

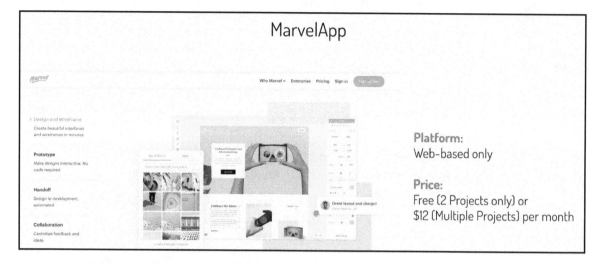

Origami.Design

Origami is a tool created and used by Facebook. Origami has similar features to the other tools we've covered, which will allow you to create interactive prototypes.

It comes with extensive documentation on how to use it and has a big community. It can easily use files created from other design software, such as Photoshop or Sketch.

Origami is mostly known for its features when it comes to testing on mobile devices, especially on iOS devices using the Origami Live extension:

Justinmind

Justinmind is a desktop app that allows you to create interactive prototypes for both web and mobile. It is really easy to use the brand identity colors and components when you work with Justinmind.

Beside this, it also generates the style guide and branding guidelines in an HTML format, which allows you to use it online for presentation to the users or for internal usage:

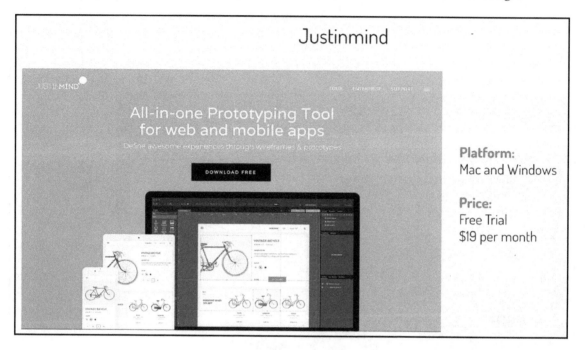

Flinto

When it comes to building prototypes, even complex ones, without any coding skills, then Flinto is it.

It is really fast to create with simple click-through prototypes and easy-to-create complex prototypes. We can reuse the same transitions and animations for different types of design components without the need to recreate them over and over again.

Flinto can be used in both ways, as an iOS app or a web-based version:

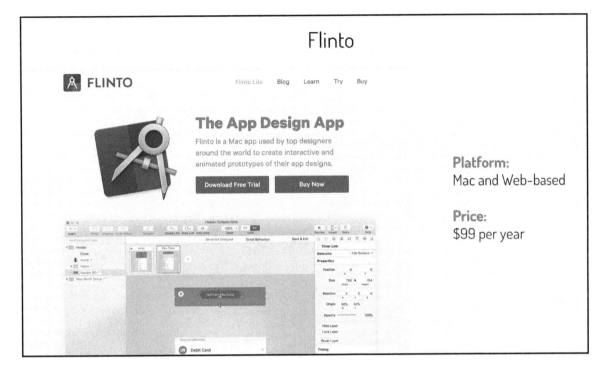

Principle

When it comes to prototyping, Principle is always my choice, not that it does more or less compared to the other tools, but because of its ease of use and its simple interface.

With Principle, it is really easy to create and design animated and interactive user interfaces.

Whether we need to design a large number of screens and connect them together to create the flow between them, or we need to create new interactions and animations, Principle allows us to create designs that look and feel amazing:

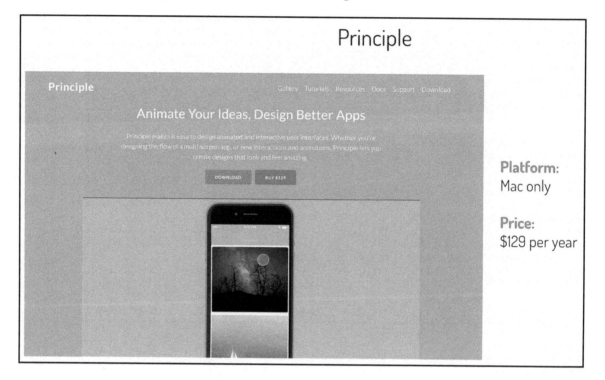

Other prototyping tools

Prototyping tools will make the process of product design much easier and faster if you do it properly. Before jumping directly into creating prototypes, keep in mind that you always need to have a process and a plan before starting to create them. For example, if you do not have the wireframes, at least, you need to sketch some pages to have a better idea of what you are going to prototype before digging directly into the tool of your choice.

Since you have made it this far, you should already know that you can create prototypes starting from the low-fidelity ones up to the high-fidelity ones throughout the entire process of your product design, starting from the UX design process, research, UI design, up to the coding part.

It is always a good idea to play with new and different tools when it comes to creating prototypes, because by doing so, you will improve your design skills and have a better idea of which tool can help you in specific situations.

Aside from the tools that I mentioned in the preceding sections, for both wireframing and prototyping, these are other well-known tools, which are worth trying:

- Proto.io (`https://proto.io/`)
- Fluid
- SketcApp
- Prottapp
- Prototypr.io (`https://www.prototypr.io/home/`)
- Atomic.io (`https://atomic.io/`)
- Webflow
- Framer

We have reached the end of this chapter. So, now it is up to you to go online, grab the tools mentioned here, try them out, and find the one, or a few of them, that will fit your type of work, or the one you think is better or easier to use, to create what you want.

Summary

In this chapter, we discussed wireframes—what they are, why we need them, where we need them, and how we can create them.

We also explained different types of wireframes, and, after that, we moved on to tools that we can use to create wireframes.

Before moving on to the next chapter, you should have a clear idea of the difference between wireframes and prototypes, and you should know which is required in the different stages of your product design process.

Also, we explained the tools and the process for creating prototypes and what we need them for.

Now, we move on to the next chapter, where we will mostly focus on the following topics: the UI design process, tools to create user interface designs, how to use Sketch to create user interface designs, how to organize Sketch when it comes to product design and preparing files for developers

UI Design and Implementation 9

With all the knowledge that you have learned so far in this book, it's now time to use it to create a user interface design. In this chapter, we will explain what a user interface design is, where it can be used, and how we can create it.

We will then explain the tools that we can use to create a UI design, such as the Sketch design tool.

All the information we've covered so far in this book, starting with UX design, to the UX design process, visual design elements, visual design principles, wireframes, and prototypes, will be the guide for us to create the user interface design. Without understanding those parts well, we cannot create a successful user interface design.

In this chapter, we will cover the following topics:

- User interface design
- UI design tools
- Designing the UI with Sketch
- Creating the Design System in Sketch

User interface design

It's time to start to use everything that you've learned so far in a practical way; this is the part where everyone can see the results of your work.

Compared to the UX design part, where we cared more about the feel of the product, we will be more focused on creating a better look for our product in the UI and presenting it better visually to our users.

UI design is the part where we design user interfaces for different computer software, mobile applications, video games, and even interfaces for different machines, such as an ATM interface, washing machine interface, car screens interfaces, or any physical and digital interface our user has to interact with.

The following is a good quote that defines the user interface design better:

> *"User interface design is like telling a joke. If you need to explain the joke, then it is not a good one."*

A good user interface design is when users do not have to waste their time, or focus too much on it, to finish a specific task.

If you want to be a good UI designer, you need to be able to connect the beautiful design with experience.

We can take an example and compare the old Mercedes cars' interiors with the new ones'; we will note great differences when it comes to user interfaces, where the old cars have physical knobs and buttons to finish specific tasks, such as controlling the climate of the car, changing the clock or date, the speed meters, and mileage, as you can see in the following image:

However, if we compare this interface with the new ones, where we have navigation, we would notice that we can accept calls from digital devices attached to the car interior, control the car climate digitally, and do tons of other things that weren't available in the old cars.

Besides the design work that is done in the interior of the new versions of Mercedes, you can also note a few digital screens that have a specific but consistent user interface design for finishing a specific task. To get a better idea, check the following image and compare it with the preceding one:

To create good user interfaces, you will always need to have two main things in mind, which we discussed in detail in Chapter 7, *Visual Design Principles and Processes*, as follows:

- Visual design basic elements: lines, shapes, colors, typography, and textures
- Visual design principles: alignment, hierarchy, balance, and repetition

You should keep these principles as a guideline when you create user interface designs.

The process of any UI design will cover a few steps. However, before that, we need the details from the research that was conducted in the earlier phase of our product design; then we need the sketches, wireframes, requirements, screen flows, and even prototypes; once all those parts are done, we move on to creating a user interface design.

We will not discuss the theory side of UI design in this chapter since we have already explained the difference between UX and UI in Chapter 1, *What Is UX?*, and covered the principles of visual design in Chapter 7, *Visual Design Principles and Processes*. So, in this chapter, it's time to put all those things into practice.

Similar to wireframes and prototypes, where we need tools to create them, we also need to use specific designing tools to design user interfaces. We will discuss the necessary steps in the next section.

UI design tools

Before we start explaining the tools that we can use to create user interface design, always remember that although a tool plays an important part in creating good interfaces, don't focus on mastering the tool – focus on mastering the skills for designing user interfaces.

For creating user interfaces, you can use different tools, such as Illustrator, Fireworks, InVision Studio, Framer, and Figma, that are available in today's market, but the main leaders in this field for a long time, and right now, are Photoshop and Sketch.

There has been a noteworthy discussion online on the tools that should be used, or which is best. I would suggest that both are useful in their own way. Surely, Photoshop has been on the market for decades, and it is a really big tool when it comes to design, but Sketch, on the other hand, its advantageous because is main focus is on building user interfaces for web, mobile, or software.

In this chapter, we will use Sketch to create the user interfaces. However, before we start using it, I will provide you with some reasons why I chose Sketch rather than Photoshop, and after that, I will explain the Sketch tool itself. Then, we will start creating the user interface.

When it comes to UI design, I prefer Sketch, but again I switch from one tool to another based on my needs. I usually combine Sketch with Photoshop during my work quite a lot since I design most of the graphical assets that I need to create on Photoshop and then export them to Sketch.

So, it would be amazing to learn both of them, but if you have limited time, start with Sketch since its main focus is on creating user interfaces.

So, the following are a few reasons why I choose Sketch and not Photoshop when it comes to creating user interfaces:

- Sketch was created for web designers and UI designers
- Sketch is lightweight, around 42 MB, whereas Photoshop requires more than 1 GB
- With Sketch, you do not have to do destructive tweaking, whereas when designing components in Photoshop, you have to go several times through the process of deleting and building the design components, especially when it comes to border radius, shadows, strokes, and so on
- In Sketch, you have advanced measuring, which helps a lot with the placing of components and makes a developer's life easier
- We can create multiple artboards in a single page using Sketch
- Sketch is much faster than Photoshop, and it requires less computer power and memory to use it
- Sketch has built-in grids, whereas we need to create our own grids in Photoshop
- Saving files on Sketch is amazing since the file size is really small compared to PSD files of Photoshop
- When it comes to rendering, Sketch is much closer to web than Photoshop
- Sketch generates the CSS code, which makes it even easier to explain the designs to developers
- The plugin community is amazing at Sketch, and, more importantly, everything in Sketch is a vector by default

The preceding are some of the reasons why I chose Sketch and not Photoshop when it comes to UI design, but remember that Sketch can never replace Photoshop. Photoshop is huge and has tons of features, which Sketch doesn't have, especially when it comes to graphic design or photo editing.

Another limitation that you will face when you will use Sketch is the operation system, since Sketch is supported only for Mac and not for Windows.

Let's start exploring the Sketch tool in detail and take a look at what it can do.

Designing the UI with Sketch

Sketch is a design tool, vector-based, that is entirely focused on designing user interfaces. It is the ultimate tool when it comes to designing user interfaces for iOS, Android, web applications, or desktop applications.

Owing to the very friendly and simple user interface design that Sketch has, it's really easy to work with it even if you have almost zero experience with it.

It can design user interface for different platforms, such as iOS, Android, or web, and it offers you the ability to design responsive user interfaces for different screens and devices, starting from the big desktop screens to the smallest ones, such as digital watches.

Sketch is considered one of the most used design tools when it comes to creating user interfaces, and it has an extremely big community, providing amazing support and plugin creations.

I have already mentioned that Sketch is really fast, and it doesn't require much computer power, such as RAM, CPU, or graphics, to start using it. Moreover, its size is so small that it barely weighs more than 45 MB in computer hard drives.

When you open the Sketch application, you will not have annoying wizards asking you different questions or requirements of what kind of screen size you want to open or what kind of design job you want to do.
When the application opens, you will simply have an infinite canvas, where you can place as many different designs and screens as you want on it.

Its user interface is divided into four main parts, where you will immediately see the following elements:

- Toolbar
- Navigator
- Inspector
- The canvas where you will do your designs

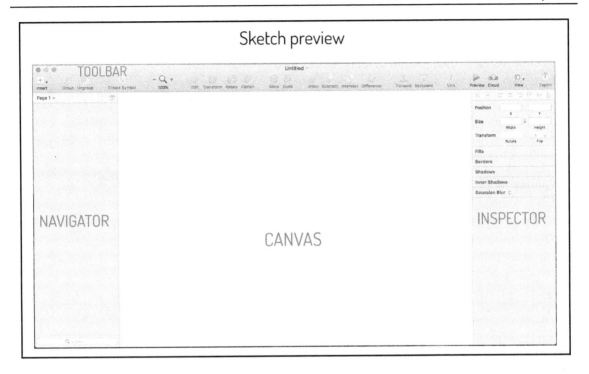

We will cover most of the features that Sketch provides to us when it comes to creating and designing user interfaces, so let's start with the first one, the toolbar.

The toolbar

The toolbar is really easy to use because of its simple user interface, flexiblity, and customizablity, so we can easily add only the tools that we need on the toolbar or order them in a way that we find easier to access.

Another thing that you have to forget worrying about when using Sketch are the units, because we will be working only with pixels on Sketch, and for the others such as centimeters, millimeters, or inches we do not have to bother.

Mostly, when using Sketch, we will use tools from the toolbar, especially lines or shapes, such as rectangles, ovals, stars, or polygons, to give a form to our design.

Here, you need to remember Chapter 7, *Visual Design Principles and Processes*, because here is the place where you start using the visual design basic elements and apply the design principles. Refer to the following screenshot:

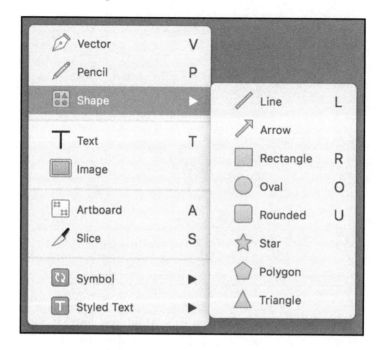

When it comes to customizing the toolbar, all we have to do is right-click on it, and then we can choose or order our favorite tools just by dragging and dropping them to the toolbar.

We can choose tools such as colors, grids, shapes, symbols, or even functions, such as converting to outlines:

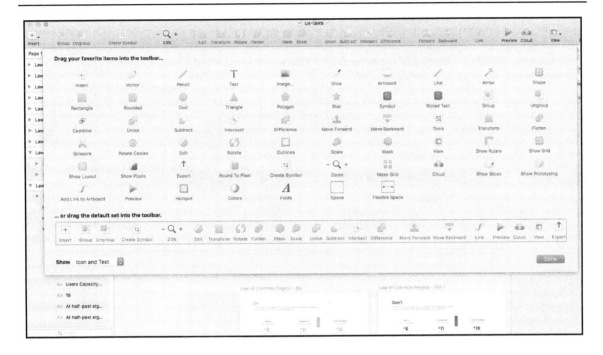

Artboards

When it comes to creating screens for web applications, websites, or mobile applications on Sketch, we use artboards.

Each artboard represents its own screen of the web or mobile app, and we can interact with those screens or create workflows with them.

Compared to the old way of designing a UI, where we had to switch between different files and tabs to design different screens of the same application, with Sketch, everything is much easier since we have all the screens on the same canvas or page, and we can easily arrange them near to each other:

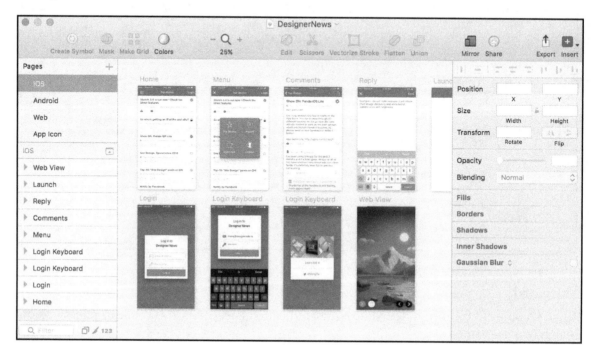

Also, when we are dealing with artboards, there is no need to hide a bunch of different layers for hiding a specific screen; we can easily hide the entire screen and focus on the other ones, and we do this specifically when we want to preview specific screens on an iPhone or other mobile devices instead of showing all the screens.

Another good thing to get yourself familiar with in Sketch is shortcuts. When it comes to artboards, we can easily duplicate them (*command + D*), rearrange them, or create a new one by just pressing the *A* key.

When we want to create a new artboard, we will have multiple options, or dozens of different available templates to choose from, as follows:

- iPad Portrait
- iPad Landscape
- iPhone 7

- iPhone 7 Plus
- Apple Watch 42 mm or 32 mm
- Responsive Web Design
- iOS Icon
- Material Design, or tons of other available templates there

Besides the available templates, as you can see from the preceding image, we can also create a custom artboard size for Dribble or Twitter, or even a specific size that we want.

Another important thing besides the artboard is pages. So, let's move to the next section and talk more about them.

Pages

We use pages on Sketch to represent a completely different platform of the web or mobile application that we are designing the user interface for.

For example, we create different pages of the same application for its user interfaces of iOS, Android, or web, or even for the Mobile Application icon, also known as the App icon.

You can see that we have all these separations, and an extremely good order and structure of our application for screens and platforms on a single Sketch file:

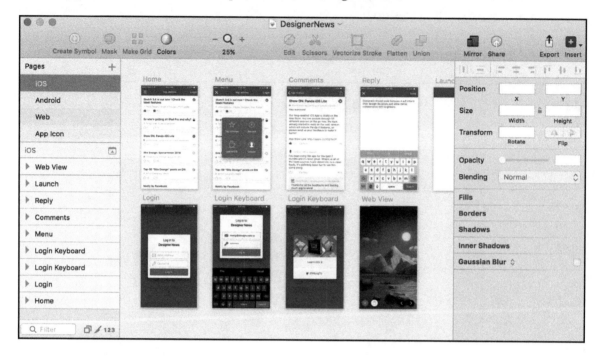

The speed when we switch between pages on Sketch is extremely fast, and it is also really easy to order the pages.

UI components templates

This is one of my favorite parts when it comes to using Sketch. The UI components for different platforms or different frameworks, such as material design or iOS design, come preloaded in Sketch and are already made for us.

To choose one of them, we need to simply go under the **File** menu of Sketch, open the **New From Template** submenu, and choose one of the available UI templates, as follows:

- **Android Icon Design**
- **iOS App Icon**
- **iOS UI Design**
- **Mac App Icon**
- **Material Design** or **Web Design**

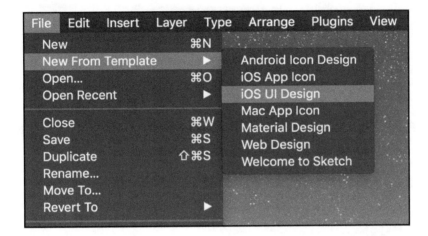

If we choose the **Material Design** or **iOS UI Design** templates, we will note comprehensive UI components there, which are great starting points for designing user interfaces, and it doesn't matter whether we are beginners or experts in the design field, they will be really handy.

If we open the **iOS UI Design** kit, we will see all the components we need, ready to be used on our new application that we want to design for iOS, as in the following screenshot:

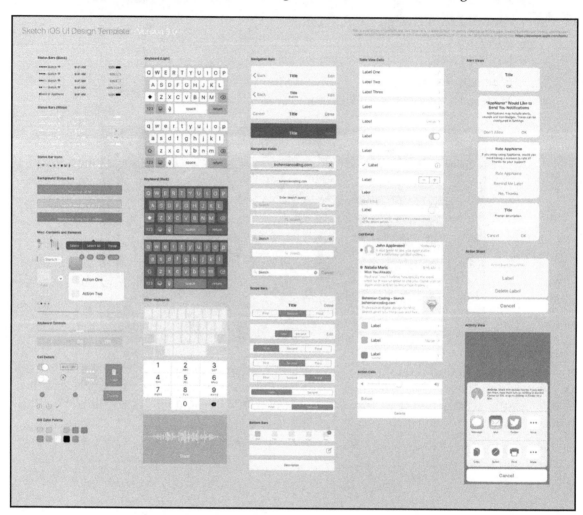

Alternatively, if we want to start building a new application using the **Material Design** UI Kit available on Sketch, we will have the UI components, as in the following screenshot:

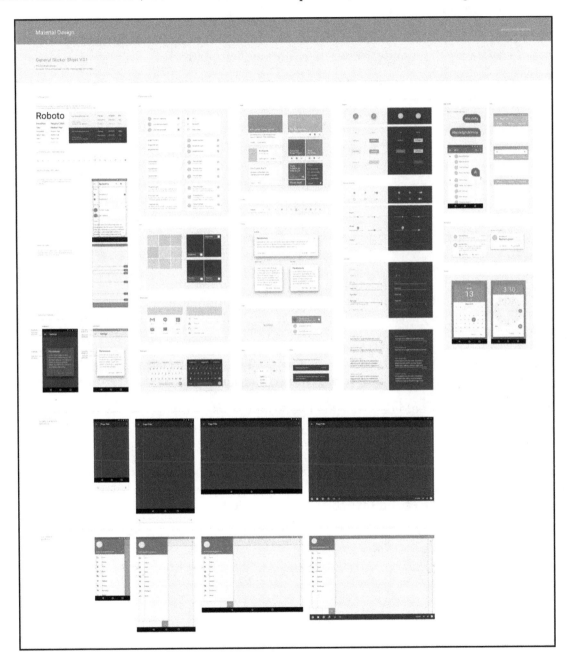

Besides the available UI templates that come preloaded on Sketch for us, we can also download different templates from online sources such as iOS 10 UI, or even the Facebook resources, which you can find at `https://facebook.design/`.

We just have to open those templates on our Sketch application, and save them as templates by navigating to **File**, rather than **Save as Template**:

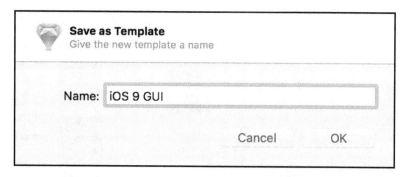

Colors

A lot of designers, including me, struggle and find it hard to deal with colors during the UI design stage; that's why it's always important to create a specific color palette for our new design.

Doing this on Sketch is really easy; we can also store our chosen colors globally and not just for a specific document, so we can access those colors later.

The best way for this would be to use the Eyedropper tool, and then we can choose the colors and create our own color palettes. The best ones to start with are Flat UI colors, iOS, or Material design ones.

Similar to what we did for the UI components templates, for color palettes, we can use the predefined ones that are available on Sketch, create new ones, or even download the new ones from online resources and save them as color palettes:

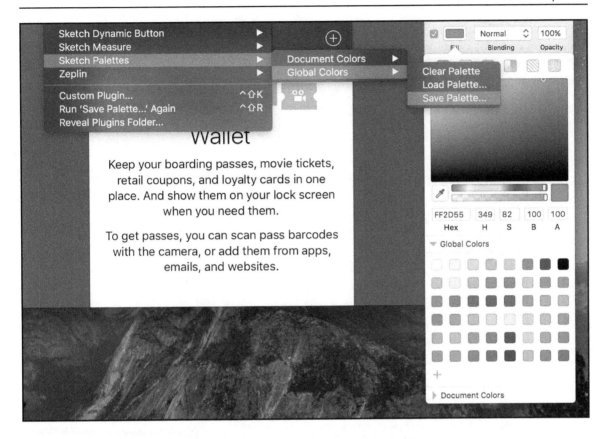

One problem we face in Sketch is the gradients, since compared to the color palettes, gradients are not easy to import, but we can easily create them manually or download them from online resources such as `https://www.sketchappsources.com/`.

Besides color palettes, dealing with applying colors on different UI components, such as buttons, shapes, tabs, backgrounds, or typography, can be easily done by selecting that specific component and applying the color from the **Inspector** panel of Sketch.

Typography

It is really easy to manage and create new text on Sketch. We can easily create the new text layer for adding text by simply clicking on the *T* key.

Then, from the **Inspector** panel, we can choose the font family, style, size, weight, or color. It is really easy for developers when they have to deal with types on Sketch, because regardless of whatever is provided on the design by Sketch, they can just copy and paste the css styles, which are generated on Sketch:

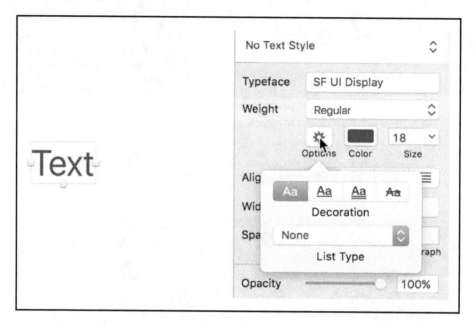

Also, it is important to go through some new fonts when you deal with web applications, especially on the Google Fonts website (`https://fonts.google.com/`), and start downloading a few new and modern fonts, which will help you a lot in creating a better and clearer user interface.

Icons and symbols

Since Sketch is a vector-based application, you can easily guess that working with icons is not a big hassle.

Icons play an important role when it comes to user interface design, so it is always nice to build their library before designing the user interface for the application.

Besides the vector format, we can simply import and use SVG icons on Sketch as well, or even edit them to the design to fit our use:

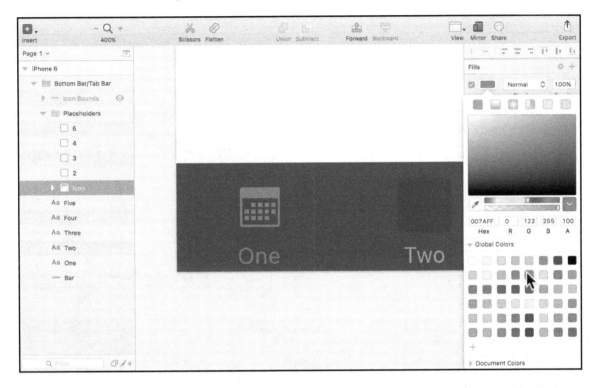

Another great feature of Sketch is the symbols, and using or creating them on Sketch is really simple. We can also share them across different screens or artboards that we have in the design.

Frequently, through the user interface design process, you will use symbols on the areas that they get repeated, for example, the status bar for mobile devices, the navigation bar, or sometimes the tab bars.

You do not have to go back and forth to edit symbols on each screen; you can change them just in one place, and they will be replaced automatically on every place or screen of the design where you used them:

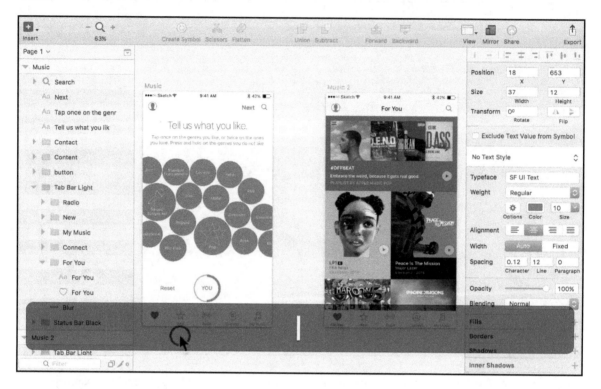

Exportation

This is one of the greatest features that comes with Sketch, especially when it comes to saving assets for different screen resolutions or platforms.

You can export the files from Sketch by just selecting specific or multiple artboards that you need, and you can also choose to export them at any kind of scale, such as **1x**, **2x**, or **3x**.

For saving the files, you can export files on six different formats using Sketch:

- **JPEG**
- **PNG**
- **SVG**
- **PDF**

- **TIFF**
- **EPS**

You will usually need a PDF format to create iOS assets, and you will use the SVG format for web application assets:

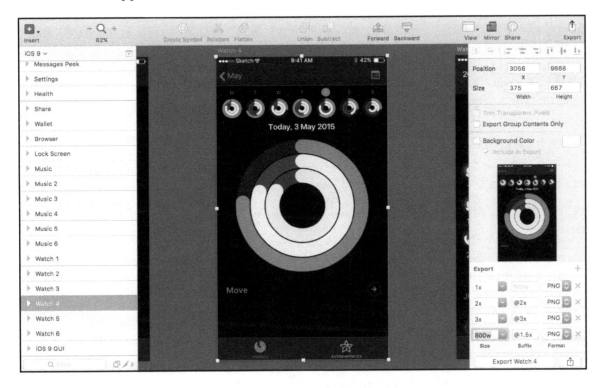

The export button is placed on the bottom-right side of the Sketch screen, and there you can customize your export result in different ways, similar to the preceding screenshot.

Preview of the UI design

Once you're done with the user interface design, it's time to test your design live. This can be easily done using the Sketch Mirror feature. All you need to do is connect your iPhone and your desktop device via a Wi-Fi or IP address and start testing the screens live on your iPhone device.

For example, if we have multiple artboards on our design, when we connect the devices using **Sketch Mirror**, we can swipe left or right between the artboards, which will give us the feeling that we are testing a live application.

Besides the swiping, we can use double-taps to zoom in and out or adjust the screen of our design. We can also scroll and expand the screens during the testing.

Before moving to the final section of Sketch, I will mention a few important plugins in the next few sections that you can integrate on Sketch to make your UI design process really productive and easy. It is important to know that migrating files between software, such as Photoshop and Illustration, to Sketch is painless, so you don't have to worry about this if you are new to Sketch.

Sketch plugins

There are almost 1,000 plugins available for Sketch nowadays, and because of the really great and active community that Sketch has, there are new plugins every week.

Plugins solve really big problems we face when using Sketch to create user interface designs.

To make our life easier during the process of UI design, we use plugins, which can speed up the user interface design process. For example, to create dynamic buttons, we can use a plugin to generate the dummy content for us; instead of writing it manually, we can use plugins to hand over our design to developers on Zeplin or InVision.

So, here, I will cover few of the best ones, which will make your UI process really easy when you get used to them.

One thing that you need to do before using any plugins is to download the plugin manager, which is **Sketch Toolbox** (http://sketchtoolbox.com/). With Sketch Toolbox, you can easily search and install specific plugins that you need without having any complications in configuring them on Sketch.

Besides this, it is really easy to manage all the plugins, especially the ones that you have already installed; you can uninstall or update them as follows:

I will not go into the details of each plugin. I will just mention the best ones, which will help you improve the process of your UI design; then, it is up to you if you want to play around with them and take a look at their benefits.

So, let's start with the plugins that are worth trying and using in Sketch:

- **Sketch Constraints**: This plugin will really help the designers and coders to be aligned with themselves, especially when they have to deal with different screen resolutions, such as iPhone 6, 7, 8, X, and 7 Plus, Android, or web. With this plugin, you will set up the constraints similar to what developers do on Xcode using Auto Layout. So, the design becomes adaptive and will fit most of the screens that developers are coding.
- **Sketch SF Font Fixer**: This plugin will be useful when you have to deal with iOS designs and will help you to adjust the character-spacing on text layers.

- **Sketch Palettes**: We have already discussed the importance of color palettes when it comes to user interface design, so this Sketch plugin will help you in generating those palettes, or you can even choose the predefined ones, such as Flat UI Palette, iOS Color Palettes, or Material Design Palette.
- **Icon Fonts**: This is an amazing plugin to choose and uses precreated fonts and icons for your user interface design. This plugin includes all the icons from popular libraries, such as Font Awesome, Material Icons, and Ionicons. Moreover, you will have the option to modify those icons and even to convert them to outlines.
- **Magic Mirror**: This is a really great and powerful tool to transform the artboards that you designed. You can also create presentable screens using it, and all you have to do is to enjoy the amazing mockups created for you by this plugin.
- **Find and Replace**: Imagine if we'd had such a tool a few years ago on Photoshop, where we can find and replace text or something else on Photoshop layers. Well, this is now possible in Sketch. This plugin will find all the text that you need in the selected layers and will replace it for you. It is a really powerful plugin, and I highly recommend that you start using it.
- **Sketch Content Generator**: When it comes to adding the content on designs, especially the dummy one, we lose too much time copying and pasting different text, avatars, names, or geolocations on our design. Well, if you use this plugin, all this hassle will be gone, because the Content Generator plugin will create all that dummy data for you in a really easy way. Besides generating plain text or avatars, you can also generate random numbers or an item from an array using this plugin.
- **Sort Me**: Usually, I use this plugin to create many pages or artboards inside my sketch file when it's become too messy; using Sort Me, I can manage the file structure and order them easily.
- **Dynamic Button**: This plugin is handy when we have to change the labels of the buttons often. So, for example, instead of reaching each button and increasing the width of the button based on the text that we provided, Dynamic Button will do this job for us.

Beside the aforementioned plugins, Sketch also contains different plugins that allow you to connect with a third-party library, or tools such as InVision, Zeplin, and Flinto.

Especially when it comes to handing over the designs to developers, this type of extension will be really handy; for example, you can transfer all your designs in one click on Zeplin using the Sketch plugin for Zeplin, and developers will have all the needed data to start coding your designs.

Before moving to the next section of this chapter, and starting to create the UI design using Sketch, I would suggest that you check these two resources on a weekly basis to find out what is happening in the Sketch community:

- **Sketch REPO**: https://sketchrepo.com/
- **Sketch App Sources**: https://www.sketchappsources.com/

Creating the Design System in Sketch

Besides all the research, testing, wireframing, and prototyping that we have done so far, designing the product is not an easy task.

That is why, instead of immediately starting to design the user interface for the product, first we need to create its Design System.

Design Systems contain the UI components, rules, constraints, and principles that will help us design the product's user interface by following the proper guidelines.

You may get it confused with style guides, but while style guides are mostly just for the styles of our product's UI components, fonts, colors, or brand attributes, the Design System is more than just visual representation – it is focused on a bigger picture of our entire project, including all the teams.

Since you're already familiar with the visual design principles and design tools such as Sketch, it's time to start creating the Design System.

Usually, to build a Design System on Sketch, I prefer the following steps:

- Creating a structure for files and folders
- Following the proper naming rules
- Choosing the colors, creating the palettes
- Choosing the fonts/typefaces
- Creating and configuring the Grid
- Creating UI components (Buttons, Tabs, Alerts, and so on)
- Building templates (Complete User Interface)

So, let's dig deeper into each of these steps.

Creating a structure for files and folders

I know it sounds basic, and you think that everyone knows it, but, believe me, I have seen great designers get lost when it comes to finding the specific components or representing the specific templates that they have designed.

So, first, it's important to organize our files and assets, and when we start the project on the right foot, everything will go well.

I would suggest that you create three different folders inside the main project folder, and those three folders should contain the following:

- `_assets`: This is the folder that will be shared internally and externally with both sides of the teams, the designers and developers. Usually, it will contain all the assets, such as fonts, brand assets, logos, images, and even the dummy content or the final content.
- `_exports`: This folder should be shared with the marketing team, because, over time, you will be exporting and screening to PNG, or social media banners, or whatever new asset you generate for the product. The marketing team will always have the latest screens with them, and they can use it for marketing purposes or planning.
- `ui-design`: Here, we will place the main files that are related to the user interface design. Since we are using Sketch as a design tool, usually, it will be only one file, but, if you need to create new ones, they will be placed here as well:

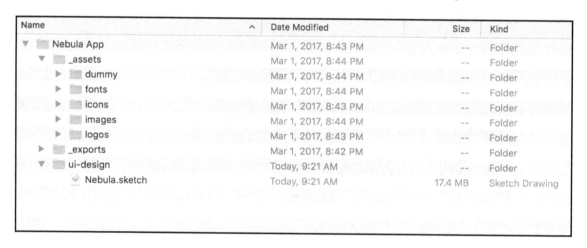

Name	Date Modified	Size	Kind
▼ Nebula App	Mar 1, 2017, 8:43 PM	--	Folder
▼ _assets	Mar 1, 2017, 8:44 PM	--	Folder
▶ dummy	Mar 1, 2017, 8:44 PM	--	Folder
▶ fonts	Mar 1, 2017, 8:44 PM	--	Folder
▶ icons	Mar 1, 2017, 8:43 PM	--	Folder
▶ images	Mar 1, 2017, 8:44 PM	--	Folder
▶ logos	Mar 1, 2017, 8:43 PM	--	Folder
▶ _exports	Mar 1, 2017, 8:42 PM	--	Folder
▼ ui-design	Today, 9:21 AM	--	Folder
Nebula.sketch	Today, 9:21 AM	17.4 MB	Sketch Drawing

You can create these folders using Finder and Automation from Mac. Also, you would notice in the preceding screenshot that I have added the underscore before the naming so that those files or folders can get ordered higher inside my project folder.

Following the proper naming convention

Similar to how the files and folder structure needs to be taken seriously when starting a new project, naming the files and folders also needs to be considered at the same level.

If we do not create a rule for this from the beginning of the project, we will have the familiar issue of filenames such as `Visual-UI.final_v5_final_new_final_final`, and imagine what will happen if the main designer who designed this project is on a vacation, and we need to find the specific file.

So, to avoid this kind of issue, you need to pick one naming convention with your team and you need to stick to it no matter what.

I suggest that you involve a few things in the filenames when it comes to the naming convention, such as the project name, the component name, and version or subversion.

So, something like this would be a proper naming convention:

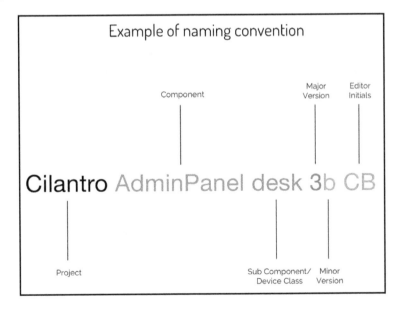

When you follow this kind of naming convention, the file and folder structure would be really easy to understand when you look for a specific file to be opened:

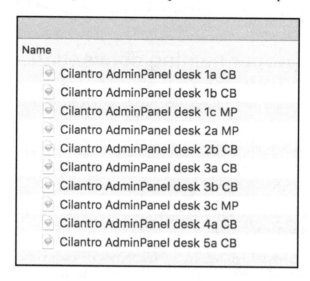

No matter what naming convention you choose, it's important that you and your team stick with it.

Choosing the colors and creating the palettes

In this stage, we need to pick the colors and create the base color palette for our project.

Picking colors doesn't seem like a difficult task, but we have to consider a few things before choosing them, especially the brand colors.

The color palette should contain a few categories of colors, as follows:

- Primary colors (usually includes the brand colors)
- Secondary colors
- Success colors
- Warning colors
- Danger colors
- Shades of gray and more shades of other colors if needed

There are different tools available online for free to create color palettes.

All the online tools, such as Colormind, MyColor.Space (`https://mycolor.space/`), or Paletton, are amazing resources to use when it comes to choosing the colors, but I prefer Coolors.co (`https://coolors.co/`) because it gives me the ability to divide the colors into five different categories and I can choose specific colors for each of them:

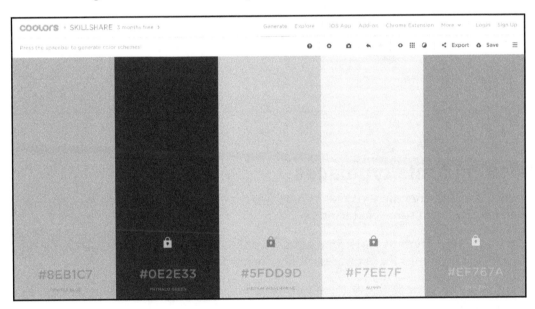

So, now that I have selected the colors, I can move them to Sketch and create the design palette that I will use through the entire process of my UI design.

We already know the Sketch tools, and using the shapes, we can create a color palette similar to what I have done in the following screenshot:

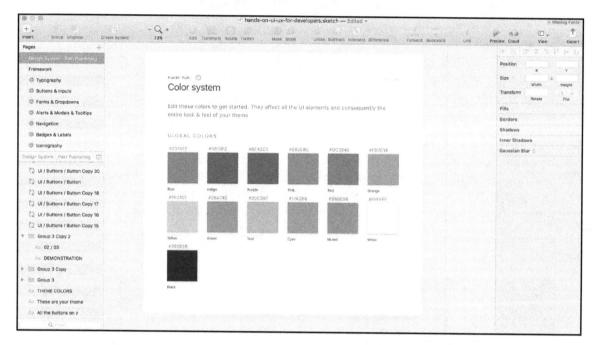

Choosing fonts/typefaces

After choosing and creating the color palette, we need to choose the fonts for our user interface to give them some character.

Similar to choosing fonts, it takes time to pick up the right and good typeface, because this is one of the main things that our user will be focused to.

The readability and scalability of typefaces needs to be considered strongly when it comes to choosing a font family.

There are different online resources from which you can get open source, licensed fonts and use them for free, such as FontPair or DaFont, but I would highly suggest that you go with Google Fonts (`https://fonts.google.com/`):

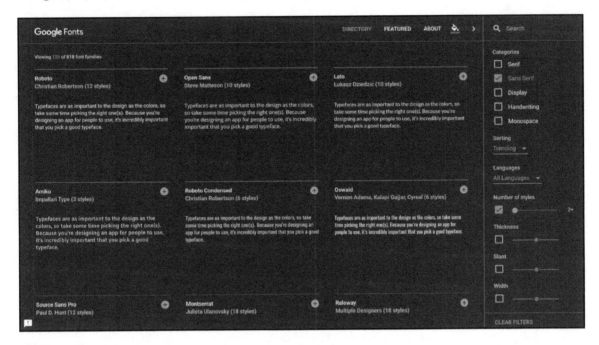

Google Fonts is an amazing resource when it comes to fonts; you can test the fonts live on black or white backgrounds, you can change their size and weight, or choose the fonts based on their categories, and once you are done, you can easily generate them for your project.

To choose the right font, don't just test them with letters, always test fonts by typing numbers and punctuation as well, so that you have a better idea how that specific font will fit inside your user interface design.

After we finally decide which typefaces we will use, we will transfer everything to Sketch and create the **Typography** guides as we did for the color palettes:

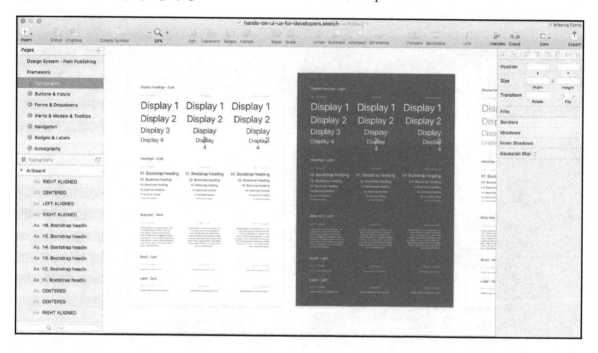

Creating and configuring the grid

Now we've got the project structure, the color defined, and the typefaces, but, before we move on to designing the UI components, we have to define and configure grids so that our application will have a consistent alignment through the entire user interface.

Often, we create grids from scratch on Sketch itself or in other specific design tools that we are using – we just need to do the right calculations.

Usually, when we have to deal with web development, and if the developers decide that they will use a specific framework for the frontend, such as Foundation, Skeleton, or Bootstrap, then we immediately start designing our UI components on that framework grid:

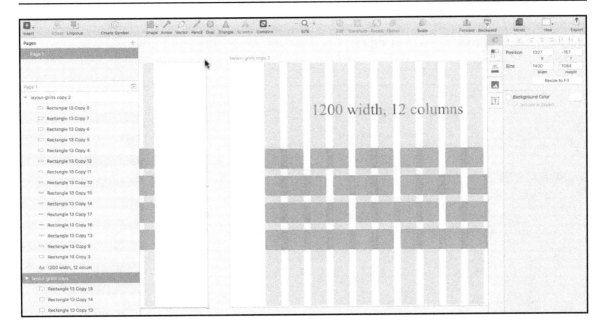

There can be different types of grids, depending on the platform that we are designing for. Also, we can have fixed-width grids or full-width grids when it comes to designing user interfaces for websites or web applications.

Once you calculate and configure the grids, it's finally time to start designing the UI components that you will use throughout the entire application.

Designing the UI components

This is one of the most exciting parts when it comes to user interface design, but we always need to create a full list of all UI components that our product user interface can contain to do it properly.

Here, we will include everything, starting from buttons, alerts, tabs, labels, forms, and input to their behaviors, such as hovers, focuses, disabled states, and different sizes and usages:

1. Colour Palette	1. Dropdown	1. Card list	1. Landing pages
2. Buttons	2. Progress indicator / bar	2. Tables	2. Dashboards
3. Text input	3. Nav bar (+ selected states)	3. Navigation header	3. Information pages
4. Radio buttons	4. Side nav (+ selected states)	4. Modal (different sizes)	
5. Checkbox	5. Table	5. Footer	
6. Switch	6. Card	6. Aside section	
7. Search bar	8. Aside	7. Mobile menu	
8. Tooltips		8. Error page	
9. Typography			
• Headings			
• Paragraphs			
• Lists			
• Bold			
• Italic			
• Links			
• Label			
10. Icons			
11. Preloader			
12. Alerts			
13. Dividers			
14. Progress indicators			
15. Table			
• rows			
• headers			
• row sections			

After we create the full list of the UI components that we have to build, we can start creating them on Sketch:

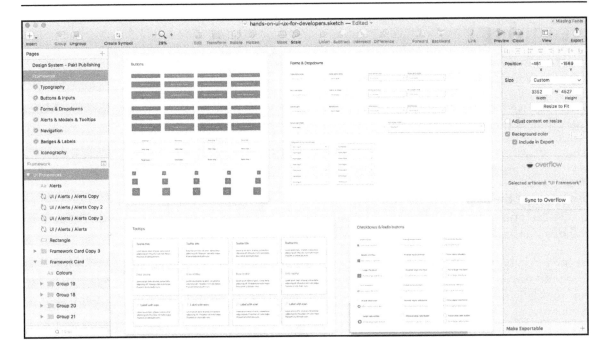

Once you've finished with the UI components comes the part that you've been waiting for from the beginning: creating the user interface.

So, with all those components in place – project structure, colors, fonts, grids, and UI components – creating the user interface design itself is going to be a much easier process, because now you have space to think more about the creativity side of the user interface design rather than dealing with small UI components, which takes a lot of time.

Summary

In this chapter, we focused on the key tools and processes that are required to build the user interface design.

We dived deeper into Sketch as a design tool, explained its features, and discussed different integrations that can be done with Sketch using its plugins.

Then, we moved on to creating a Design System using Sketch and explained the simple process for creating the Design System.

We covered the entire process of UI design – choosing the colors and fonts, configuring the grids, designing the UI components, designing the entire user interface, and handing over the designs to developers using tools such as Zeplin or Invision.

In the next chapter, we will cover the coding area of the user experience design and discuss frontend development best practices. We will also look at different grid systems that we can use for CSS and for the css framework, such as Bootstrap – see you in the next chapter!

10
Frontend UI Implementation and Process

It has been a long journey till now. This is the last stage we need to finish before our product moves to the development stage.

Here, we will have to do the development, but our main focus is on the development of the UI, not including backend functionalities, servers, or databases.

In this chapter, we will start explaining the process of how to hand over the product design to the frontend development team, what kind of assets should be provided to them, and what kind of tool we can use to make the process easier for both sides, that is, for design and frontend development.

After that, we will explain the frontend development discipline—what languages and tools they use, and what areas of development they cover.

We will cover the following topics in this chapter:

- UI handover process
- Tools that make the handover process easier
- Frontend development process
- Overview of CSS layouts such as float, flex, and grid
- CSS preprocessors and postprocessors
- CSS methodologies for maintaining code
- CSS frontend frameworks
- JavaScript role in UI development

UI Design handover

Similar to the UI Design process, where we needed information such as client requirements, clear planning documentation, research, user personas, wireframes, and prototyping for building user interfaces, when it comes to frontend development, developers need to know how you think the user interface that you designed will work, alongside the assets that are included on your user interface design, layout, grids, and UI components and all other required documentation, so that they can start the user interface development process.

The best way to provide all the required assets and data to developers is by having a proper handover process from the design stage to development stage, and to achieve that we need to involve the development team in the design process from the beginning.

Before I move on and explain the steps for handing-off the UI design, let me first explain the product development process in a classic way; a simple product development process involves the following three stages:

- **Design Stage**: Where we do the complete UX research; build wireframes, user personas and prototypes; and design user interfaces
- **Frontend Stage**: The stage where we convert UI designs into code and connect the design with backend services
- **Backend Stage**: All the functionalities of the product are built here, including the data that gets stored on the database, the services provided to the frontend team so that they can interact with them, server configurations, and everything that is happening behind the scenes with product functionalities:

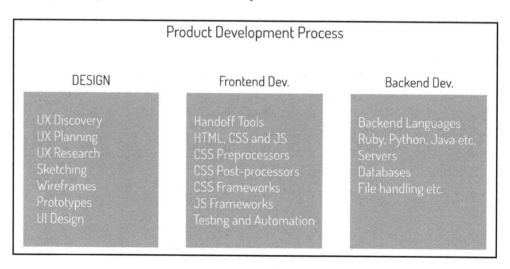

The frontend is the part that connects the designing and the coding sides of our project. To get good results for the final product, frontend developers need to be involved on both sides, the design and backend, from the beginning, so that when it comes to connecting these two areas, their expectations will be clear:

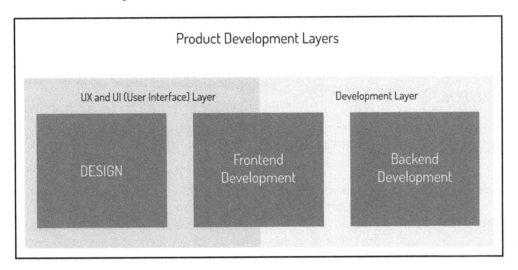

We will discuss details for the frontend in the next section of this chapter—I just wanted to give you a clear idea of what a frontend developer's job is.

To have good results for UI implementation on the frontend side, there needs to be great collaboration between the design team and the frontend team.

In the preceding chapter, we explained the process of designing the user interface, and now we need to hand over these designs to frontend developers so that they can start implementing and coding these screens.

To make the process of handing over the designs to frontend developers smooth, you need to follow these steps:

- Start communicating with the frontend team from the early stage a of design
- Explain to the developer how you expect the design to work
- Share the mock-up/user interface that you designed
- Share the prototype
- Share the design specification, assets, and the design system
- Status checklist

Communicating with the frontend team on the early stages of design

Right from the first stage where you start planning, it's good to involve the developers as well, because they will be the ones who will bring your idea to life through their coding skills.

Having a frontend developer involved from the early stages of the design process will help you understand what can be done in the coding stage and what not to do in the UI design that you will now create.

Moreover, both designers and developers will better understand the ins and outs of the product, which will allow them to avoid mistakes that could happen through the product design and development stages.

Getting insights into the product from the early stages will give frontend developers time to research different kinds of frameworks that they can use through the development process, such as Bootstrap, Skeleton, Material Design, or Foundation. They can also easily prepare the workspace for the development process by deciding on different tools, such as CSS, preprocessors such as Sass or Less, automation tools such as gulp or grunt, and even JavaScript frameworks such as Angular, React, or Vue.

So, always involve the developers from the beginning stage of the product design to achieve better results and avoid mistakes that could happen later on the development side.

Explaining to the developer how you expect the design to work

It's best to explain to the developer how you expect your design to work, not just when you finalize the user interface design, but from the time when you do the wireframes or even sketches on paper.

This will help you get a better idea of whether the specific design or animation that you are trying to achieve is doable in the development stage or not and whether it will take too much time for the developer to achieve it or not.

Moreover, developers can easily explain the good and bad things to do for a specific design, so they can help you improve it.

Involving the developers at this stage in the design process will make them understand the user goals better, and they can empathize with you; so, when it comes to the development stage, they will be much more careful and will always have the user and your suggestions in mind through the development process.

Sharing the mock-up/user interface designs

During this stage, the developer will get a clear idea of the product that they have to develop because they will be able to see the user interface that you designed.

When you provide the user interface design mockup to developers, it will be easier for them to start creating the workflow for development. Looking at the design that you provided to them, they will have a clear idea of whether the design is for full screen or if it has a fixed screen, how to develop the design for different platforms, what the behavior on responsive screens will be, and how many different platforms or browsers they will be able to support during the development process.

Often, you will have to use tools such as InVision or Marvel to provide the mockups to developers, but if we are talking just a few screens, then you can send them in the form of a presentation in a PDF file, just to give them some insight into how the user interface design is coming along.

This will be an ongoing process till the user interface that you designed is final and it contains all the required UI components, and only then can the developer begin the development process.

The final user interface design will be provided using different handover tools, but I would suggest Zeplin or Sympli.

We will cover the Zeplin tool in detail in the next section of this chapter, and you will get a clear idea of how it can help us and the developers.

Sharing the prototype

When you provide mockups, it is also a good idea to provide prototypes to developers as well, because they can easily take a look at how specific components behave when a user is interacting with them.

Prototypes will give them a better understanding of how you expect the user interface of the product to work.

Another benefit from providing prototypes to developers is that they will understand the screen flow, know what screen they have to develop next and how they are connected, and they will get a better picture of the user's journey through the screens that they are developing.

The prototype can be from a different fidelity, low or high, but what matters is that the developers understand how they can interact with the design that you provided and what the flow of the screens is.

Also, the main idea of sharing prototypes with them is that they can document interactions and can create a small framework or libraries so that they can reuse them later on different pages if that specific interaction or animation is repeated through the user interface design.

Besides all of the preceding points regarding sharing prototypes, don't forget to allow them to comment on the screens and brainstorm these screens in a real meeting. This will help better organize the team and allow them to solve problems faster.

Sharing the design specification, assets, and the design system

When it comes to starting the implementation of the design on code, the critical elements that we will mention in this section will be required immediately.

By this, I mean that, besides the user interface design, a developer will need all the assets that you used inside the UI design such as branding assets, logos, images, and fonts.

By having these kinds of data, they can prepare the structure of the project before starting the development. The next stage is creating a style guide, where they will use ready-made components such as buttons, tabs, inputs, and grids, and many more other design elements.

The best way for them to achieve this is by having the design system that we discussed and explained in the preceding chapter.

By having the design system, developers will be able to understand what grid system you have used in the design stage, and it will be easier for them to decide whether they should go with some ready-made frameworks, such as Bootstrap, or create something new from scratch.

The design system will also give developers more insights by making them understand what kinds of UI component will be included inside the user interface, for example, any unique component compared to standard ones (buttons, inputs, forms, tabs, and so on), any unique layout, or whether there are extra design components for upcoming features.

When you are providing assets to the developer, always ensure that you provide optimized ones. For example, if the image is big, you have to optimize it on the smaller side; provide the proper type of file, for example, fonts, SVG icons, or compressed PNGs.

After the developer gets all these kinds of data and designs, it will be easy for them to create a specific framework, especially a CSS one, that will fulfill their needs for UI developmen. Also, you should clarify with the developer side what the exact naming convention should be, and how best to organize assets packages for them.

Status checklist

This part is where you create a list of all the UI components, UI screens, and features that are or will be included later on in the product, so both you, as a designer, and the developers can check the status of these components, features, and screens.

Usually, the status checklist document is divided into five different columns, and each column represents the data related to that task.

For example, in this document, you have the **Action Item**, the link to the design (from Zeplin, Sympli, or Invision), the **Dependency** that tells you whether it is a backend task, frontend, or design, the comments column, and also the status:

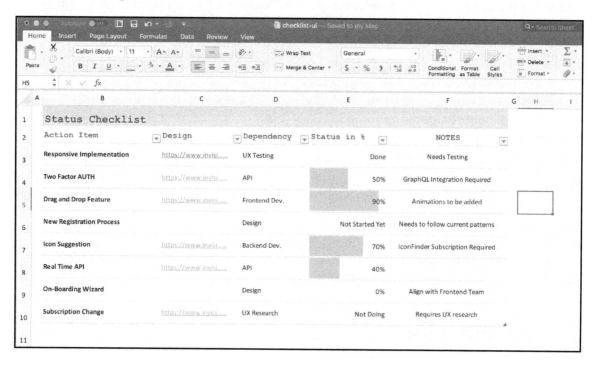

If any feature or component is missing from the status list, then the developer will not consider themselves accountable for missing the implementation of a specific page or feature because you didn't mention that to them through the status checklist, so everything that needs to be provided by the developer for a release of the product needs to be written there.

Using a handover design tool

To make the process of handover design to developers easier, we need to use handover design tools such as InVision, Zeplin, or Sympli.

In this section, I will explain this process using both Zeplin and Sympli.

We have kept the developers updated for the entire process of UI design, from the sketches, wireframes, and prototypes. Now that they are updated about the structure of UI files, the components, and design system, it is time to hand over the final design to them.

Handover of the design can be done in different ways, such as providing the design on PDF with an explanation, Sketch files, or Photoshop files, but this will be more complicated for developers because they need to learn this tool first. That is why the best suggestion when it comes to providing the files to developers is to use handover design tools.

While using handover design tools such as Zeplin or Sympli, developers do not have to think much about assets, fonts, CSS colors, shadows, and so on because they can easily access all information inside those tools.

There is a new tool for design handover from Google, called Gallery (`https://material. io/tools/gallery/`), but since it is still new and in its beta version, Zeplin is my preferred variant. Let's start by explaining how we can provide a UI design to developers using Zeplin as a handover design tool.

Handing-off UI design using Zeplin

It doesn't matter with which software you designed the user interface. It can be Photoshop, Sketch, or even Adobe XD. When it comes to Zeplin, all you have to do is choose the extension or the plugin that's specific to the design software in which you designed the user interface and transfer the design to Zeplin.

Zeplin, as a tool, does much more than just help us with the design workflow and design handover—it is a collaboration tool that is used between designers and developers, specifically between UI designers and frontend developers.

It allows UI designers to transfer their designs directly from Photoshop or Sketch to Zeplin folders online and generates all the necessary CSS code for developers such as font sizes, colors, spaces, shadows, and borders.

Since in `Chapter 9`, *UI Design and Implementation*, we used Sketch as a UI design tool, in this chapter, we will explain how we can connect Sketch with Zeplin to hand over designs to developers.

So, the process to follow for handing over designs to developers using Zeplin is really simple; just follow these steps:

1. Download the Zeplin plugin for Sketch and install it.
2. Create your project on Zeplin and choose the platform that the design is for—it can be for the web, Android, or iOS.
3. Create a proper name for the project so that the developer team will understand which project those designs are meant for.
4. After that, navigate to Sketch and select individual objects that you want to export and make them exportable, and this will allow developers to download all these components or assets through Zeplin.
5. Next, select the page and then all the artboards that you want to transfer to Zeplin.
6. After you select the artboards, just navigate to the main menu of Sketch, choose **Plugins**, then **Zeplin**, and then just click on **Export Selected Artboards**.
7. Select the project name that you created in step 2 of this process and click on **Import**:

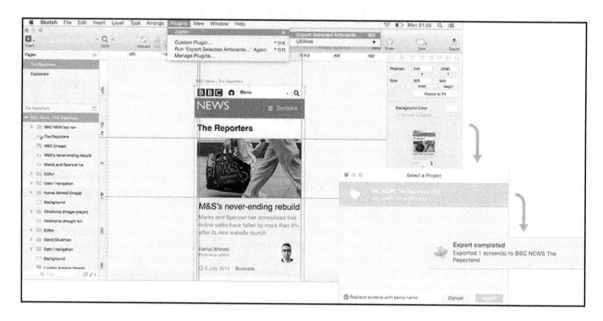

Now, you are all done with the process of transferring designs from Sketch to Zeplin. From now on, it's up to the developers to use Zeplin and start implementation on code from the design that we provided.

When developers open Zeplin to access designs, they will have everything that they need there, starting from the workflow pages so that they can choose which page needs to be implemented on the code side first. When they open the page, they can select any element or component that they want and take a look at all the CSS details related to that component.

The design will be placed on the left-hand side, and, on the right-hand side they will have the information column, which will show all the details related to the specific design component that they select, even the font family, image assets, or CSS attributes.

You can get a better idea of this in the following screenshot:

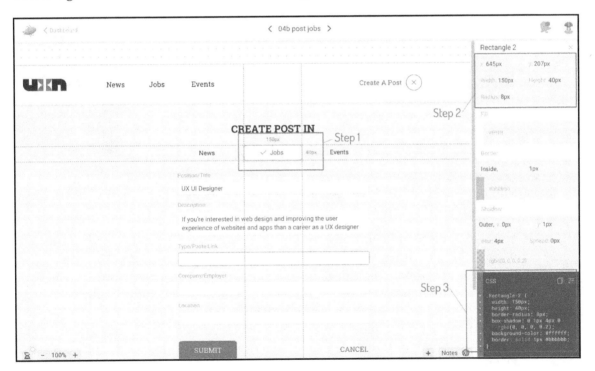

When it comes to downloading or copying attributes, just select the object of the design that you want, check the right-hand column where you will note the details of font styles, colors, assets, or other CSS attributes, and all you have to do is just copy the generated CSS or click on the Download icon when you have to download any image or SVG asset:

As you should note, using a handover design tool has many advantages, and you will see the following benefits, especially when you use the combination of Sketch and Zeplin:

- You will not lose time building specific documentation for colors, styles, assets, or fonts, because these will be generated by Zeplin for you.
- Designers can update their designs in real time when it comes to adding a new design or editing an existing one, and, every time, the developers will be automatically updated about those changes.
- You can create exportable designs, which developers can easily access and download, ranging from image assets, such as PNG or JPEG, up to SVG assets when it comes to icons.
- You can easily create a style guide on Zeplin, which developers can follow during their development process.

- There are different integrations that can be done using Zeplin. You can integrate Zeplin with Slack so that the entire team will be updated about new changes or for the process of design.
- You can provide feedback or comments through Zeplin with regard to the design, and you can also communicate with developers about the changes, as to what can or can't be done.

Handing over design using Sympli

You can find the same features that you have on Zeplin on Sympli. Sympli is also a great collaborative tool between designers and developers when it comes to design handover.

I prefer Zeplin when I am dealing with a single big project, but I would choose Sympli when I have to deal with multiple different projects, and each project has a different team or developer assigned to them:

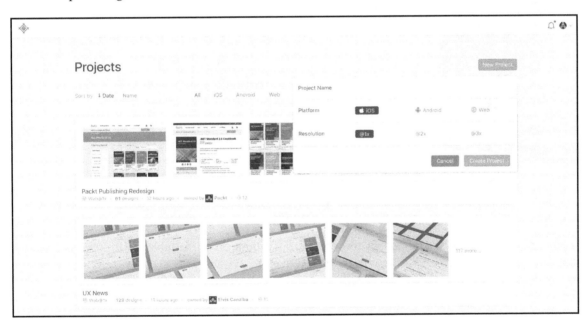

It is almost the same process as with Zeplin. All you have to do is to go to the Sympli website, choose the extension that you need—it can be Photoshop or Sketch—download it, and install it on your computer.

The next step is to make your file exportable, select artboards, and export them on Sympli using the Sympli extension.

The user interface is familiar to Zeplin, so the design will be placed on the left and at the center of your screen, whereas you will have all other details such as font styles, color, asset download links, and CSS attributes, such as shadows or borders, on the right-hand side:

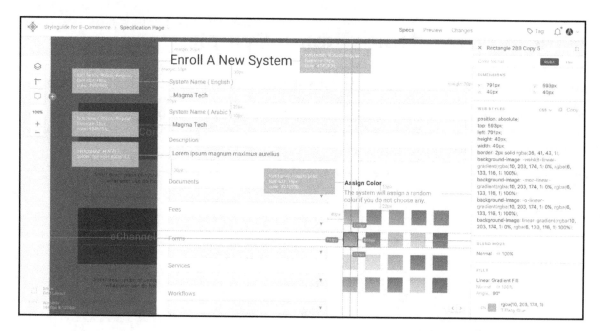

Also, on Sympli, you will have different features such as Rulers, Layers, and the ability to choose different resolutions when it comes to web or mobile devices.

You can add comments and assign them to a specific member or designer if needed; once the design is updated, everyone will be notified:

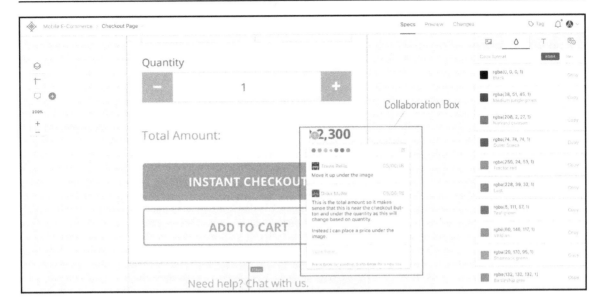

When it comes to handing off the design, I would always suggest that you use these kind of tools, not only for developers, but also for different departments such as marketing, design, development, and even management.

Everyone can collaborate with the user interface designer through Zeplin and Sympli, which will make the process of feedback for the UI really easy, and it will be even easier to get their opinion once the designs are updated since they will be notified.

Now that we have handed over everything that was required to developers, it is time to start the development process. So, in the next section, I will go into detail and explain what a frontend developer task is, which tools they use, and what they are expected to deliver as a final result, so let's move there immediately.

Frontend development/UI development

After we've designed the final user interface, and everything is handed over properly to developers, it is time to convert the design to a real-world application that our user can interact with, and the person who does this job is a frontend developer.

A few companies and individuals like to separate frontend development into two areas, the UI developer and frontend developer, but, actually, these mean the same thing, so it doesn't make sense to do this kind of separation.

Based on a few articles that you can find online, you will see that they suggest that a UI developer is a person who is mostly focused on only user interface implementation using HTML and CSS, while they avoid JavaScript as much as they can, and the frontend developer is more focused on JavaScript itself and its framework.

As much as it sounds good to separate these things, it is a wrong approach. UI development falls under frontend development, so whoever is implementing the user interface design has to also connect that UI with the backend, so do not confuse yourself with these special titles; just focus on one, which is the frontend developer.

A frontend developer deals with everything that has to do with the client side of mobile or web application. Three main skills of the frontend developer are *HTML, CSS*, and *JavaScript*.

In order to be a good frontend developer, you need to have at least the basic skills of UI design, because the main task of a frontend developer is to create convenient user interfaces which will fulfill user or customer needs; to do that properly, they need to have a sense of how user interface design works.

Frontend developers have to deal more with logical thinking, so it is understandable that they cannot always be creative like designers, but when they are aligned together, then extremely good results can be achieved.

I always like to separate the frontend development process into two stages:

- The first stage is to integrate the user interface design that is provided by the design team into code. Here, we will need to make the interface functional and convenient and it also needs to be beautifully implemented, similar to what the design team expected when they designed it.
- The second stage is to connect that user interface design with backend services such as kind of UI components API and bring the user interface to life by adding real data and functionalities there.

Before we go deeper into the process and tools of the frontend development, I would like to clarify and explain the differences between frontend and backend development.

Frontend development covers all parts that have to do with the client side of the website or application, meaning that it covers everything that we as users can see or interact with inside an application or website. The frontend development area is responsible for how our application looks and feels when we interact with it.

Backend development, on the other hand, caters for everything that has to do with the server side, so communication between the application and database through servers is done on the backend:

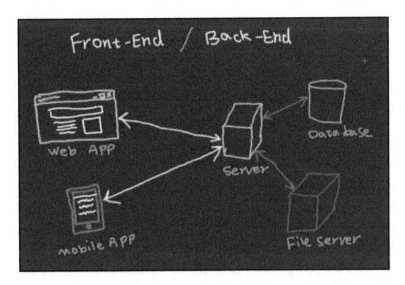

A simple way to explain this would be to take the example of the process of doing a search on Google; for example, when we navigate to the Google URL using the browser, the request goes to the server side, and then the main Google page opens on the client side, which is our browser.

So, on the client side, we see the user interface of Google, and when we type something into the search and click on the Search button, the request goes to the server side again, and it provides us with a new page with results on the client side.

We cannot see behind the scenes of this process when we search, because it is the backend side of development handling. Whatever appears for us on the browser is the frontend side of development, or, simply put, the client side. Frontend developers just connect the data layer with the presentation one.

So, let's get back to the frontend side and talk about the tools and frameworks that can be used before starting the development process.

We already know that to become a frontend developer, we need to be good at the following three main skills:

- **HTML**: Like human body attached to a skeleton, HTML is the user interface skeleton for websites or applications, and it gives structure to all components and pages.
- **CSS**: After we build the skeleton with CSS, we will start to add colors, shapes, alignments, and hierarchy to our website or application structure. In other words, we make our application better looking and easier to use.
- **JavaScript**: Using JavaScript on our web application allows us to add interactivity between the HTML and JavaScript. We can create sliders, modals, or popups. Moreover, we can use JavaScript to connect our UI with backend services using Ajax calls or specific frameworks such as Angular, React, or Vue.

We will not go into the basics of any of the previously mentioned skills since that is not our priority, but we will cover best practices, frameworks, layouts, and tools that you can use to make the frontend development process as smooth as possible, which follows the latest and modern practices from the frontend world.

When we're comes to development on the frontend, first we need to choose the process, workflow, and the tools that we will use before starting development.

For example, when we deal with responsive design or creating design system components, we can decide what framework we should go with—it can be Bootstrap, Material Design, or even a custom one created from scratch.

When it dealing with CSS, we will need to make a lot of decisions before starting a project, especially on the following points:

- CSS layouts
- CSS preprocessors
- CSS postprocessors
- CSS methodologies
- CSS frameworks

So, let's discuss more about each of them in the next section.

CSS layouts

In the early stages of HTML, CSS layouts were mostly used to create plain documents instead of dynamic websites. Using a table layout, especially, to represent something using HTML was difficult since when it came to changing the layout to something different, it took a ridiculous amount of time to delete and rewrite all the HTML just to change the layout view.

This thing changed entirely when CSS came into the game. It's quite similar to HTML. The early incarnation CSS was not so advanced at its first release, and it took a long time for it to be where it is today.

Today, with the latest CSS feature, you can create anything that you can imagine inside your website or web application, such as drawing canvas, generating shadows, borders, animations, and even 3D animations.

The first thing that we create during user interface development using CSS is the layout of the website or application.

To explain CSS layouts in the best way, let's create a folder that will include two files: HTML and CSS. We will have `index.html`, where we will add the structure of the page, and `style.css`, where we will provide the styling of the page.

In the HTML page, we will place basic code, where it will generate the header, content, and footer for us:

```
<!DOCTYPE html>
<html lang="en">
<head>
 <meta charset="UTF-8">
 <title>CSS Layouts - Packt</title>
 <link rel="stylesheet" href="style.css">
</head>
 <body>
  <header>Header part goes here.</header>
  <main>
   <h1>Main title goes here and it's content is added below.</h1>
   <p>Lorem ipsum dolor sit amet, id ac, nonummy sit mauris. Ut nibh cras
beatae    diam...</p>
  </main>
  <nav>
   <h4>Navigation section is here.</h4>
   <p>Lorem ipsum dolor sit amet, id ac, nonummy sit mauris.</p>
  </nav>
  <aside>
   <h4>Aside section / Sidebar here</h4>
```

```
    <p>Lorem ipsum dolor sit amet, id ac, nonummy sit mauris.</p>
  </aside>
  <footer>Footer area goes here.</footer>
 </body>
</html>
```

Without CSS, an HTML page in the browser would look something like this:

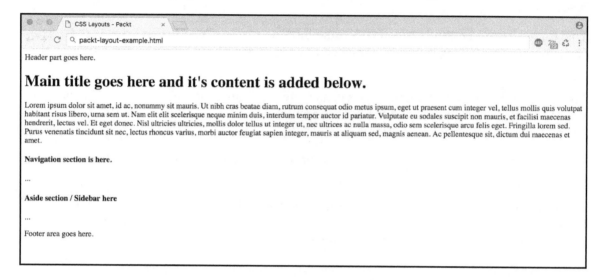

However, after we add some basic styling to the CSS file, it will look as follows:

```
body {
 margin: 0;
 padding: 0;
 max-width: inherit;
 background: #fff;
 color: #4a4a4a;
}
header, footer {
 font-size: large;
 text-align: center;
 padding: 0.3em 0;
 background-color: #e7692c;
 color: #f9f9f9;
}
nav {
 background: #eee;
}
main {
 background: #f9f9f9;
```

```
}
aside {
  background: #eee;
}
```

Then the layout of the page will look like this:

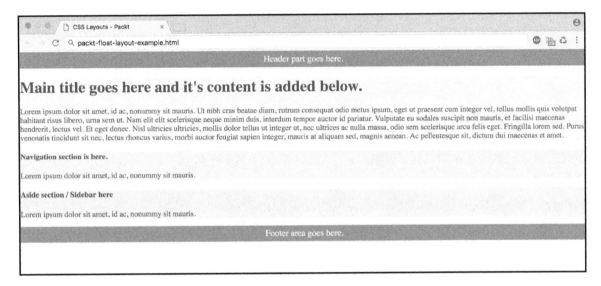

There are different approaches to how we can create layouts using CSS. We can even combine different layout approaches to achieve a design layout that we want, but it would not be a preferred thing to do.

So, one of the first things before we start the development stage would be to choose the CSS layout that we will follow through the entire stage of the user interface development.

When it comes to CSS layouts, three of the most preferred approaches are as follows:

- Float-based layout
- Flexbox-based layout
- Grid-based layout

In the next section, we will explain each of the preceding layouts, and you will have a better idea which of the CSS layouts will fit your development process better, and which of them will make it easier to achieve results from the user interface designs that you have received from the UI design stage.

Float-based layout

The float layout is an old approach to CSS layout, which was introduced in the first half of 2000. At the beginning, it was meant to be used for images to float right or left inside text columns.

Recently, it has been used to float `divs` with the entire content inside them to the right or left. You can still find a lot of website nowadays using this approach.

There is nothing wrong with using this approach to CSS layout, but there are too many bugs since the float wasn't designed for this purpose, so you need to use different tricks to achieve a specific required layout based on the user interface that is provided by designers.

Let's take an example and create it using the float layout. Say we need a full-width header, which has three columns below it—two sidebars at the left and right with content that will be in the middle, and a full-width footer below. To do this using a float-based layout, our CSS will have to look something like this:

```
body {
  padding-left: 200px;
  padding-right: 190px;
  min-width: 240px;
}
header, footer {
  margin-left: -200px;
  margin-right: -190px;
}
main, nav, aside {
  position: relative;
  float: left;
}
main {
  padding: 0 20px;
```

```
 width: 100%;
}
nav {
 width: 180px;
 padding: 0 10px;
 right: 240px;
 margin-left: -100%;
}
aside {
 width: 130px;
 padding: 0 10px;
 margin-right: -100%;
}
footer {
 clear: both;
}
* html nav {
 left: 150px;
}
```

We will get the following result when we open the HTML page in our browser:

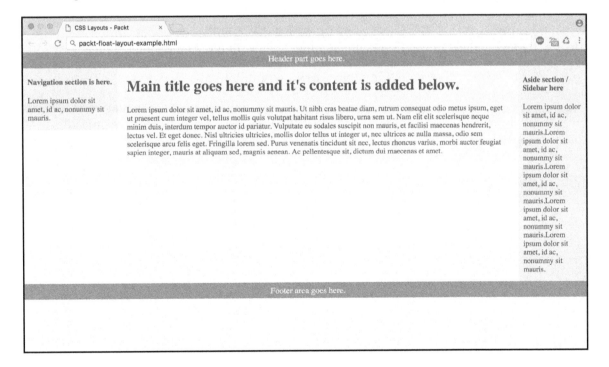

As you may have noticed, the preceding layout is not bad, but the sidebar columns do not have the same or equal height yet; also, the page starts from the center column and the footer is not filling the full height of the page.

We can do some workarounds such as providing a fixed height for the columns to make them look the same, but these issues will still start appear when we open the website on different screens and different platforms.

There are other tricks that can be done to fix this issue, but other problems can occur when we apply a specific CSS style to `div` tags; that is why, a few years ago, the new CSS flexbox-based layout was introduced to solve these kinds of issue.

Flexbox-based layout

The CSS flexbox-based layout was first introduced in 2009, but it took almost 6 years, till 2015, to be fully supported by all of the latest major browsers.

Instead of using floats, with flexbox-based layout we can easily define the distribution of space across columns or rows.

When this approach to CSS layouts came into the game, finally developers didn't need to use any hacks or tricks to create specific layouts that were required by designers.

So, let's try to achieve the same thing that we did with float-based layout with the flexbox-based layout.

First, we will need to add an extra `div` to our HTML page to wrap all the three middle columns together into one, which will be the left sidebar, right sidebar, and the center content.

Our modified HTML page will now look like this:

```
<body>
 <header>Header part goes here.</header>
 <div class="container">
  <main>
   <h1>Main title goes here and it's content is added below.</h1>
   <p>Lorem ipsum dolor sit amet, id ac, nonummy sit mauris...</p>
  </main>
  <nav>
   <h4>Navigation section is here.</h4>
   <p>Lorem ipsum...</p>
  </nav>
  <aside>
   <h4>Aside section / Sidebar here</h4>
```

```
   <p>Lorem ipsum...</p>
  </aside>
 </div>
 <footer>Footer area goes here.</footer>
</body>
```

Our CSS styles in the `css` files will be as follows:

```
body {
 min-height: 100vh;
 display: flex;
 flex-direction: column;
}
.container {
 display: flex;
 flex: 1;
}
main {
 flex: 1;
 padding: 0 20px;
}
nav {
 flex: 0 0 180px;
 padding: 0 10px;
 order: -1;
}
aside {
 flex: 0 0 130px;
 padding: 0 10px;
}
```

As you can see in the preceding code, there is less CSS code compared to the float-based layout, but it looks a bit confusing at first sight when you look at the code for the CSS flexbox properties.

Do not worry because once you get used to it, you will see the benefits of avoiding the many hacks and tricks that you needed to use on float-based layouts.

You will see the following result when you open the HTML file on your browser:

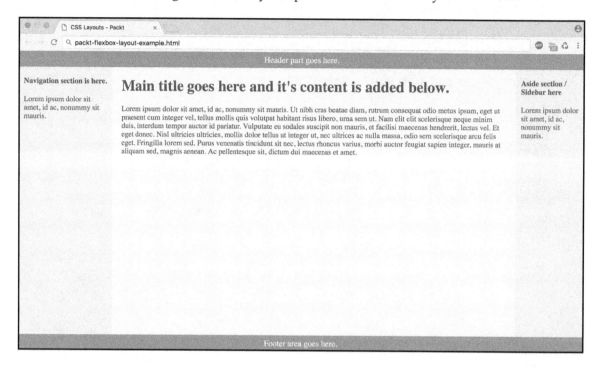

Well, the result of using a flexbox-based layout is much better than the float-based layout. As you can see, the sidebars and content in the middle all have equal heights and the page is on the full height with the footer placed at the bottom of it.

One of the cons of using the flexbox layout browser support. Although flexbox-based layout is fully supported on all the latest browsers, it has really small support in old ones and is not supported in most of them.

It is good for developers and companies that are developing browsers such as Chrome, Firefox, or Safari to end support for older browsers and force people to download the latest ones.

Another downside is that it requires you to add an extra div to wrap the elements so that you can apply the CSS styletoor them, for example, in our case, we added a new div called `<div class="container">`. This is not a downside when it comes to creating a new web application from scratch, but, it is counted as a downside for existing websites that want to move from float-based layouts to flexbox-based layouts.

One of the biggest downsides of flexbox-based layouts is the CSS code itself. It takes time to understand it because it doesn't have expressive CSS properties for defining CSS layouts.

However, in my opinion, the CSS itself is both one of the easiest and hardest languages to learn, because it is really easy to start with but gets complicated when you dive deeper to use all of its features; once you get used to it, though, everything becomes really simple.

Similarly, creating a simple layout in the flexbox-based layout is easy, then it gets a bit hard, but once you understand all the ins and outs of it, you will know its value and use it to solve a lot of different problems.

As I mentioned at the beginning of this section, the flexbox-based layout was primarily designed to manage space within a single column and row, not for creating CSS layouts for the entire page of our website or web application.

It is not that you cannot manage to create the layout for entire pages, especially when you can see that it does a much better job than the float-based layout, but when it comes to managing multiple columns and rows with CSS, then there is a better approach of CSS layouts to do it; using the grid-based layout.

Grid-based layout

Only 2 years after the flexbox-based layout was introduced, the grid-based layout was introduced in 2011, but it took almost 7 years to be supported on almost all major browsers.

In 2018, the work for supporting grid-based layouts underwent a huge improvement, and it is supported on most well-known browsers.

Compared to flexbox-based layouts where we needed to add an extra div to use it, we do not need to add anything extra to the HTML in the grid-based layout, so we can easily remove the extra div that we added to the flexbox-based layout, that is, `<div class="container">`.

We can easily start adding just CSS without the need to change the HTML structure or classes.

So, the new CSS using the grid-based layout properties will look like this:

```
body {
  display: grid;
  min-height: 100vh;
  grid-template-columns: 200px 1fr 150px;
  grid-template-rows: min-content 1fr min-content;
}
header {
  grid-row: 1;
  grid-column: 1 / 4;
}
nav {
  grid-row: 2;
  grid-column: 1 / 2;
  padding: 0 10px;
}
main {
  grid-row: 2;
  grid-column: 2 / 3;
  padding: 0 20px;
}
aside {
  grid-row: 2;
  grid-column: 3 / 4;
  padding: 0 10px;
}
footer {
  grid-row: 3;
  grid-column: 1 / 4;
}
```

When we open the HTML page on the browser, the result will be totally the same as it was on the flexbox-based layout, but the CSS code will be improved, and it will be really easy to understand when you read it. It also makes more sense when you are writing it to create and define page layouts.

The main code line, which can cause confusion when you read grid-based layout CSS, is the `grid-column` property, but once you understand that it is used for defining the starting and the ending points of the columns, it will be much easier for you to use it.

In our example, we have three columns, but in CSS we use a range of numbers from 1 to 4. Take a look at the following screenshot, and you will note that numbers 1 and 4 define the starting and ending points of the column:

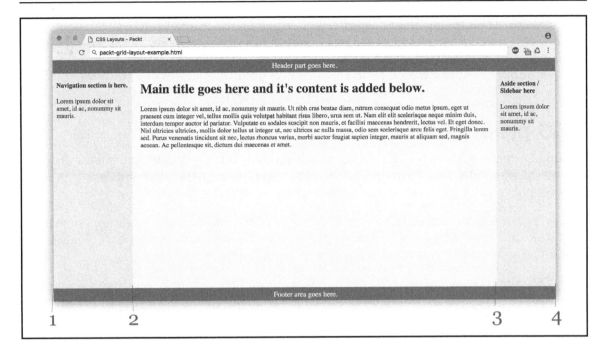

As you may have noticed, using the `grid-column` CSS property, we define the starting and ending points of each column that we have.

After you learn the grid-based layout and get used to it, it will become the best approach for creating CSS layouts for your websites or applications.

The only main downside from using the grid-based layout is browser support, but even this issue will go away in a while because browsers implement their support for it nearly every month.

The grid-based layout is counted as one of the first and real tools which is actually designed specifically for creating page layouts. So, my suggestion would be to grab it and learn it as soon as you can, because the time will come really fast when this CSS feature will be totally supported by all major browsers. It will make your life as a frontend developer much easier.

The world of CSS is changing really fast. In just a few years, we have had different features released, such as animations, flexbox layouts, grid layouts, or variables known as custom properties. So, without doubt, another fancy CSS layout approach will be released next, but since the grid-based layout is the best one that we have till now, now is the time to dive into it and learn it.

When it comes to implementing user interface design on the frontend side, CSS layouts are just one part that we need to consider before starting the development. There are a few other sides options we have to choose on the CSS side before starting the development process, and the next one would be to choose a CSS preprocessor, so let's move there.

CSS preprocessors

Around 10 years ago, when CSS was not so advanced as it is nowadays with all these new features, it was really hard to maintain CSS code when we were dealing with big applications.

CSS preprocessors were created to extend the CSS, which would include features such as variables, functions, operators, and other different assets, which at that time were missing on the CSS side.

With CSS preprocessors, we extend the functionality of CSS and make our lives as developers much easier by doing different math calculations to achieve specific layout results or UI component results.

Besides math calculations such as subtraction, addition, division, and multiplication that we can do using CSS preprocessors, we can also use different built-in functions to create or achieve specific results that we need on CSS. An example can be taken from `percentage()` built-in functions, which we use when we need to convert any number into a percentage value on CSS.

Another cool thing with preprocessors is variables, where we can define different CSS properties using variables and use them all over our website application. The use of variables can best be explained with colors, so instead of repeating colors over and over again on CSS files, we can declare palette colors using variables, and then just use the variable names based on the color that we need to use through all CSS files:

```
@dark-color: #4a4a4a;
@light-color: #f9f9f9;
@side-color: #eee;
body {
  color: @dark-color;
}

header, footer {
  background-color: @dark-color;
  color: @light-color;
}
```

```
main {
  background: @light-color;
}
nav, aside {
  background: @side-color;
}
```

When it comes to more advanced features of CSS preprocessors, we can also use the if/else condition or loop through our entire application. For example, we can use the if/else condition to deal with some kind of toggling of CSS through styles by switching a button on and off or by toggling the active and passive states.

It is important to know that most CSS preprocessors features are still missing on pure CSS. The new features are often based on CSS, but there is still much work to be done before they can achieve what that CSS preprocessors can do.

When we write code on CSS preprocessor files, the code gets converted to pure CSS so that the browser will understand it and apply the generated styling to the entire website or application for us.

Other features that come included with CSS preprocessors include mixing, nesting, inheritance selectors, selectors, and a lot more. By having access to these kinds of features makes the maintenance process for our CSS really easy, and when it comes to new developers being included on the team, the code has better readability, and it will be really easy for them to see and understand the structure of our CSS.

There are a lot of benefits that we get when we use CSS preprocessors, but the most important ones that are worth mentioning are as follows:

- You do not need to repeat code, so instead of writing the same CSS over and over again, all you have to do is just call specific variables, and you are all set
- When it comes to changing colors, fonts, or other UI aspects, you can create and reuse modules
- It saves a huge amount of time compared to hardcoded CSS
- Another benefit of CSS preprocessors is that you can start working with them immediately if you know CSS since the syntax is really easy to get started with
- The code maintained is much easier process compared to pure CSS

You probably got the idea that CSS preprocessors are just an extension of the CSS language and that their main goal is to speed up the development process to save time and have a better style structure.

There are a few CSS preprocessors available for developers online, but the three most popular ones are as follows:

- Sass
- Less
- Stylus

Sass

Sass is one of the most popular and most widely used CSS preprocessors. It contains a lot of features and is extremely compatible with CSS.

Sass was introduced for the first time in 2006, and it is completely built in the Ruby programming language. It is cross-platform, so you can use it on any platform that you prefer.

It has a huge number of features, starting with variables, mixins, nesting, inheritance selectors, functions, imports, and tons of other features that make the life of developers really easy when it comes to coding on CSS.

There are two available syntaxes on Sass: you can choose SCSS or SASS one. The syntax is really similar to pure CSS; two things that you can ignore from the pure CSS side when you are using SASS syntax are semicolons and curly brackets.

If developers are from the Ruby or Python side of development, it will be really easy for them to get used to Sass syntax since it is similar to both of those languages.

In the following example, you can see what simple CSS code looks like when we write in pure CSS in Sass:

```
Pure CSS
#skyscraper_ad
{
 display: block;
 width: 120px;
 height: 600px;
}

#leaderboard_ad
{
 display: block;
 width: 728px;
 height: 90px;
}
```

```
SCSS:
#skyscraper_ad
  display: block
  width: 120px
  height: 600px

#leaderboard_ad
  display: block
  width: 728px
  height: 90px
```

We will not go into the details of how to use and install Sass because their documentation is really extensive and straightforward; go to the official Sass website at `http://sass-lang.com/` to find out more.

The main purpose of this section is to make you aware of the CSS tools that you can choose and pick before starting the development process.

Less

Less was introduced 3 years later than Sass, in 2009, and similar to Sass, Less was also built in the Ruby programming language.

If we compare these two CSS preprocessors, they have almost the same features, but Less's idea was to create as much similar syntax with as much pure CSS as it could. They actually achieved it, and what is more interesting is that you can even write pure CSS on Less, and everything will work fine since Less accepts any pure CSS code as valid.

You can see the similarity between pure CSS and Less in the following example:

```
@dark-color: #4a4a4a;
@light-color: #f9f9f9;
@side-color: #eee;
body {
  color: @dark-color;
}

header, footer {
  background-color: @dark-color;
  color: @light-color;
}

main {
  background: @light-color;
}
```

```
nav, aside {
  background: @side-color;
}
```

Compared to Sass, you can see that Less uses @ with variable prefixes instead of $.

Later, in 2012, Less was rewritten completely in JavaScript or, specifically, using the JavaScript framework known as Node.js, instead of the Ruby programming language for compiling.

By rewriting it completely in Node.js, Less CSS preprocessors became much faster, and it made the workflow of developers who were using Node.js more appealing and easy.

So, compared to Sass where you need the Ruby language to compile Sass code to CSS, to use Less, you will need Node.js installed to compile the code to pure CSS.

Both Sass and Less have a big community, so support for both platforms is great, and you will barely get stuck somewhere and not be able to get help.

As we did for Sass, we will not go into the details of how you can install Less on your project since the process is really simple; just follow the steps provided on their official website, http://lesscss.org/.

Stylus

Stylus is a newer CSS preprocessor compared to Less and Sass. It was first introduced in 2010, and its intention was to provide a much easier and cleaner syntax compared to what Less and Sass were providing.

Besides all the standard features that you have in Sass and Less, using Stylus you can create your own functions to create and manage new CSS parameters.

Another different advantage of Stylus compared to the two other CSS preprocessors is transparent mixins, where you can avoid specifying a list of different parameters, but you will able to define your functions.

Stylus is completely written in the JavaScript framework, Node.js, similar to Less.

All three CSS preprocessors are really similar to each other, and they all provide almost the same features, so whichever one you choose for your project won't be a mistake, but life will become easier when you start the development process.

Like I stated for Sass and Less, the installation process for Stylus is really simple, and getting started with it is really easy. To check it out so that you can have a better idea of what options Stylus provides for you, just navigate to their official website at `http://stylus-lang.com/`.

CSS postprocessors

CSS postprocessors are tools which we use after the files are compiled to pure CSS from CSS preprocessing tools, such as Sass, Less, or Stylus.

By adding postprocessors, we minify our CSS in a proper way; for example, all the comments, white spaces, and unnecessary declared properties around our CSS files will be removed, and the CSS gets organized in a better way so that browsers can load it faster.

We can take an example of margins or paddings. Let's say that after compilation to pure CSS from preprocessing tools, we get CSS properties such as margin: 0px 0px 0px 0px; or padding: 0px 0px 0px 0px;. Postprocessors will organize these properties in a minified and organized way, so the final results on CSS will be margin: `0;`, and padding: `0;`, and these new CSS results will be saved to a smaller new CSS file, which can be something like `styles.min.css`.

To achieve a better understanding of this process, check out the following diagram, which shows the entire process from the preprocessing side up to the postprocessing result of the CSS file:

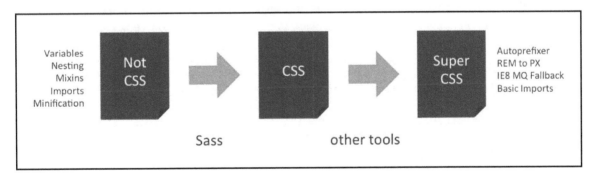

The postprocessing tool will do a job that developers do not much care for. Also, for the latest CSS features, which are not fully supported by all browsers, they need vendor prefixes—these will be automatically added by our CSS postprocessors, so we do not need to add prefixes such as `-moz-`, `-webkit`, `-o-`, or `-ms` manually.

On the CSS preprocessing side, we learned that we can do things that are only possible with pure CSS-like variables, functions, nesting, or mixins, whereas CSS postprocessor tools do everything that is possible with pure CSS, but optimize in a better way and perform automation for developers.

Postprocessors use JavaScript to analyze our compiled CSS code, and they transform it into valid CSS as a result.

The following are a few tools that are available online to do the CSS postprocessor job:

- **PostCSS** (https://postcss.org/)
- **Pleeease** (http://pleeease.io/)

You can check out more about both these tools, and you will see that it is really easy to set them up and configure them on your projects. Doing this, you will be good to go.

When it comes to frontend tools, most of the time which you use is a matter of choice, but the good thing is that these tools are available for use.

CSS methodologies

Working with CSS tools such as preprocessors and postprocessors makes a big difference in helping us write and maintain CSS code.

However, they do not solve the entire problem when we have to deal with a bigger code base of CSS in bigger projects. The biggest issue with CSS itself is its nature—how it works—for example, every style that we define is globally applied to every website or web application page we have as long as our CSS file is included there.

To solve this problem, usually we have to apply different and longer class names, which becomes a big mess when it comes to maintaining that code.

To avoid these issues during our development process, we have to follow some guidelines or rules that will allow us to have control over CSS, such as class names, ID, properties, prefixes, and all the other parts that are connected with it.

The best way to do this is by using CSS methodologies. CSS methodologies will guide us in how to write CSS in a structured and organized way; as a result, the code will be easier to maintain by everyone who will be involved on the development team since they will have a documentation and convention that they need to follow when it comes to CSS.

There are a lot of CSS methodologies available online, but the following are a few that we will cover:

- **Object-Oriented CSS (OOCSS)**
- **Scalable and Modular Architecture for CSS (SMACSS)**
- **Block, Element, Modifier (BEM)**
- **Atomic CSS (ACSS)**

Object-Oriented CSS (OOCSS)

This CSS methodology was first introduced in early 2009, and it has two main principles when it comes to organizing CSS.

The first one is to properly separate the entire structure of our CSS code from themes styles or, sometimes known on CSS as, the skins.

Using this approach, we divide CSS that has anything to do with the layout of the pages, such as floats, flexbox, or grids, from styling skin components such as colors, fonts, shapes, and animations.

So, using OOCSS, we have the following two groups where we write the CSS:

- Structure (CSS Layouts, grids, alignments, and hierarchy)
- Skin (colors, backgrounds, fonts, and shapes)

This CSS methodology is a great approach, and it provides a log of guidelines on how to use it, but when it comes to dealing with specific components or areas of websites or web applications, it is as very perspective as other CSS methodologies such as SMACSS.

Scalable and Modular Architecture for CSS (SMACSS)

This CSS methodology was introduced 2 years later, after OOCSS, and compared to OOCSS, where it was decided on two groups: the SMACSS CSS methodology split on five different categories, as follows:

- Base rules
- Layout rules
- Modules
- State rules
- Skin (theme) rules

Beside these five categories of rules, the other good thing is that it comes with some naming conventions that should be followed when developers are writing CSS.

For example, over time when developers have to deal with layouts, they should name classes used for layouts with prefixes such as `l-` or `layout-`, and also, when it comes to dealing with component stages, if it is hidden, collapsed, or clicked, they should use classes such as `is-hidden`, `is-clicked`, or `is-collapsed`.

By using this CSS methodology approach, you will have much better organized code, and there are no big cons included. So, when it comes to dealing with projects that will have a big CSS codebase, it is worth using SMACSS.

Block, Element, Modifier (BEM)

This approach was first introduced by Yandex in 2010, and the focus of this CSS methodology approach is to identify three main components of CSS: block, elements, and modifiers.

The main idea behind this CSS methodology is to divide user interface components into small pieces and independents blocks.

For example, a block inside this CSS methodology can be a FORM that we create into a HTML page, and the elements are the small parts which can be included inside the form, such as BUTTONS or INPUTS.

A modifier inside this approach is usually referred to as an entity defining the behavior, appearance, or the state of a block or an element.

The BEM CSS methodology approach is really easy to get started with and understand since it follows a specific naming convention and has proper guidelines on how it should work. So, by including new team members on a project that is following the BEM approach, it would be really easy for them to understand what is going on with the project's CSS.

All of these CSS methodologies are great approaches to follow, but when it comes to newer CSS methodology such as Atomic CSS, then it takes us to a whole new level of how we should organize and use CSS inside our projects.

Atomic CSS (ACSS)

This CSS methodology was first made famous by Yahoo!, and was popular in 2014. Its main approach was to focus on small atomic components, where you create classes for each of them and provide visual functions for those tiny components.

Atomic CSS is different in that it is known as a functional CSS, and compared to previous CSS methodologies that we discussed in previous sections, such as BEM, OOCSS, or SMACSS, the Atomic CSS approach is the complete opposite of them.

This approach received a negative reaction at first. No one wanted to follow it; consider an example of what a button looks like in the previous approaches:

```
<button class="search__button">Search</button>
```

Let's explore the preceding code in Atomic CSS:

```
<button class="f1 br1 ph3 pv4 white bg-red hover-bg-light-
red">Search</button>
```

It looks like a disaster with all of these mixes of classes that are included inside one UI component, but when companies started adopting and using this approach, their job effectiveness on the CSS side had amazing results.

If you would like to go deeper into this approach, I would highly suggest that you read the following article by Adam Wathan, which explains this approach in an amazing way. Follow `https://adamwathan.me/css-utility-classes-and-separation-of-concerns/` to read more about this article.

Lately, we are seeing a lot of different and new approaches in CSS methodologies, especially the famous one known as *CSS in JS*, which brings new questions to the game besides the Atomic CSS approach discussion. It is known as one of the most controversial CSS methodologies available.

Anyway, the important point is to choose a CSS methodology before you start a development process so that your life will become much easier when you handle and maintain the code. It is a matter of choice and is dependent on the type of project that you are working on.

So, going deeper into these CSS methodologies, read more about them, and find out which one would suit your project and start using it.

CSS frameworks

Before I start to explain what a CSS framework is, let's get you back to Chapter 9, *UI Design and Implementation*, where we talked about design system.

The design system was a system where we placed all the components—such as buttons, inputs, and tabs—and defined grids, style guides, color palettes, fonts, and guidelines. Similarly, when it comes to the CSS framework, we have all of these points covered—just compare it to the design system. The CSS framework contains everything that we can reuse to build our application for the final stage before going live.

The best way to understand it would be to know that the design system contains elements and components and guides that are only available visually to us, so we use them to create the user interface design. However, the CSS framework contains all of these components ready-coded for us, and we can use them throughout our entire product to build a working user interface that users can interact with.

CSS frameworks contains UI components such as table, buttons, forms, grids, colors, and types, and many more predefined components:

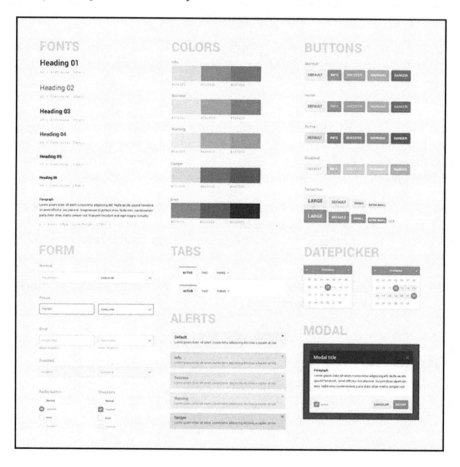

In the frontend world, usually a CSS framework contains a structure of files and folders, which contains files with valid code for HTML, CSS, and JavaScript.

All of the CSS frameworks come with an extended document, which clearly explains for what purpose the framework was created, what components it contains, and how you can use those components.

Using CSS frameworks simplifies all the required hard work which developers should have done while creating layout, grids, UI components, best practices, and more. They also remove two of the biggest pains when it comes to frontend development: browser support and responsive design.

Most of the CSS frameworks were built keeping in mind the different browser supports and platforms, starting from small devices such as phones and tablets up to bigger screens for desktops.

So, consider that sometimes it is not worth creating something from scratch and waste a lot of time when you have everything ready and built for you.

There are tens or even hundreds of CSS frameworks available nowadays online for developers, but the leader for almost a decade has been Bootstrap.

Just because it is the most popular framework doesn't mean that other CSS frameworks are not better than Bootstrap. That is why I am going to suggest a list of the most popular frameworks of 2018. It is worth spending a bit of your time checking them out.

The following are the most popular CSS frameworks in 2018:

- Bootstrap (http://getbootstrap.com/)
- Foundation (https://foundation.zurb.com/)
- Bulma (https://bulma.io/)
- UIkit (https://getuikit.com/)
- SemacticUI (https://semantic-ui.com/)
- Materialize (https://materializecss.com/)
- Skeleton (http://getskeleton.com/)

Do not take this to mean that every time you have to start a project on the frontend side you need to choose a CSS framework.

You have to understand that all of these depend on your project's needs; for example, if you are not going to use most of the components that are provided by CSS frameworks, then it is not worth taking them. Instead, create your own.

What I mean by creating your own is to create a framework which only contains the components, rules, and guides that will fit your project's needs, which will make the life of other developers involved in it easier.

The purpose of this section was to tell you that there are various CSS frameworks that you can use. It is up to you to check their advantages and disadvantages, and to check whether they will fit your development process or your project's needs.

However, one thing is for sure: if you won't one, you will have to create one. It is a must that you have the proper guidelines for all the UI components, principles, and guides when it comes to frontend development, because without it, sooner or later, your project will become a mess, get out of control, and will be impossible to maintain.

Summary

This has been a long chapter but with really important lessons that you need to know about when it comes to the implementation of user interface design on the code side. You should have a clear understanding of the process of handover design to developers, what files and data you need to provide to developers, and what kind of tools you can use to hand over the designs.

Besides that, we discussed the development process, especially for CSS tools such as preprocessors, postprocessors, methodologies, frameworks, and animations. When it comes to frontend development, you should now have a better idea of the tasks and tools that fall under the aegis of frontend development.

It has been a great journey—now, it is time to see what a UX designer does after launching the product. We will explain this part in greater detail in the next chapter.

11
Post-launching UX Activities

We have now come to the final part of UX. In this chapter, we will explain the next steps that we, as UX professionals, can take when we launch a product.

After we launch a product, we will need to learn more about the customers that will be using the product; we will need to reach out to them, listen to them, and improve the product for them.

We will elaborate on the kinds of metrics we should get from our customers, which parts of these metrics are important for us to know, and how we can use metrics to our benefit.

We will cover the following points in this chapter:

- Steps to take after a product launch
- Gathering feedback from users
- Performing A/B testing
- Gathering and using metrics
- Performing user interface accessibility testing
- Creating and analyzing conversion funnels

Post-launch UX activities

We have come a long way. After following the proper UX process, involving planning, researching, analyzing, designing wireframes, prototypes, and the user interface, and developing the design, we launched the product.

However, even after launching the product, we will have to do another round of testing, to check that everything works properly.

This round of testing can be done by different groups of users, listed as follows:

- Our team itself, which knows how the product should work
- New users that know the concept of the product that we built, but have never used it before
- New users that have no idea about our product, but have decided to give it a try

This is a good thing, because we can gather feedback from the different user groups and create a plan for what we should tackle next, in order to improve our product.

This post-launching step is one of the best, because we will have time to collect and test reviews from our users. During this time, we can focus on fixing bugs and improving the speed of our product, and we can also plan new features, based on user comments.

This process of testing the live product is ongoing, and every time we gather new feedback (based on its importance), new improvements can be released in the next version of our product.

Although we came to the end of most UX processes by launching the product, you can see that the UX design job is far from being finished, since there will be ongoing work to improve the product every day.

In spite of all of the actions that we took in the pre-launch of the product, the post-launch UX process can help us to create a much a better user experience, through gathering the correct data from our real users and solving any troubles that they might face when using our product.

The idea of a post-launch UX process is to build a product that users will get addicted to, because it will solve their problems and make their lives easier.

Compared to the pre-launch UX process, on the post-launch side we have better insights into our product, better metrics, real user feedback, and, most importantly, we can understand what we implemented incorrectly inside of our product, so that we can fix it.

By having all of this data, we will always be one step closer to building a great user experience for our users; also, it will not be as difficult as the pre-launch UX process, when we had to assume or research about what our users would need, without having a final product to test.

The first area that we need to tackle after a successful product launch is the onboarding area. The best way to improve it is to collect all of the metrics based on the users' behavior when they use our product, create qualitative analytic data from those metrics, and prepare a plan in order to design a better onboarding experience for the users.

We will have to check our users' locations and devices and the time they spend on the product; also, we will need to obtain answers to the following questions:

- Why are users using our product?
- Where are they accessing our product from?
- Who is using our product?
- When are the users using our product?
- How are they using our product, and how do they behave with it?

The best way to answer all of those questions, and to improve their user experience, is to follow some steps to gather different information on the users and analyze the product itself.

The post-launch process that I prefer to follow to collect this kind of metric is as follows:

- Collecting the correct user feedback
- User accessibility testing (UI testing)
- A/B testing
- Tracking and recording UI sessions from users
- Creating and analyzing conversion funnels

Now, let's look at each of the preceding steps in detail.

Collecting the correct user feedback

In this section, we will start to collect feedback directly from the users that are using our product.

The best way to understand where the users are struggling with our product is by asking them directly - not just in general, but for every specific feature of our product.

By gathering feedback from our users, we can create a better and clearer path for our product's road map, including the following:

- The fixes and improvements that we will implement for the next release.
- New features that users are asking for, and whether they really need them.
- A clear vision of our product's future.

The main benefit will be customer satisfaction, because we will have a better idea of how our users feel about our product, what their expectations are, and how we can make them happy by improving the product.

There are different ways to collect user feedback; in this section, I will cover a few of them, which you can use on your website, in a web application, or in a mobile application.

However, before we start using these methods, first, we need to consider a few things and take a look at which method will be the best fit for gathering feedback.

The points that we need to consider are as follows:

- We need to know what part of our product we want to improve. Is it a specific feature of the product? Is it the onboarding experience? Is it the content marketing side of the product?
- We need to have a clear idea of what we will do with the data that we collect for each specific area. We have to be prepared to improve an entire part of the product, if needed. For example, it could be confusing content, a non-friendly user interface, or a confusing onboarding experience. So, we need to have the resources to cover those areas, such as a content writer, a UI designer, or a developer.
- We need to know what method we can use to gather information from our users. The best way to convey this point is to explain each of those methods separately, so that you will have a better idea about them and can decide which one to use.

The following are the three methods that I prefer to use, in order to gather data from users:

- Customer feedback surveys
- Emails and contact forms
- Social media

I did not include any analytical tools or recording sessions; those types of feedback fall under a different category in the post-launch process.

At this point, we will only gather data that is provided directly from users; then, we will filter the information based on the number of users that request certain changes on our product's roadmap plan.

So, let's start with the first method for gathering user data: implementing customer feedback surveys.

Customer feedback surveys

Creating a good and useful customer survey form is not an easy task to achieve, even though it looks simple.

Besides all of the different questions that we can ask our users, we need to be careful to choose a proper way to approach the users. If we annoy them by showing the surveys everywhere around our product, they will get bored with it, and may even start disliking the product itself.

A simple method for collecting user feedback that you are probably familiar with is showing a simple slider or box at the bottom of a website after the user has finished a specific task or filled in a specific form.

Usually, this short survey contains questions about your experience when using a specific feature of the product, or whether you were happy with the process, or something similar to that.

The following screenshot shows an example of this type of survey, created using the Qualaroo tool, which looks like a poll and asks the user simple questions:

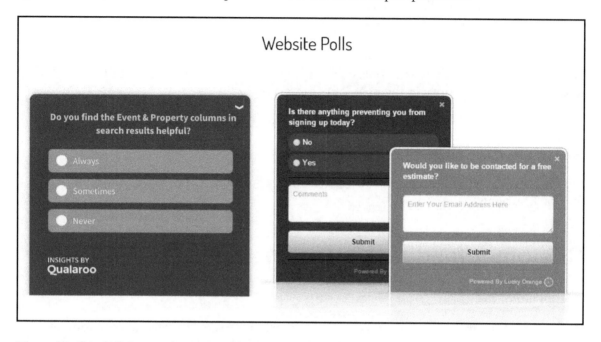

These kinds of slider can be created internally by developers, or by using external tools, such as Qualaroo, Survey Monkey, GetFeedback, or Typeform.

Besides short and small surveys, we can also create an extended survey and can provide this information to the users when they submit their responses; they can also take a look at what others think about the product, as shown in the following screenshot:

Longer surveys – Stats

My most important support metric is...

1	Customer satisfaction rate	**44%**
2	Speed of first response	**21%**
3	Time to resolution	**16%**
4	Contact rate per customer	**5%**
5	Customer effort score	**5%**

To create a good and not-so-annoying survey, and to get the best out of it, you will have to follow the following rules:

- Only ask questions that matter for your product, through which you can achieve your end goal
- Ask smart and short questions, for which users can provide a precise answer.
- Do not ask more than one question at a time
- Avoid mixing different topics in one survey, as the survey needs to be focused on one topic at a time
- Use direct answer options, such as yes or no; that way, you can avoid assumptions and have clear answers
- For a better user experience, do not create long surveys

Follow the preceding rules to create a better user experience with your surveys. It will be really interesting for users if you provide some kind of a bonus for them at the end, such as a thank you for taking the time to fill in your survey.

Emails and contact forms

We are used to seeing emails as a marketing tool, but they play an important role when it comes to collecting feedback from users.

Usually, users will contact you through email when they find a major issue in your product; for example, they may have a specific problem when using the product, such as a subscription model issue or a payment system problem.

I know it looks like a difficult task to open an email, write it, and send it, but we can make this process easy for our users by creating useful contact forms, which make it easy for them to write to us.

The following are some reasons why a contact form is a much better way for us to receive emails:

- **Security**: This way, we can avoid receiving too much spam in our email account, since we add protection to the email that we use to receive the requests.
- **Reachability**: It will be a really easy process for our users to fill in a simple form and submit it, compared to the standard method, where they have to search for our email, then open another application, such as Gmail or Outlook, to write to us.
- **Clarification**: We can collect extra information when they fill the form in, by asking which department they want to address their email to or stating that they will be able to attach a screenshot of their issues.
- **Engagement:** Besides talking directly to the users through emails, we can also ask the user to provide us with different ways of reaching them, such as a phone number. Also, we can add a function: unsubscribing from emails, which is very important for users that are looking for control. If we add this feature, communications from those users will increase.

If you implement all of the preceding points inside a contact form, you can achieve something similar to the following Packpub contact form, where you can get the adequate information that you need from the user:

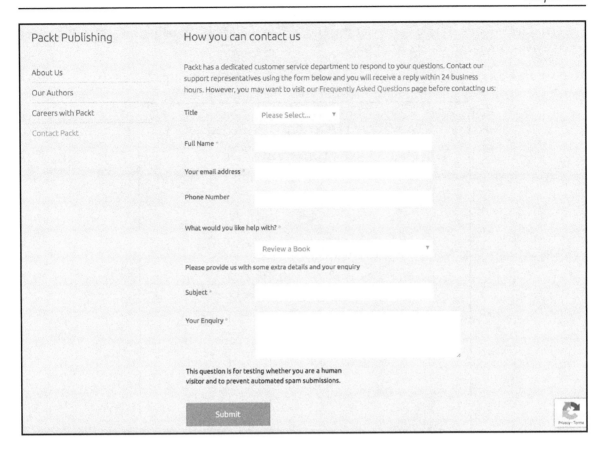

When we create a contact form to obtain proper data from the users and to give them a good user experience, we have to keep the following points in mind:

- Customer Support needs to be fast in responding to user emails, with clear steps taken
- The system for customer feedback needs to be well-organized
- Customer support needs to follow up on each issue separately

After all of those implementations and considerations, the final step is to get feedback from users on their experience with the Customer Support.

We can implement a simple survey at the end, when their ticket is being resolved, and can receive some final comments from them.

To do so, we can implement something simple, such as the following:

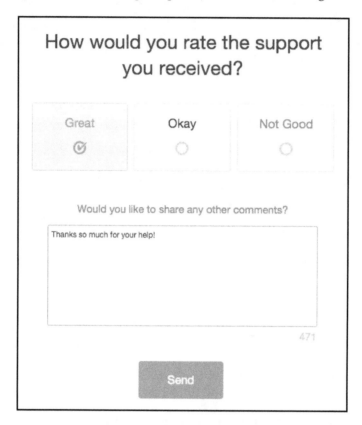

This section discussed another method for getting feedback from our customers, related to the product that they are using. Now, let's move on to the last method: social media.

Feedback through social media

It may sound confusing, but there are tons of information that we can gather from our users through social media.

Aside from the direct messages, comments, and mentions that we can get from our users through social media, we can also create different surveys or polls there, where we ask our users specific questions related to the product.

Let's look at an example of a poll that we can create on Facebook, where we can ask our customers for their opinion on a feature or issue that we are trying to resolve for them:

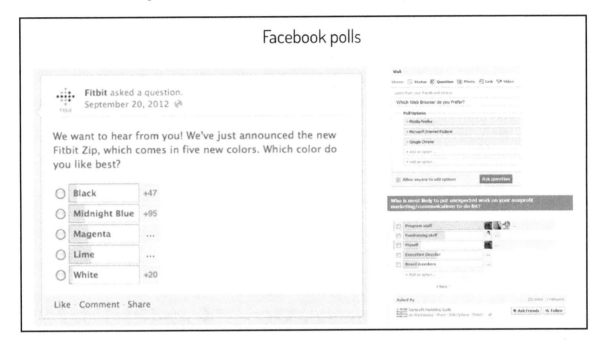

As you can see, it is a really short poll, and we can get tons of metrics from the users about our product. To facilitate this, we can make available an online subscription to the group, such as a Facebook link to our product, so the poll is visible the next time users are on Facebook.

User accessibility testing (UI testing)

When it comes to accessibility testing, we will need to spend much more time on up-front planning, and implementing this will take more time, but we will have better insights and feedback, compared to all of the methods that we have discussed up until now.

With accessibility testing, we can discover new problems that users are facing and struggling with when they use our product—things that we were unable to discover through the previous methods.

Accessibility testing is a common method, used mostly for website or web application testing, but its principles can be applied to any kind of product, online or offline.

In this testing, we can discover how users interact with our user interface, and take a look at their struggles. We can find out what part of the product they spend most of their time on, and we can also see what part of the product they are failing to complete specific tasks on.

To gather the proper data for accessibility testing, we need to use different external tools, such as Google Analytics or heatmap tools, which can provide us with information to check where the users are navigating inside our product, which buttons they are clicking on frequently, and at which point they are leaving our product.

A simple example of using a heatmap tool in a mobile application is shown as follows:

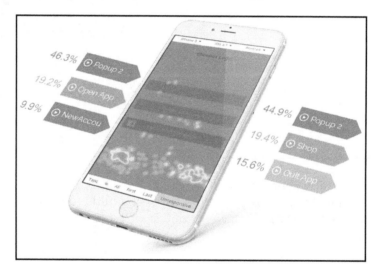

As you can see, the preceding image shows areas where users are touching the screen the most when they use our application; also, we can track all kinds of different gestures, such as swiping, tapping, double-tapping, and pinching.

These types of tool are essential when it comes to testing the product after we launch it and gathering feedback from our users all of the time.

A/B testing

A/B testing is a traditional tool, which we have been using on UX for a long time in order to track the performance and conversions of our product design.

We have to create two UI designs, which are not totally different; they may have some consistencies, but we can track both of them to check which one is performing better.

The main thing that we check when we perform A/B testing is the conversion rate—which means identifying the most preferred UI design

In the following screenshot, you can take a look at an example of two different mobile UI designs and tracking their conversions. Based on that, you can get a clear idea of the UI design that is performing better:

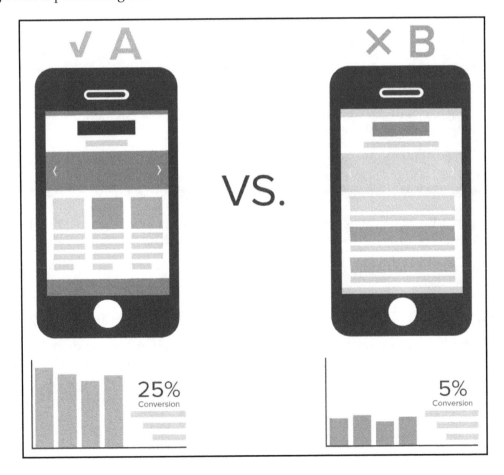

To clarify, A/B testing can be used both before and after launching the product. It can be an ongoing process, even after we decide the final UI design, because we can perform A/B testing for new features that we will implement in our product in upcoming releases.

When performing A/B testing, we record both designs, analyze them, check their heatmaps, and structure all of that information in a proper way, taking a look at which one is performing better and then going with that UI design.

During this process, all we care about are the metrics and the design that is performing better. Although some designers state that certain metrics limit their creativity when it comes to UI, the main thing that we care about is improving the design so that our users find it easier to use, not improving the creativity or fanciness of the design.

As for accessibility testing where we use external tools, when it comes to A/B testing, we have to use tools such as Google Analytics and Kissmetrics or even Mixpanel, to track heatmaps.

Using these tools, we can get information on both designs, such as what areas are clicked on frequently, from which online sources users visit our product, what tasks users are performing, and where users fail or struggle.

Especially when it comes to critical flows, such as registration or payments, we can easily track where the users are failing to finish those steps.

If we adopt the habit of performing A/B testing every time, we will always have the possibility of providing a better UI design to our users, because we will know what design converts better, and what design is a better fit for our business and users.

A/B testing metrics will always help us to improve the product, but in the end up to it is the designer to convert those metrics into a meaningful design that will meet user and business needs.

Tracking and recording user UI sessions

When it comes to tracking sessions from users, there are different ways to do it. We can do it by asking some of our teammates or other departments to record their sessions when they use the product, or we can use external tools to track user sessions.

The main point is to track shorter and longer sessions, to check the differences between them.

For shorter sessions, we will check why the users are using the app for such a short time, and why they are leaving immediately, whereas for longer sessions, we will check what is making the users stay in the app for a longer period of time.

Once we have figured out these things, it is easy to combine lessons from both sides and start to improve the UI in such way that we can avoid losing users.

To get better results from session records, we need to choose a specific task that our user can perform from start to finish, such as the following:

- Registering
- Adding a product to the cart
- Changing the password
- Subscribing
- Payment
- Other tasks that send a user from point A to point B

After we gather the preceding information from different users, we can start to compare why it took longer for some users to register than others. We can then find the issues, and can start to tackle those parts of the design to provide a better solution for the next release.

Creating and analyzing conversion funnels

Similar to tracking UI sessions, here we need to track conversions: Where do users find our product, and how do they start using it?

To achieve this, we should first set some goals. What do we want the user to do when they arrive at our product? Do we want them to register, subscribe, play games, buy something, or some other specific action?

We will create funnels for these kinds of tasks, and we will track the entire process, from the time that users enter our app to the final stage where they buy something or take an action that we expect them to take.

We collect all of the data together in one place, and then start analyzing it. This can also be done with an analytics tool, and we can track each goal separately, as in the following screenshot:

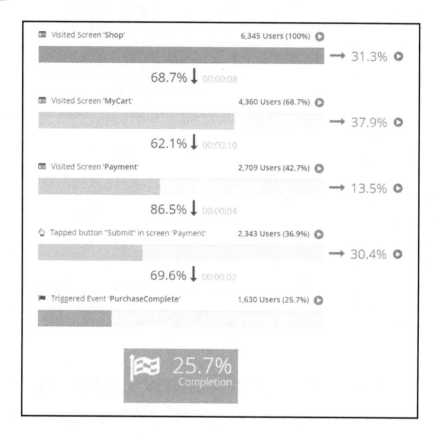

Via these reports, we can check why users are not engaging with specific screens, reasons for some screens better at conversion, or what is stopping the user from finishing a specific action when they start it.

Creating a friction-less user experience for our customers is not an easy task. It takes time and effort, but by following a proven process and using the right tools, amazing results can be achieved.

The process that I like to follow when it comes to creating and tracking conversion funnels is as follows:

1. Decide the main goals—list and prioritize those that best suit the user's need.

2. Create the process that the user needs to follow, from start to finish, for each goal—the process for buying a product or registering, for example.

3. Choose an analytics tool and track the entire process from start to finish.

4. Analyze the feedback gathered from analytics tools, weigh the pros and cons of the current design, detect whether the users are struggling to finish a process from beginning to end, and figure out what we can improve to make the process easier.

5. After tracking several goals separately, create a bigger picture for the entire product, its future, and what can be improved.

6. The final thing to note before we move on to the next section is that data, metrics and analyzing them, are always better than assumptions, and this is 100% correct.

So, to create a better product, even after its launch, always track every single part of it—what users are doing, how they are behaving, and what their product feedback is. Gather the data, always have metrics for your product, analyze every part of the metrics, and start to improve your product.

Summary

In this book, we have mentioned several times that UX is an ongoing process, and we have to design the interface in a way that makes sense to users.

Having a successful product involves not only launching it, but also having a post-launch process in place; because to create a great user experience, we have to design the right features for our users, research our users' problems, and build designs that solve those problems.

The best way to do this is to gather as much data as we can from our users, and then form our product by following suggestions and making improvements.

We have already covered a few steps that need to be taken after the launch of the product, to start applying the ones that fit your process.

In the next chapter, we will discuss big data and how we can provide a better user experience when we are dealing with it, the role that UX plays in it, and what big data means to UX. So, see you in the next chapter!

12
Designing for Big Data

Today's world is experiencing a growing amount of big data, which is being collected from different sources, such as e-commerce business, social network platforms, search engines, and even from small online business.

With all this data, we need to know how to display it to our users, the best way to use it, and how it can help us develop a better product.

By the end of this chapter, you will have a better understanding of those points, and the role of big data in the user experience.

In this chapter, we will cover the following points:

- Big data and its role on UX
- How to design products using big data
- The role of big data in mobile design
- Why big data matters for user experience

UX Design with big data

Let's start this chapter by explaining the meaning of big data. By the name itself, you can tell that we are talking about really big data—data that can't be processed using traditional methods.

It usually starts with a small amount of data, data we collected from different sources; but then we start storing a large amount of it, and exceed storage volumes in terabytes, petabytes, or even the exabytes. Information inside this data can be structured or unstructured, and this large volume of data is known as big data.

So, with all this data on our hands, by using it in the right way, we can create much better designs and provide a more improved user experience to our users.

UX can be a bridge between big data and the users, and by showing our users the right data, we improve the product itself.

Let's take an e-commerce business as an example. When we buy something on their website, it always suggests other related things we can purchase, or it suggests what other users have bought in conjunction with the item that we want.

Here, the biggest part is being played by UX and the proper use of big data, which uses information to suggest actions the users can take, this also improves business.

You experience similar cases every day on websites such as AliExpress, Amazon, and eBay. Here is an example of how Amazon uses these suggestions:

However, a lot of even startups or stable companies, especially those that collect a lot of data from their users, have so much data that they can't tell what's important for their users and what's not.

To make use data properly, we need to find better ways to process and use it, which is where UX plays a vital role.

By designing custom data visualization through UX and creating better reporting solutions, companies can reach their goals much more easily, and can revolutionize the product they offer to users.

UX design is a key factor in analyzing, displaying, and using big data in a way that will add value to the business and to its customers.

The role of big data in UX design

We explained big data and the importance of UX in it, but let's look at a better example of the role that UX plays in big data. As an example, let's explore how data for the same product is displayed across different platforms, such as desktops devices, tablet devices (iPad, Kindle), and mobile devices (iPhone, Android).

Bigger devices will always show more data, where users can easily navigate through it thanks to larger screen sizes. When it comes to small devices, we will only display the most important data.

Since we used the Amazon website as example in the previous section, in the following screenshot you can see the differences in how data is presented on Amazon, depending on whether users are using a desktop or mobile application:

We do this because we don't want to overwhelm users with unnecessary amounts of data. Instead, we want to provide them only with the data that is important to them and to our business, so that we can guide them to take the steps that we want, by avoiding the confusion that too much information can cause.

When it comes to mobile UX, here are some benefits of handling big data in the right way:

- Developers get a deeper understanding of the customers, and big data helps them to optimize the user experience for a targeted audience
- When it comes to user interaction, big data can tell us more about user behaviors, which means developers can implement more meaningful user-interface interactions
- big data also helps marketing departments create better marketing campaigns by using information such as users interests, preferences, behaviors, and location

UX design helps us to put this data into graphic visualizations, or graphical images, which will provide the users with clear information, or even trigger them to take the specific actions we want.

Big data is incredibly complex, and by employing proper UX designs, we simplify that data and provide users with a clear picture of what they need to know.

We already know that the main goal of UX is to provide a better user experience of the product, keeping the business needs in mind, but with all the rapidly-changing data and information, we need to be sure that, as UX designers, we are aware of those changes and are always bringing the best experience to both the users and the business.

Simply put, when it comes to mobile applications, the role of UX design is to filter all this data into something useful to our users.

Data visualization

With all this data at our disposal, UX design and big data are both concerned with data visualization.

Data visualization is just a form of visual presentation that shows the information collected from big data to the users.

Most of the time, the term big data is used for data that is extremely large and complex. This is where we need data visualization, to extract that data in better and simpler ways for us and our users.

We are all aware of the famous quote that a picture is worth a thousand words. This can also be the case when it comes to visualizing data for our users. Displaying the data in graphical assets can provide our users with meaningful information for each piece of data that we add inside the product's user interface.

A key concept of big data is to analyze the data and just put the information we need inside the product. Most of the time, we only need to deal with a deep analysis of the data when we create dashboards.

A dashboard is the first page our users will see when they subscribe to different services on web or mobile applications. Do not confuse dashboards with reports; dashboards are not just reports, other things get placed inside dashboard user interfaces, such as summaries, trends, charts, diagrams, and analytics.

A good example of the elements the dashboard contains are shown by Google Analytics in the following screenshot:

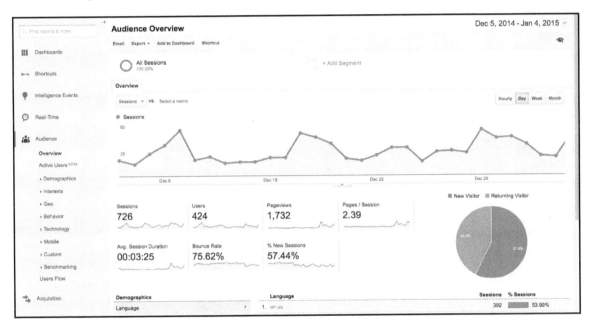

You can see similar dashboards on different web applications, this image is just to give you better understanding of what kinds of elements are placed inside.

As you can see, all the information on the Google Analytics dashboard is important, and this data is displayed visually to the users in an easy-to-understand way.

The main purpose of designing dashboards is not to show analytics reports, charts, or diagram data, but to make it possible for the users to interact with that data to achieve their goals.

For example, inside Google Analytics, we can filter the traffic based on different dates in a specific month or year. We can also check which countries the users are coming from and the sources of the traffic.

WordPress offers a better example of a dashboard. Besides displaying reports and statistics, this dashboard also lets users take immediate actions, such as drafting a post:

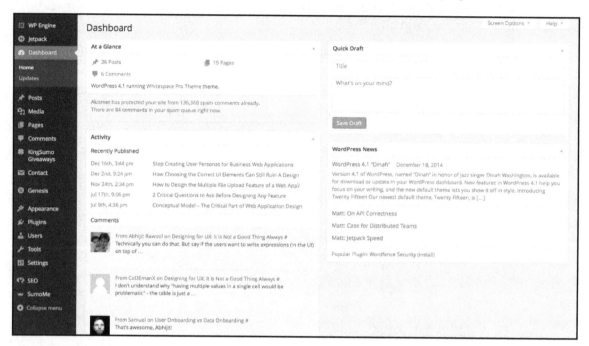

On this dashboard, we can change or edit existing pages, or post inside the WordPress platform without moving away with from the dashboard. A good dashboard user interface is one that both displays data and lets users interact with that data immediately.

When we deal with UX in big data, and especially when we have to create user interfaces for dashboards or something similar, we need to keep the following in mind:

- What kind of data we need to show to the users
- How we will present that data visually inside our design
- What actions users can take with the data available to them

But before providing the users with data, we need to know the users. We already talked about this in Chapter 3, *User Behavior Basics and User Research*, of this book, when we discussed knowing our users and their behaviors.

Once we decide on the data that we want to display to our users, it is really important to create a good visual design for it.

The design should be easy to read and to use, since our users will spend most of their time on the dashboard or similar reporting pages.

Another important element when we are designing dashboards and displaying data to our users, is allowing them to customize their user interface and display only the data that they want or need. Since not all the data will be important to our users, enabling customization will create much better user experience for them.

This book was designed to help you create interactive and positive user experiences. We started with the UX process, and progressed through planning, research, wireframes, user behaviors, prototypes, design principles, and the UI design. By understanding all these parts of the process, and dealing with and displaying the data properly, you will be able to create an engaging and user-friendly design.

Big data is a complex task, but it is our job as UX designers to simplify it; just because big data is complex, doesn't mean UX has to be.

There will be always complexity in processing big data into small pieces of information to finish a specific task, that is why UX is critical when it comes to dealing with data. Be sure to keep track of your data throughout the product design process, right from the very beginning; making data-maintenance an on-going process will help with future improvements.

A final tip before closing this chapter, when you are dealing with big data, be sure to take a step back to get a bigger view of the data and what you can do with it, then start analyzing and filtering the data that makes sense to the business and its customers, and avoid adding unnecessary data to the user interface design.

Summary

You have come a long way, and have finally reached the end of this book. This was the last chapter, and its purpose was to explain big data, the role of UX in big data, and how we can use it to create a better user experience.

Data is what makes UX work better. Learn how to deal with big data, research user behaviors, and display what matters to your users.

To create an engaging user experience, always follow all the steps in the UX process, perform research as often as you can, analyze all the data that you gather, and always incorporate new data to help your product evolve.

Other Books You May Enjoy

If you enjoyed this book, you may be interested in these other books by Packt:

UX Design for Mobile

Pablo Perea

ISBN: 9781787283428

- Plan an app design from scratch to final test, with real users.
- Learn from leading companies and find working patterns.
- Apply best UX design practices to your design process.
- Create low and high fidelity prototypes using some of the best tools.
- Follow a step by step examples for Tumult Hype and Framer Studio.
- Test your designs with real users, early in the process.
- Integrate the UX Designer profile into a working team.

Fixing Bad UX Designs
Lisandra Maioli

ISBN: 9781787120556

- Learn about ROI and metrics in UX
- Understand the importance of getting stakeholders involved
- Learn through real cases how to fix bad UX
- Identify and fix UX issues using different methodologies
- Learn how to turn insights and finding into practical UX solutions
- Learn to validate, test and measure the UX solutions implemented
- Learn about UX refactoring

Leave a review - let other readers know what you think

Please share your thoughts on this book with others by leaving a review on the site that you bought it from. If you purchased the book from Amazon, please leave us an honest review on this book's Amazon page. This is vital so that other potential readers can see and use your unbiased opinion to make purchasing decisions, we can understand what our customers think about our products, and our authors can see your feedback on the title that they have worked with Packt to create. It will only take a few minutes of your time, but is valuable to other potential customers, our authors, and Packt. Thank you!

Index